Psychoanalyses/Feminisms

SUNY series in Feminist Criticism and Theory
Michelle A. Massé, editor
and
SUNY series in Psychoanalysis and Culture
Henry Sussman, editor

Psychoanalyses/Feminisms

edited by
Peter L. Rudnytsky and Andrew M. Gordon

State University of New York Press

Published by
State University of New York Press, Albany

© 2000 State University of New York

For information, address State University of New York Press
State University Plaza, New York 12246

Production by Dana Foote
Marketing by Dana E. Yanulavich

Library of Congress Cataloging-in-Publication Data

Psychoanalyses/feminisms / edited by Peter L. Rudnytsky and Andrew M. Gordon.
p.   cm. — (SUNY series in feminist criticism and theory) (SUNY series in
psychoanalysis and culture)
Includes bibliographical references and index.
ISBN 0-7914-4377-9 (alk. paper) — ISBN 0-7914-4378-7 (pbk. : alk. paper)
1. Psychoanalysis and feminism—Congresses. I. Rudnytsky, Peter L. II. Gordon,
Andrew, 1945– . III. Series. IV. Series: SUNY series in psychoanalysis and culture
BF175.4.F45 P79 2000
150.19'5'082—dc21   99-045447

10   9   8   7   6   5   4   3   2   1

To
Bernard Paris
and
Kathleen Woodward

Contents

INTRODUCTION

Peter L. Rudnytsky

The essays in this volume stem from a conference that took place April 7–10, 1994, and was sponsored by the Institute for Psychological Study of the Arts (IPSA) at the University of Florida.[1] By calling the conference *Psychoanalyses/Feminisms,* our intention was not simply to juxtapose these two preeminent intellectual movements of the twentieth century, but to highlight the manifold natures of each. If we took for granted that psychoanalysis and feminism have much to say to one another—and that each may be indispensable to the other's continued vitality—we likewise understood that neither psychoanalysis nor feminism is a monolithic entity and that the resulting dialogue must involve a plurality of voices on both sides.

To bring together psychoanalysis and feminism is necessarily to call into question the basic assumptions of each. If feminism has insisted that "the personal is the political," psychoanalysis reminds us that no realm of human life is impervious to unconscious motives, which often subvert—or at least complicate—an individual or collective subject's avowed intentions. Conversely, no one influenced by feminism can persist in looking upon Freud as a sovereign authority whose writings have the status of holy writ. Rather, as feminist critics from Karen Horney to Luce Irigaray have argued, Freud is no less important as a symptom of the crises of Western patriarchal culture, which are everywhere apparent in his work, than he is for any of his epoch-making theoretical ideas.

If, therefore, psychoanalysis and feminism are each other's antitheses, an encounter between them must result in the transformation of both. Such confrontations do not take place without friction and conflict, although the alternative to the often painful process of growth is a stagnation that leads to death. But by virtue of their dialectical relation, psychoanalysis and feminism are also mirror images, not least in the way that each is at once a theoretical discourse and inseparably tied to forms

1

of social practice: for psychoanalysis, the new kind of human relationship between analyst and patient that may well be Freud's greatest invention; and for feminism, the quest for more equitable gender arrangements than have prevailed throughout history. In thus melding theory and praxis, psychoanalysis and feminism resemble Marxism, which, whatever its defects, is likewise animated by a vision of a better life for suffering humanity that has changed the face of the world as we know it.

Both psychoanalysis and feminism are at their best when they are used as methods of critical interrogation that put received ideas to the test, and at their worst when they are allowed to harden into dogmas that furnish their adherents with *a priori* answers to every question. Because feminism and psychoanalysis unsettle each other's complacencies, and thereby rekindle their own radical potential, what it may not be unseemly to term their marriage has—despite the storminess of the courtship—proven to be both enduring and fecund.[2]

The essays gathered here capture the spirit of the IPSA conference in several respects. Since one of the aims of both feminism and psychoanalysis is to make structures of authority less oppressive, this should foster a collaborative approach to learning and a distrust of the academic star system that pays greater heed to status than to substance. Accordingly, this volume features the work of twelve scholars at different stages of their careers, from graduate students to those whose achievements have earned them eminence. Organized into four sections, the essays engage a satisfying range of texts and topics and display the full force of the plural on both sides of the slash mark in the title. Just as the proffered visions of psychoanalysis are multifarious and critical—not only *using* but *interrogating* Freud and Lacan, as well as object relations theory, self psychology, and Horneyan theory—so too the iconoclasm of our contributors does not shrink from raising a hammer (which, as Nietzsche observed, may also be a tuning fork) against feminist pieties. Above all, I believe each essay possesses an intellectual distinction that will both instruct and entertain the reader.

No confrontation between psychoanalysis and feminism can afford to bypass the primal father, and the three essays in our opening section, "Rereading Freud," undertake indispensable tasks of ground-clearing. Madelon Sprengnether's "Mourning Freud" sets the stage for this volume by imagining how psychoanalysis would be different if a woman had promulgated its founding concepts. It seems a good bet that the Oedipus complex would be dislodged from its position of primacy, and, as in *The Spectral Mother* (1990), Sprengnether argues that the experience of mourning is far more central to the formation of selfhood than the castration complex. Dissecting Freud's response to the death of his father in 1896, Sprengnether contends that he highlighted his identification with Oedipus as a way of defending himself against even more disturbing resemblances to Hamlet. By an independent route, she thus seconds Harold Bloom's conclusion that "Hamlet did not have an Oedipus complex, but Freud certainly had a Hamlet complex" (1994, 376).

Narrower in scope, my essay, "'Mother, Do You Have a Wiwimaker, Too?': Freud's Representation of Female Sexuality in the Case of Little Hans," looks at this first recorded instance of child analysis, in which Freud seeks to provide an empirical foundation for his emerging theory of the Oedipus complex. Despite its concern with masculine identity, I argue that the case history crystallizes Freud's views on female sexuality and hence calls for feminist scrutiny along the lines afforded the better-known fable of Dora. Although I dispute Freud's premise that children of both sexes believe in the ubiquity of the penis and are ignorant of the vagina, I credit him for having provided the clinical data that enable us to refute his theories.

My critique of Freud's phallocentrism is carried forward by Ranita Chatterjee in "Of Footnotes and Fathers: Reading Irigaray with Kofman." Given the similarities between the overarching projects of these two French feminists, Chatterjee is struck by the ferocity of Sarah Kofman's attacks on Luce Irigaray. She argues that Kofman sees Irigaray as an elder sister or mother with whom she must compete for the father's love. Kofman's anger is contrasted with Irigaray's laughter, and Chatterjee defends Irigaray against the charge of essentialism by arguing that her image of woman's two lips "is not referring to a *real* biological female body, but to an alternative representation of the female body within the Symbolic order."

To what degree gender identity is essential or constructed is further explored by the three contributors to "Fashioning Femininity." In "Marlene, Maggie Thatcher, and the Emperor of Morocco: The Psychic Structure of Caryl Churchill's *Top Girls,*" Patricia Reid Eldredge employs Horneyan theory to analyze the gender-encoded issues of dependency and dominance in Churchill's play. Agreeing with Marcia Westcott (1986) that dependency is "the core problem in women's personality development," Eldredge regards the various characters in *Top Girls* as mimetic representations of the protagonist's "interpersonal and intrapsychic conflicts." But whereas the guests at Marlene's phantasmagoric dinner party act out her struggles between expansiveness and detachment, compliance and rage, Eldredge suggests that the "central absent presence" in the play is Marlene's "real self." Although this Horneyan concept is anathema to postmodernists, few readers are likely to quarrel with Eldredge's advocacy of "empowered caring" as an ideal to guide us in the pursuit of psychological and social change.

David Galef's "Dishing It Out: Patterns of Women's Sadism in Literature" exemplifies the iconoclasm of this volume by broaching the eyebrow-raising subject of women's sadism and taking seriously the idea that there are "universal gender differences" grounded in "brain physiology." The forms taken by women's sadism, however, are perforce culturally determined, the most typical manifestation being "passive-aggressive" behavior. Galef illustrates his theses with an array of apt examples drawn from modern fiction and poetry and with equally wide-ranging references to psychoanalytic theory.

Among Lacanian literary critics, Joan Riviere's "Womanliness as a Masquerade" (1929) has served as a touchstone for thinking about gender. Exposing its vacillations, Véronique Machelidon proposes in "Masquerade: A Feminine or Feminist Strategy?" that Riviere's text itself be regarded as a rhetorical performance designed to curry the favor of her father-figures, Ernest Jones and Freud. By assuming the guise of a faithful daughter, Riviere enacts the duplicities of femininity and occludes the elements of rivalry in the father-daughter relationship. For Machelidon, as for Judith Butler, both gender and heterosexuality are socially constructed; and her Irigarayan quest for a definition of femininity not bound by phallocentrism leads Machelidon to indict the conflation of the phallus with the penis in Riviere, Lacan, and Michèle Montrelay.

The metaphor of the mirror has been central to Lacan as well as to object relations theory and self psychology. A feminist slant on the interplay of self and other in narcissistic experience animates the three essays in "Gendered Mirrors." In "Sadomasochism as Intersubjective Breakdown in D. H. Lawrence's 'The Woman Who Rode Away,'" Barbara Schapiro anatomizes the conflicting desires for reciprocity and domination in love relationships depicted in Lawrence's story. Schapiro's allegiance to Winnicottian object relations theory, which gains support from the empirical research of Daniel Stern (1985) on the development of attunement in infancy, leads her to concur with Jessica Benjamin (1988) that "domination and submission result from a breakdown of the necessary tension between self-assertion and mutual recognition that allows self and other to meet as sovereign equals." Schapiro thus depicts Lawrence not as a chauvinist writer who "celebrates male domination," but rather as one who makes manifest its "tragic consequences." Whereas part of Lawrence succumbs to "defensive splitting" and a "rigid gender polarity," another part of him exhibits "a capacious, flexible imagination," and the unresolved tension between these pathological and healthy components of his psyche—which carry the burden of cultural as well as personal meanings—constitutes for Schapiro the abiding fascination of Lawrence's work.

A complementary female version of the self-same predicament emerges from Michelle A. Massé's "'He's More Myself Than I Am': Narcissism and Gender in *Wuthering Heights.*" Integrating the theories of Freud, Horney, and Kohut, Massé takes Catherine Earnshaw as a prototype of "the female narcissist who attempts to achieve the masculine aims of *Bildung.*" Rejecting romantic readings of Brontë's novel that glorify Catherine's passion for Heathcliff, Massé presents her as a character doomed not by fate but by "the *in*ability to love, where love is understood as intersubjective reciprocity." Neither with Edgar Linton nor with Heathcliff can Catherine, scarred not only by her parents' early deaths but also by a lack of acceptance by her father, surmount her sense of entitlement and enter into a genuine love relationship.

A Lacanian perspective on narcissism is afforded by Maureen Turim's "Looking Back at the Mirror: Cinematic Revisions," an essay in film studies. Combining autobiographical retrospection with theoretical sophistication, Turim extends the line of argument first advanced in her "The Place of Visual Illusions" (1980). In contrast to the widespread tendency among Lacanian film theorists to devalue both the Imaginary realm and avant-garde cinema, Turim recovers a ludic dimension of Lacan and invokes Christian Metz to celebrate the power of both mirrors and movies to grant their beholders access to an always unforeseen space. Turim remarks on the recurrent tendency in both Western and Japanese films to equate narcissism with femininity, although the stereotypically female fears of aging and loss of beauty are offset by male fears of infantilization and maternal domination. In her conclusion, Turim recognizes that gender boundaries are being redrawn at present and voices the hope that the changes may be for the better.

The title of the concluding section, "Voyages Out," is taken from Virginia Woolf's first novel, *The Voyage Out* (1915), which serves as the destination of Claire Kahane's "The Woman with a Knife and the Chicken without a Head: Fantasms of Rage and Emptiness." Kahane obliquely approaches Woolf's novel by exploring the cultural obsession with the specter of the castrating woman as she has been incarnated through the ages from the biblical Judith to Lorena Bobbitt. Kahane's leitmotif of "male fear and female rage" has been encountered elsewhere in this volume. Like Madelon Sprengnether, Kahane dwells on Freud's insistence on castration as the master trope of loss, by which he explains defloration and decapitation. She does so, however, not to debate its merits but simply to lay bare the workings of the patriarchal imagination. Complementing Michelle Massé's reading of *Wuthering Heights,* Kahane treats *The Voyage Out* as "a female *Bildungsroman*" in which—as the theory of Melanie Klein helps to elucidate—"the object of female vengeance is not a male but a female figure." But when, as often happens, women's anger is repressed, it "leaves only fantasms of emptiness in its place," and the most poignant loss proves to be "the loss of rage itself."

Both feminism and psychoanalysis rely on personal narratives as a mode of knowledge and history-telling. David Willbern's "Playing Scrabble with My Mother" returns the reader to the Kansas of his childhood to recreate the primal scene of the "ludic and lascivious" relation to language that is the hallmark of his critical style. In addition to restaging that mythic encounter, Willbern treats us to a specimen of his "supersonic" mode of reading, which produces meanings by breaking sound and syntax barriers, taking *Measure for Measure* as a test case.

Finally, the need for greater dialogue between scholars and clinicans of psychoanalysis is met by Lynne Layton in "Trauma, Gender Identity, and Sexuality: Discourses of Fragmentation." At once erudite and clinically informed, Layton weighs the divergent views of fragmentation advanced by postmodern theory and humanistic versions of psychoanalysis, probes the disintegration in Kathy Acker's *Blood and Guts in High School*, and adduces case material concerning a young woman who was sexually abused in childhood and now suffers from a multiple personality disorder in which different parts of the self are coded as male and female. In Layton's sane view, "some experience of a cohesive 'I,' of a sense of sameness that unites even the most disparate fragments," is "necessary to good mental health," though "the experience of a core self" permits one to "experience this self as evolving and changing in its interactions with the world and with others." By making room for postmodernism within a humanist framework, Layton's essay makes palpable her ideal of therapy as a process that "deconstructs binaries." She thereby "creates a sense of cohesion"—in the reader, as in the patient—"that does not obliterate diversity and is not oppressive, but rather is liberating." Such, we hope, is likewise the collective achievement of *Psychoanalyses/Feminisms*.

Our conference was cosponsored by the Women's Studies Program of the University of Florida and supported by financial assistance from the Division of Sponsored Research, the Dean of Liberal Arts and Sciences, and the Department of English at the University of Florida. Our thanks go to all who made (and continue to make) such an interdisciplinary venture possible: Elizabeth Capaldi, Willard Harrison, Elizabeth Langland, Patricia Craddock, Ira Clark, Norman Holland, Helga Kraft, and Sue Rosser. Henry Sussman and Michelle Massé honored this volume by including it in the series of which he or she is the general editor; invaluable assistance was anonymously rendered by the four scholars who read the manuscript for SUNY Press. Tai-Won Kim adroitly prepared the index.

Notes

About the front cover: The magazine held by the girl in Rockwell's illustration has a photograph identifiable as that of Jane Russell. The display of Russell's bosom in *The Outlaw* (1943), directed by her paramour Howard Hughes, sponsored a worldwide craze. The conjunction of this cultural icon of femininity with the Lacanian mirror and the Winnicottian transitional object in the mind of a girl serves as a visual representation of the issues explored in this volume.

1. For an informative report on the proceedings of the conference, which mentions many of the papers presented at the various seminars, see Layton (1995). In addition to Madelon Sprengnether, whose paper is included here, the keynote speakers were Jessica Benjamin, Teresa Brennan, Juliet Flower MacCannell, Diane Middlebrook, Bernard Paris, Ellen Handler Spitz, and Valerie Traub. Kathleen Woodward organized a seminar on "Psychoanalysis and the Emotions."

2. As John Forrester reminds us, the first wave of feminist theory in the 1970s—exemplified by Betty Friedan, Kate Millett, and Germaine Greer—was marked by an antagonism to psychoanalysis "as splenetic and furious as any of the present entanglements" (1997, 2). It is a remarkable feature of the ensuing decades that feminists have largely surmounted the stumbling block imposed by Freud's misogynistic attitudes to appreciate the indispensability of psychoanalytic instruments, just as devotees of psychoanalysis have outgrown Freud's parochialism and recognized a common cause with feminism.

References

Benjamin, J. 1988. *The Bonds of Love: Psychoanalysis, Feminism, and the Problem of Domination.* New York: Pantheon.

Bloom H. 1994. *The Western Canon: The Books and School of the Ages.* New York: Harcourt Brace.

Forrester, J. 1997. *Dispatches from the Freud Wars: Psychoanalysis and Its Passions.* Cambridge: Harvard Univ. Press.

Layton, L. 1995. Report on Conference at the Institute for Psychological Study of the Arts. *Psychoanal. Q.* 64:209–14.

Riviere, J. 1929. Womanliness as a Masquerade. *Int. J. Psychoanal.* 10:303–13.

Sprengnether, M. 1990. *The Spectral Mother: Freud, Feminism, and Psychoanalysis.* Ithaca: Cornell Univ. Press.

Stern, D. N. 1985. *The Interpersonal World of the Infant.* New York: Basic Books.

Turim, M. 1980. The Place of Visual Illusions. In T. de Lauretis and S. Heath, eds., *The Cinematic Apparatus.* Bloomington: Indiana Univ. Press, pp. 143–50.

Westcott, M. 1986. *The Feminist Legacy of Karen Horney.* New Haven: Yale Univ. Press.

Part I
Rereading Freud

Chapter One
Mourning Freud

Madelon Sprengnether

Freud had a way of telling stories—of telling
stories about others and of telling others
stories about himself—that made history.
—Shoshana Felman,
Jacques Lacan and the Adventure of Insight

OEDIPAL POLITICS

Suppose, for a moment, that Freud had managed to invent psychoanalysis without reference to Sophocles' *Oedipus Rex*. Or, even more radically, that a woman had created the founding concepts that underlie
psychoanalytic theory and practice. How might our discussions of the
relationship between psychoanalysis and feminism be different under
these circumstances?

I raise these questions heuristically: in order to highlight the
centrality of Freud's oedipal construct to his entire theoretical labor, to
signal the chief area of difficulty that feminism (on both sides of the
Atlantic) has encountered in its critique of psychoanalytic culture, and to
raise the possibility that psychoanalysis might have been conceived of
differently, if not by a woman, then by Freud himself, pursuing alternative clues in his self-analysis.

An outgrowth of Freud's intense introspection following his father's death in 1896, the oedipal construct acquired its status as the
"nuclear complex" of the neuroses when Jung began to challenge
Freud's libido theory through a variety of "complexes" of his own invention. Freud first referred to the "Oedipus complex" in his 1910 essay, "A

An earlier version of this chapter appeared in *Psychoanalysis in Contexts*, ed. Anthony Elliott
and Stephen Frosh (London: Routledge, 1995).

Special Type of Choice of Object Made by Men," where he connects it to the boy's anguish at discovering his mother's sexual activity (and hence unfaithfulness) with his father. Once he had settled on this term, Freud tied it to a more ambitious project, that of explaining the evolution of human civilization. In *Totem and Taboo* (1913), Freud's rejoinder to Jung's equally ambitious *Transformations and Symbols of the Libido* (1911–12), Freud locates the Oedipus complex at the very origin of human culture.

In Freud's fanciful anthropology, there was once an all-powerful father who not only dominated his sons but also claimed possession of the available women. The sons rose up against this father, killed him, and ate him. Later, filled with remorse for this deed and recognizing the necessity of making alliance with one another, they collectively atoned for their crime by forbidding the killing of a totem animal and renouncing the women they might have possessed. Freud comprehends these "two fundamental taboos of totemism" in terms of the "two repressed wishes of the Oedipus complex": to kill one's father and marry one's mother (1913, 143). What the sons of the primal patriarch accomplished through a voluntary act of renunciation, subsequent generations achieve by acceding to the castration complex, to the prohibition or the "law" of the father. Systems of ethics, religion, and civilization itself, Freud claims, are built on just such a father-son dynamic.

The obvious problem in this fable is the role it accords women—as passive objects of men's fantasies and desires, as nurturers, rather than creators of human culture. Although Freud (following the lead of J. J. Bachofen) struggled to find a place for matriarchy in his scheme, the best he could do was to imagine it as a transitional stage between two father-dominated periods.[1] Freud treats mother-right as regressive, something like a dark age preceding the restoration of father-rule, which for him signals the highest level of social organization. "The family," he claims,

> was a restoration of the former primal horde and it gave back to fathers a large portion of their former rights. There were once more fathers, but the social achievements of the fraternal clan had not been abandoned; and the gulf between the new fathers of a family and the unrestricted primal father of the horde was wide enough to guarantee the continuance of the religious craving, the persistence of an unappeased longing for the father. (1913, 149)

In Freud's rough sketch of patriarchal social organization, mother goddesses, mother-right, even mothers themselves, quietly disappear.

One reason for the success of the Oedipus complex as a structural concept is the ease with which it explains the social status quo. From this perspective, many feminists have found in Freud an ally, one who can help to elucidate the social system we hope to transform.[2] To the extent that the Oedipus complex is considered a universal and immutable phenomenon, however, it seems unlikely that any other outcome than the one Freud describes is possible. Certainly he himself did not imagine such.

While post-Freudian theorists have focused on areas Freud neglected, such as female sexual development and mother-infant relations, few have directly questioned the existence of the Oedipus complex. The preoedipal researches of the early object relations theorists, for instance, were meant to supplement, rather than to displace, Freud's primary oedipal construct. An argument could be made that contemporary psychoanalysis does not depend very heavily on interpretations based on the hypothesis of an Oedipus complex, yet the term remains intact—less as a sign of its intrinsic appeal, perhaps, than as a tribute to the founding father of psychoanalysis himself.[3] Even feminist theory, I believe, has been hampered by its assumption that the Oedipus complex must somehow be gotten around, rather than interrogated at its core. Ingenious arguments have been proposed for situating women differently within this general structure, yet the structure itself does not permit much flexibility.

Feminist psychoanalytic theorists, while displaying considerable verve and ingenuity in manipulating Freud's oedipal construct, have been unable to alter its bedrock implications.[4] As long as the father (or his function) remains identified with the achievement of language and culture, the position of women will be marginal to both. The Oedipus complex guarantees the perpetuation of this system (in theory at least) by requiring the submission of both men and women to its patriarchal logic.

FROM MOURNING TO OEDIPUS

"In My Own Case Too"

I suggest that the Oedipus complex has enjoyed a privileged status in psychoanalytic theory, not because of its self-evident universality, but because of its capacity to reflect men's place in the prevailing sex/gender system in a relatively positive, even at times, heroic light. In formulating the Oedipus complex, Freud put the best possible face on his own position within a social order that served him personally and whose rightness he never questioned. That he first arrived at this hypothesis through a painful labor of introspection should not only alert us to the personal nature of this achievement but also raise the possibility of alternative constructions. What many theorists tend to forget is the specifically autobiographical ground of Freud's foundational concepts, praising him instead for the unprecedented nature of his discoveries.

Freud's standard biographers take his self-analysis at face value, as if to do otherwise would jeopardize his entire life's work.[5] To question Freud's autobiographical effort, they imply, would raise doubts about the foundations of psychoanalysis itself. Yet this position relies on a strikingly fallible assumption—that Freud had unmediated access to the contents of his own unconscious. Freud alone, in this view, was free of the wish-fulfilling distortions of fantasy and desire. Given that psychoanalysis rests on the supposition of individual blindness in these matters, it seems contradictory, at the very least, to exempt its founder.

It makes more sense, I think, to scrutinize the process by which Freud arrived at his major insights, considering whether other self-representations might have served him (and us) as well. If, for instance, we suspend judgment about the validity of Freud's self-analysis, we may discover new theoretical prospects in the material he brought to light. Specifically, by remaining open to biographical constructions other than the Oedipus complex we may clear the way for a more fruitful alliance between psychoanalysis and feminism.

Contemporary theories of autobiography suggest that self-writing offers a means of shaping an inner world of coherence out of an inherently contradictory and unstable psychic mix.[6] They tell us that we cannot trust solely to memory, which is notoriously unreliable, a creator as well as a transmitter of evidence. Nor can we hope to comprehend the multitude of social factors that comprise our historical moment, giving rise to the particular vocabulary of our self-construction. Whatever narrative we arrive at will of necessity be a product of conscious artifice, partial and self-serving. As a result, the test of an autobiography lies less in its fidelity to truth than in its use value, the extent to which it satisfies our need for meaning in the context of lived experience.

I propose that we read Freud's formulation of the Oedipus complex as autobiography, as an attempt to stabilize an unstable subject in both culturally mediated and personally invested ways.[7] From this perspective we may see how Freud's choice of the Oedipus story as a foundational myth was consonant not only with his culture's values but also with his individual needs.

Freud's fascination with Oedipus (encouraged by the preoccupation of German Romanticism with the culture of ancient Greece) predated his self-analysis, reaching as far back as his adolescence, when he made a careful study of *Oedipus Rex* in preparation for his *Matura* examination.[8] Writing to his friend Emil Fluss at this time, Freud laid out his program of study: "I have a good deal of reading to do on my own account from the Greek and Latin classics, among them Sophocles's

Oedipus Rex." Evidently his preparation paid off; as he later reported to Fluss, "The Greek paper, consisting of a thirty-three-verse passage from *Oedipus Rex,* came off better. [I was] the only *good.* This passage I had also read on my own account, and made no secret of it" (E. Freud 1975, 4). Not long after this, Freud formed a fantasy that he did not reveal until the occasion of his fiftieth birthday, when he was presented with a medallion bearing an image of Oedipus confronting the Sphinx accompanied by the words from Sophocles' play: "Who divined the famed riddle and was a man most mighty." "When Freud read the inscription," Ernest Jones recounts, "he became pale and agitated and in a strangled voice demanded to know who had thought of it. He behaved as if he had encountered a *revenant,* and so he had" (Jones 1955, 14). Freud offered the explanation

> that as a young student at the University of Vienna he used to stroll around the great arcaded court inspecting the busts of former famous professors of the institution. He then had the phantasy, not merely of seeing his own bust there in the future, which would not have been anything remarkable in an ambitious student, but of it actually being inscribed with the *identical* words he now saw on the medallion. (Jones 1955, 14)

Early in life, it appears, Freud formed a powerful identification with Oedipus as heroic investigator. Given his attachment to this figure, it is hardly surprising that he should have returned to it during the period of inner turmoil that coincided with his self-analysis. The oedipal analogy was ready to hand, so to speak, available for Freud's creative use.

One might argue that Freud did not so much discover Oedipus in his unconscious as finally acknowledge the extent to which he had already assimilated this figure into his self-image through his daydreams of heroic achievement. Yet the psychodynamic nature of Freud's interpretation remains at issue. On this level, I believe that the Oedipus myth offered Freud a means of mediating the crisis of mourning precipitated by his father's death.

"You Are Requested to Close the Eyes"

Freud was in the midst of a profound reexamination of his professional and personal identity when Jacob Freud died in 1896. In the preceding year, Freud's last child, Anna, had been born (leading to a decline of sexual relations with his wife Martha); his patient Emma Eckstein had been operated on (with unfortunate consequences) by his friend and correspondent Wilhelm Fliess; and he himself had produced the dream of Irma's injection, the "specimen dream" of psychoanalysis, in which he questioned his efficacy as a physician of nervous diseases. While struggling to theorize the origins of his patients' neuroses, moreover, Freud was actively investigating and combatting his own. He suffered variously from headaches, heart palpitations, sinusitis, fatigue, depression, and the occasional episode of impotence. During this time he, like Emma Eckstein, submitted to nasal surgery at the hands of Fliess, otherwise treating his sinus symptoms with cocaine, while anxiously attempting to calculate his "good" and "bad" periods according to a complex Fliessian mathematics of male and female cycles. Gloomily, he anticipated an early death.

Though fully aware of his father's failing health, Freud appears to have been devastated by his actual death. Writing to Fliess within three days of this event, he first praises his father's dignified acceptance of the inevitable, "He bore himself bravely to the end, just like the altogether unusual man he had been," then admits to his own feelings of depression, "All of it happened in my critical period, and I am really quite down because of it" (Masson 1985, 201). A week later, he writes with greater emotional urgency:

> By one of those dark pathways behind the official consciousness the old man's death has affected me deeply. I valued him highly, understood him very well, and with his peculiar mixture of deep wisdom and fantastic lightheartedness he had a significant effect on my life. By the time he died, his life had long been over, but in [my] inner self the whole past has been reawakened by this event.
>
> I now feel quite uprooted. (202)

Freud describes a condition of being overwhelmed and exposed: first caught offguard by "one of those dark pathways behind the official consciousness," then flooded by memories "reawakened by this event," and finally left feeling "uprooted." This last statement stands alone, as if to emphasize Freud's sense of isolation. It also seems to mark some limit of his capacity to think along these lines, as he turns in the next paragraph to matters of professional concern.

Toward the end of this letter, Freud returns to the subject of his father's death, in a partially coded way, however, through reference to a dream. "I must tell you about a nice dream I had," Freud states, "the night after the funeral. I was in a place where I read a sign: You are requested to close the eyes."

Freud recognizes the location of the sign as the barbershop he visits every day. "On the day of the funeral," he explains, "I was kept waiting and therefore arrived a little late at the house of mourning. At that time my family was displeased with me because I had arranged for the funeral to be quiet and simple, which they later agreed was quite justified. They were also somewhat offended by my lateness" (202).

The cryptic injunction to close the eyes, Freud claims, has two meanings, both of which carry a reproach, that "one should do one's duty to the dead (an apology as though I had not done it and were in need of leniency), and the actual duty itself" (202). Although Freud effectively chastises himself through his interpretation of this dream, he does not probe more deeply into his motives for his disappointing his family twice—first by arranging a type of ceremony they do not approve of and then by arriving late. Instead, he implies that he had good reasons for both and hence no real need to feel sorry. If there is an "inclination to self-reproach" embedded in this dream, Freud concludes, its meaning may be found in the feeling-state "that regularly sets in among the survivors" (202).

In *The Interpretation of Dreams* (1900) Freud offers a somewhat different analysis of this dream, where he reports it as an example of the divergent meanings contained in alternative verbal constructions. Here, he tells us that the dream occurred the night *before* his father's funeral and that the printed notice took the following form: "You are requested to close the eyes" or "You are requested to close an eye" (317). "Each of these two versions," Freud maintains, "had a meaning of its own and led in a different direction when the dream was interpreted" (318). The meaning that Freud pursues is the one that indicts him for negligence in his management of his father's funeral. "I had chosen the simplest possible ritual for the funeral," he explains, "for I knew my father's own views on such ceremonies. But some other members of the family were not sympathetic to such puritanical simplicity and thought we should be disgraced in the eyes of those who attended the funeral. Hence one of the versions: 'You are requested to close an eye,' i.e. to 'wink at' or 'overlook'" (318).

Reading these two dream interpretations in tandem suggests that Freud indeed felt some guilt or remorse at having settled on a simple funeral for his father. It also opens the possibility (assuming that this dream occurred *before* the ceremony) that his lateness was partly intentional, as though he were begging indulgence for an act he had yet to commit. While the "filial duty" Freud mentions in the letter to Fliess may refer to the actual closing of the dead man's eyes, there is a further likelihood that Freud was in some sense closing his own—that is to say, not fully acknowledging his own reactions.

In consciously choosing a less than full ritual, and in (unconsciously perhaps) arriving late, was Freud expressing some reluctance to deal with his own grief? Both acts elicited his family's disapproval, as though he were slighting the occasion. In the preface to the second edition (1908) of *The Interpretation of Dreams,* Freud refers to his father's death as "the most important event, the most poignant loss, of a man's life" (1900, xxvi). Yet his scanting of his father's funeral suggests a more conflicted and evasive response.[9] What might account for this?

"To Be Cheerful Is Everything!"

Freud's correspondence with Fliess in the aftermath of Jacob Freud's death deals with the symptomatology of his patients (which he continues to attribute to sexual seduction in childhood), his own physical complaints, and his darkening mood. Late in November, he writes: "What I am lacking completely are high spirits and pleasure in living; instead I am busily noting the occasions when I have to occupy myself with the state of affairs after my death." Freud's reference to his own death is somewhat cryptic, as if he had merged his identity with that of his father in the process of disposing of the deceased man's estate. At the very least it suggests that he is still preoccupied by the thought that he will die young, "a topic," he confesses, that "one should not deal with too extensively if one loves one's friend and only correspondent" (Masson 1985, 204). However discreetly, Freud seems to be acknowledging a death wish.

In subsequent letters, Freud offers evidence from his clinical practice confirming his seduction theory, culminating in the personal observation that "unfortunately, my own father was one of these perverts and is responsible for the hysteria of my brother (all of whose symptoms are identifications) and those of several younger sisters. The frequency of this circumstance often makes me wonder" (231). His entire family, Freud seems to conclude, is sick. We know, of course, that Freud abandoned the idea that every neurosis conceals a history of sexual seduction, overcoming his own nervous depression in the process of defining himself as an oedipal subject. So triumphant, in fact, was Freud's emergence from this period of personal crisis that few have thought to question its dynamics. Yet it is not altogether clear why his formulation of the Oedipus complex should have released him from his physical symptoms, his anxiety, and his deepening melancholy.

In abandoning his seduction theory, Freud foreclosed certain lines of investigation while opening and pursuing others. The most immediate effect of his change of heart was to exonerate his father from the charge of abuse.[10] "Then the surprise," as Freud states to Fliess on this occasion, "that in all cases the father, not excluding my own, had to be accused of being perverse—the realization of the unexpected frequency of hysteria, with precisely the same conditions prevailing in each, whereas surely such widespread perversions against children are not very probable"

(264). In a single stroke, Freud dispenses with the "paternal" etiology of his siblings' hysteria—not to mention his own complex of nervous symptoms. From this perspective alone, Freud's expression of relief makes sense. "Here I am again," Freud begins his momentous September 21, 1897 communication to Fliess, "refreshed, cheerful, impoverished, at present without work, and having settled in again, I am writing to you first" (264).

Freud's tone elsewhere in this letter is almost jubilant. Far from being daunted by this newest discovery, he feels relaxed and confident. "If I were depressed, confused, exhausted, such doubts would surely have to be interpreted as signs of weakness," he allows. "Since I am in an opposite state, I must recognize them as the result of honest and vigorous intellectual work and must be proud that after going so deep I am still capable of such criticism." He eagerly anticipates a few days "idyl for the two of us" in his friend's company, claims that he is "in very good spirits" and concludes that he has "more the feeling of a victory than a defeat" (265).

Freud's evident good humor at encountering this latest stumbling block in his theoretical work suggests that something more than an intellectual conviction is at stake. His upbeat mood signals an emotional shift, as though the process of mourning instigated by his father's death has finally run its course, releasing him from the weight of his depressive feelings. Yet, "cheerful and refreshed" as Freud professes himself to be, he also makes an odd allusion to Hamlet at the moment of the hero's recognition of his impending death. Adapting Hamlet's statement, "The readiness is all," in response to Horatio's warning about Laertes, Freud pronounces "'To be in readiness': to be cheerful is everything!" hence neutralizing Shakespeare's meaning (265). Even more significantly, Freud ignores the implications of his identification with Hamlet's tragic fate.

In a draft statement included in a letter to Fliess on May 31, 1897, some months before his dismissal of his seduction theory, Freud speculates on a disturbing thought process, evidently discovered in the course of his self-analysis. "Hostile impulses against parents (a wish that they should die)," he offers, "are also an integrating constituent of neuroses." Pursuing this idea further, he links it with a meditation on mourning. "These impulses are repressed," he observes, "at periods when compassion for the parents is aroused—at times of their illness or death. On such occasions it is a manifestation of mourning to reproach oneself for their death (so-called melancholia) or to punish oneself in a hysterical fashion, through the medium of the idea of retribution, with the same states [of illness] that they have had" (250). Freud as much as admits that he has wished his father dead, yet in the face of his actual death turns this thought inward, punishing himself for his murderous desires through the medium of his neurotic symptoms and depression. In this way the idealized image of the father remains intact, while the guilty son gets his due.

It is tempting to speculate that if Freud was unable to sustain a theory of the neuroses that pointed the finger at a "perverse" father, it was at least in part because he could not allow himself such an act of filial impiety in the face of his father's death.[11] Trashing his father's memory in this way would be the equivalent of killing him twice over. Like Hamlet, Freud leaves his father's reputation intact, choosing to vent his hostility elsewhere.

Although Freud's comments on death wishes against parents suggest that they emerged from his observations of his own mourning, he does not pursue this train of thought. His abandonment of the seduction theory, by curtailing the question of his father's complicity in his children's neuroses, also appears to cut off his investigation into the dynamics of the grieving process. As a result, the reasons Freud may have had for wishing his father dead remain largely opaque. By the time Freud chose to theorize them (in his oedipal construct), he had abstracted these impulses beyond the point of individual guilt or reproach.

Freud's dream containing the injunction "You are requested to close the eyes" acquires even greater resonance in this regard. It is as though Freud chose to turn away, at the very moment of his father's death, from the full psychic impact of this event. Emotionally he seems to have come to an impasse until the momentous decision to jettison the troublesome seduction theory, at which point he began to emerge from mourning and to forge a new identity. Yet Freud leaves clues, I believe, to the fate of his grieving process in his interpretation of *Hamlet,* beginning with the piece of revisionary self-help advice, "To be cheerful is everything!"

"The Whole Past Has Been Reawakened by This Event"

Perhaps the most striking parallel between Freud and Hamlet is their experience of father loss. If Shakespeare's play is about anything, it is surely about grief. Yet Freud passes over this obvious source of identification, reading the play instead as a disguised version of *Oedipus Rex.* In superimposing the oedipal plot on the Shakespearean text, Freud indicates the extent to which his heroic identification with Oedipus took precedence over his sympathy with the mourning Hamlet.

Near the first anniversary of his father's death, Freud announced his breakthrough discovery to Fliess: "A single idea of general value dawned on me," he states. "I have found, in my own case too, [the phenomenon of] being in love with my mother and jealous of my father, and I now consider it a universal event in early childhood." Immediately the analogy with Oedipus springs to mind. "If this is so," he continues, "we can understand the gripping power of *Oedipus Rex*. . . . [T]he Greek legend seizes upon a compulsion which everyone recognizes because he senses its existence within himself. Everyone in the audience was once a budding Oedipus in fantasy and each recoils in horror from the dream fulfillment here transplanted into reality, with the full quantity of repression which separates his infantile state from his present one" (Masson 1985, 272).

Freud's secondary train of association concerns *Hamlet*, which he interprets as a repressed version of *Oedipus Rex*. Although Shakespeare's plot does not portray father-murder and mother-son incest, Hamlet's actions make sense, Freud maintains, if understood as expressive of his unconscious desire. Hence Freud reads Hamlet's delay in avenging his father's death as the product of "the torment he suffers from the obscure memory that he himself had contemplated the same deed against his father out of passion for his mother," concluding that Hamlet's "conscience is his unconscious sense of guilt" (273).

In his focus on the "unconscious" substratum of the play, Freud deliberately ignores the surface construction of the plot, which is at least as relevant to his situation as the oedipal interpretation he provides. If we look, for instance, at the material from his childhood that Freud was investigating immediately prior to his pronouncement concerning himself and Oedipus, we may discern other lines of identification with *Hamlet* that he was either unable or unwilling to pursue. To have done so, I maintain, would have led him in the direction of a less optimistic construct than that of oedipal desire, which (however much based in tragedy) manages to obviate the question of death.

Shakespeare's Hamlet suffers not only from feelings of loss concerning his father's death, but also from resentment at his mother's remarriage, which offends him on multiple grounds. She has chosen the wrong person (her brother-in-law Claudius), at the wrong time (within two months of her husband's death), for the wrong reasons (to satisfy her lust). In Hamlet's eyes, her relationship with Claudius is incestuous, adulterous, and possibly even murderous. So deeply does he feel the betrayal of his father's memory that he has the Player Queen speak the lines: "A second time I kill my husband dead,/ When second husband kisses me in bed" (II.ii.194–95), posing a question about Gertrude's complicity in her husband's murder to which the play provides no answer.[12] We, like Hamlet, are left pondering Gertrude's desire, wondering how much she knows.

Among the flood of memories awakened by Freud's grieving process, the most striking ones relate to the period of his earliest childhood. Although Freud separates these figures in his imagination, their images blur around issues of sexuality, betrayal, and loss. These reminiscences seem called to life, moreover, in the absence of a paternal figure, much as Hamlet's torment about his mother's desire is elicited by his father's death. It is as though Freud's present loss speaks to older, deeper wounds. Yet the questions he poses about his early relationship to his mother (and mother-surrogate) are foreclosed in his oedipal construction of family dynamics, which effaces the issue of maternal desire.

The first of Freud's startling discoveries concerns his childhood nurse, whom he refers to as "the 'prime originator' " of his sexuality, "an ugly, elderly, but clever woman who told me a great deal about God Almighty and hell and who instilled in me a high opinion of my own capacities" (Masson 1985, 268). This woman, Freud claims, who washed him in reddish water in which she had previously washed herself and who persuaded him to steal, "was my teacher in sexual matters and complained because I was clumsy and unable to do anything." Freud's recollections of this figure are clearly mixed. Although he associates her with feelings of humiliation and impotence, he also credits her with bolstering his self-esteem. She provided him, he avows, "with the means for living and going on living," so that even now he can feel "the old liking breaking through again" (269).

When Freud asked his mother, Amalie, about this woman, she confirmed his memories of her religious influence on him, correcting him, however, in one particular. Whereas Freud had thought that he was induced by his nurse to steal, it was in fact she who took "shiny new kreuzers and zehners" from him. When this was discovered, Freud's half-brother Philipp fetched the police, and she was sentenced to ten months in prison. Freud's distortion of memory is based on a dream interpretation. "For the dream picture was a memory of my taking money from the mother of a doctor—that is wrongfully. The correct interpretation is: I = she, and the mother of the doctor equals my mother" (275). At midlife, in his dreams, Freud and his nurse are one.

It seems that Freud's nurse treated him badly on several accounts: by sexually seducing him, casting doubt on his abilities, sexual and otherwise, taking money from him, and finally leaving him. Yet Freud cannot suppress an "old liking," even to the point of identifying with her in his dreams. What might he have felt as a child at her sudden, unexplained departure?[13]

Freud asks himself a similar question: "if the old woman disappeared from my life so suddenly, it must be possible to demonstrate the impression this made on me. Where is it then?" The scene he recalls in response introduces a number of considerations that suggest further parallels between his situation and that of Hamlet.

"My mother," Freud relates, "was nowhere to be found; I was crying in despair. My brother Philipp (twenty years older than I) unlocked a wardrobe [*Kasten*] for me, and when I did not find my mother inside it either, I cried even more until, slender and beautiful, she came in through the door." The meaning of this puzzling memory fragment now seems clear. "When I missed my mother," Freud explains, "I was afraid that she had vanished from me, just as the old woman had a short time before." Thinking that his mother has been "boxed up [*eingekastelt*]," like his nurse, Freud looks to his brother for help. "The fact that I turned to him in particular," Freud offers, "proves that I was well aware of his share in the disappearance of the nurse" (272).

Even in its reconstructed state, the scene is fragmentary, yet it evokes powerful trains of association, as Freud reveals in *The Psychopathology of Everyday Life* (1901), where he elaborates on this memory. Here he maintains that his mother was pregnant with his sister Anna at the time that his nurse had committed her thefts. Because of the role his half-brother had played in her dismissal, the boy Sigmund turned to him for clarification when he subsequently missed his mother. "I suspected that my naughty brother had done the same thing to her that he had done to the nurse," Freud explains, "and I forced him to open the cupboard [*Kasten*] for me" (51). He interprets his mother's slimness as an indication that she had recently been delivered of his baby sister.

In a footnote added in 1924, Freud offers a further association to these events. "The wardrobe or cupboard," he now reveals, "was a symbol for him of his mother's insides," hence his insistence on opening the cupboard. "Besides the well-founded suspicion that this brother had had the lost nurse 'boxed up,' there was a further suspicion against him—namely that he had in some way introduced the recently born baby into his mother's inside." Freud's clever brother, who dispatches his nurse and confuses the child with his punning manner of speech, here takes on a more sinister aspect. In the boy's imagination, Philipp "had taken his father's place" through an illicit liaison with his mother—thus aligning his position with that of Claudius in the analogy with *Hamlet*. Instead of a sexual triangle, moreover, as described by the relations among Oedipus, Laius, and Jocasta, we have something more like a quadrangle composed of an absent (or ineffectual) father, an adulterous couple, and a son who feels both confused and aggrieved.

It appears that in the days and weeks preceding his formulation of the oedipal model, Freud was exploring not his childhood rivalry with his father and desire for his mother, but rather his feelings of being displaced or betrayed in an evolving family dynamic that included a dismissed nanny and a mother whose attention was given elsewhere—if not to the distraction of an affair, at least to the very real demands of pregnancy and confinement. In this field of force, the powerful figures appear to be the seductive nurse, sly brother, and enigmatic mother, rather than the classic forbidding father and libidinous son of oedipal theory.

Just as Hamlet senior's death raises questions in the mind of Hamlet about the bounds of his mother's sexuality, Jacob Freud's death seems to have opened a space for his son to explore the question of Amalie Freud's desire. Did she, in fact, as Freud fantasized, betray his father? If so, how could Freud himself rely on her love? These are the kinds of questions that plague Hamlet, who expresses as much emotion over his mother's misdeeds as he does over his uncle's crime. Yet Freud glosses over these issues in his interpretation of Shakespeare's play, choosing a more convoluted explanation of Hamlet's anger and despair.

The image that torments Hamlet and that finally goads him into action (in killing Polonius) is that of Claudius and Gertrude making love. At the same time he spends much of the play repressing (or displacing), not his fantasied desire to kill his father, but his rage against his mother, an emotion that Freud in his long life never admitted to personally and that he scrupulously avoided discussing in theory. Freud's oedipal construct effectively banishes such an unfilial response. Yet the circumstances of his early life suggest more than one reason why the boy Freud might have felt resentment, if not outright anger, at the failure of maternal care.

Between the ages of one and a half and four, Freud suffered a number of potentially traumatic losses, most of which he alludes to (in condensed form) in his letters to Fliess. The first major shock was the birth, followed quickly by the death, of his brother Julius, whom Freud "greeted . . . with adverse wishes and genuine childhood jealousy" and whose death "left the germ of [self-]reproaches" in him (Masson 1985, 268). A circumstance, which Freud does not mention and may have complicated his reactions to the death of Julius, is the fact that his mother's brother, also named Julius, had died the preceding month.[14] That Amalie named her second son after her brother suggests some degree of sisterly affection. Although we have no evidence concerning the nature or extent of her grief, it is likely that her second mourning was compounded by the first. Under these circumstances, Freud may well have felt her unavailability or removal.

At the time of Julius' death in the spring of 1858, moreover, Freud's mother was already pregnant with her third child, Anna, who was born in December of that year. The following month, Freud's nanny was caught stealing and dismissed. Then, in August 1859, Freud's family relocated from Freiberg to Leipzig, a move evidently prompted by the failure of Jacob Freud's business. In less than a year, the family was on the road once again, this time to Vienna, where at last they set down roots. The mere chronology of these events suggests a high degree of disruption in Freud's early life: through death, the arrival of unwanted siblings, the departure of his nurse, the breakup of his extended family system, and loss of their Freiberg home. The reawakening of memories from this period is more than likely to have renewed old feelings of distress.

Freud's memories of his early years touch on other significant themes, such as paternal failure (in business), and maternal sexuality (including nursery seduction and adult infidelity), in addition to sudden unexplained loss and death.[15] So powerful are these issues and so various the possibilities for interpretation that no single narrative seems adequate to frame them. If we compare the plots of the two plays Freud offers as analogues of his psychic life, however, the events of *Hamlet* appear to be more resonant. Yet Freud chose *Oedipus Rex* not only as a means of comprehending his own experience but also that of humankind. What purpose could this momentous decision have served?

"I Now Feel Quite Uprooted"

If we examine Freud's self-analysis in the light of his grieving process, we may achieve a fresh understanding of his oedipal identification. That Freud felt profoundly ambivalent toward his father is clear not only from his handling of the details of his funeral, but also from his self-reproach and accompanying death wishes. That he suffered specifically from feelings of sexual rivalry with him in childhood is much less evident. Rather, Freud's early memories chiefly concern the ambiguous and disturbingly seductive behavior of his mother and his nurse. In this confusing environment, moreover, Freud's own needs for love and reassurance appear to have been overlooked. The emotional tone of these memories is primarily one of anxiety—in response to the multiple dislocations of Freud's early life. So painful was Freud's reaction to his family's departure from Freiberg, for instance, that he associated the gas jets at one of the railway stops with his nanny's description of the fires of hell. His lifelong travel anxiety was evidently due to the effects of this trauma.[16]

Freud's "uprooted" feeling in the aftermath of his father's death speaks to the period in his childhood when he was literally uprooted from his familiar family setting and perhaps similarly distraught.[17] The memories that Freud produces from this time suggest, in addition, that his mother was emotionally preoccupied or unavailable, thus compounding his feelings of anxiety and bewilderment. In this way, Freud's current state of mourning appears to have touched on ancient griefs and fears. Yet these issues do not inform his oedipal theory, which posits a passionately desiring son in relation to conventionally gendered, and otherwise idealized, parental figures.

What is missing from this formulation is an awareness of loss. As Freud later (and here implicitly) rewrites *Oedipus Rex,* for instance, no one has to die. The father's authority will prevent the son from enacting his incestuous desire, hence instilling in him the habit of renunciation necessary for participation in culture. If the mother is unavailable, moreover, it is not because of any wayward desire of her own, but rather because of the son's deference to his father's authority. In such a scenario, there is no weak, ineffectual or dying old man to reckon with, no mother capable of enacting her own will.[18] From this perspective, it appears that Freud did less to uncover than to obscure the intimate dynamics of his family life. If anything, he closed the door on the earliest period of his childhood when he chose the figure of Oedipus to represent his psychic life.

THE SHADOW OF THE OBJECT

The cornerstone position of the Oedipus complex in psychoanalytic theory has made it difficult, if not impossible, for subsequent critics to examine its appropriateness to the material from which it springs.[19] Yet if we consider this construct in the light of Freud's mourning process it appears less transparently self-evident than artfully imposed. In recreating himself as an oedipal subject, Freud clearly found relief from his personal crisis. Yet the Oedipus complex, in displacing questions of early childhood loss, occludes the most critical issues to emerge in the aftermath of Jacob Freud's death.

Freud's construction of an authoritative "oedipal" father not only prevented him from exploring the multiple trajectories of desire within his family system, but it also barred him from conceptualizing maternal eroticism and aggression, while rendering meaningless his childhood anxieties and ambivalences about the adequacy of maternal care. Perhaps most importantly, it created the illusion that social and cultural life begins with a child's recognition of his father's commanding presence in the private sphere of the family, as in the world.

While critical of Freud's reasoning, most feminist psychoanalytic theorists do not seek to dislodge the Oedipus complex per se.[20] Their achievements, as a result, fall short of their radical political aims. A focus on the preoedipal/Imaginary period, however useful in rescuing the figure of the mother from the shadowy background of Freud's theory, does not alter her position within the overall structure that absents her from culture. I believe that feminist theory will remain obstructed by this problem as long as it fails to question the foundational status of the Oedipus complex.

If, however, as I have argued, Freud's oedipal construct serves to displace and occlude a profound crisis of mourning, then we may be free to consider other theoretical prospects in his self-analysis and hence alternate scenarios for the genesis of psychoanalytic theory. We may speculate, for instance, on how psychoanalysis might have developed had Freud chosen to theorize mourning (that is to say, the dynamics of loss), instead of Oedipus.[21] Freud himself offers hints along these lines in his essay "Mourning and Melancholia" (1917), where he picks up threads of his earlier communications with Fliess.

In "Mourning and Melancholia," Freud returns, so to speak, to the scene of mourning, probing more deeply into its painful dynamics than he was evidently capable of doing in the aftermath of his father's death. As if to signal this awareness, Freud also returns to Hamlet, referring to him this time, not as an oedipal subject, but as a classic victim of melancholy. Like the melancholic, who suffers from a disturbance of self-regard, Hamlet sees himself as "petty, egoistic, dishonest, lacking in independence, one whose sole aim has been to hide the weaknesses of his own nature" (1917, 246). Indeed, Freud's whole interest is fixed on this syndrome, which he contrasts with so-called "normal mourning."

Whereas in normal mourning the ego gradually detaches itself from the lost object, releasing affective energy, the melancholic ego, according to Freud, holds on to the loved object through a process of identification.[22] This mechanism derives from "the preliminary stage of object-choice," or the oral phase. "The ego wants to incorporate this object into itself," Freud explains, "and, in accordance with the oral or cannibalistic phase of libidinal development in which it is, it wants to do so by devouring it" (249–50). "By taking flight into the ego," as Freud states poetically, "love escapes extinction" (257).

Yet the love preserved in this way is full of conflict. "The loss of a love-object," Freud allows, "is an excellent opportunity for the ambivalence in love-relationships to make itself effective and come into the open." In melancholia, especially, "the occasions which give rise to the illness extend for the most part beyond the clear case of a loss by death, and include all those situations of being slighted, neglected or disappointed, which can import opposed feelings of love and hate into the relationship or reinforce an already existing ambivalence." Because the subject has incorporated the loved object, moreover, anger or hatred will be directed against the self. In this way, the melancholic's rage "comes into operation on this substitutive object, abusing it, debasing it, making it suffer and deriving sadistic satisfaction from its suffering" (251).

Freud's understanding of melancholic identification as a psychic mechanism inherited from the oral phase suggests that he is thinking about the earliest stages of love and loss, and hence the period in his own life when he was most vulnerable to disruptions of maternal care. If this is so, Freud may well have been describing the residue of his childhood reactions to his mother and his nurse, neither of whom died, yet both of whom disappeared temporarily or permanently and evoked ambivalent emotions. While Freud's nurse aroused him, shamed him, and left him, his mother simply (and perhaps of necessity) turned her attentions elsewhere. Although Freud does not directly address the issue of maternal loss, it hovers in the background of his description of melancholia, as a kind of shadow text.

A powerful metaphor, moreover, links Freud's discussion of melancholia with his thoughts on the same subject in 1895, indicating that Freud was preoccupied with this subject *before* his father's death and hence prior to his mourning for that loss. In a draft statement to Fliess (included in an envelope postmarked January 1895), Freud offers a neurological explanation of the dynamics of melancholia.[23] As a result of "a very great loss in the amount of excitation," he states, "there may come about *an indrawing, as it were, into the psychic sphere,* which produces an effect of suction upon the adjoining amounts of excitation." This giving up of excitation produces pain. Next, "there sets in, as though through an *internal hemorrhage,* an impoverishment in excitation," which "operates like a *wound.*" Comparing this process to neurasthenia, in which excitation runs out, "as it were, through a hole," Freud concludes that "in melancholia the hole is in the psychic sphere" (Masson 1985, 103–4).

Freud's imagery of sucking in anticipates his description of oral incorporation in "Mourning and Melancholia," where the wound metaphor also recurs. Here he states that "the complex of melancholia behaves like an open wound, drawing to itself cathectic energies . . . and emptying the ego until it is totally impoverished" (1917, 253). This account, while less graphic than his earlier one, portrays the same dynamic. Evidently attached to this idea, Freud repeats it toward the conclusion of his essay where he tries, rather unsuccessfully, to explain how melancholia comes to an end. "The conflict within the ego," he suggests, "which melancholia substitutes for the struggle over the object, must act like a painful wound which calls for an extraordinarily high anti-cathexis" (258). Whereas the mourner gradually accepts the fact that "the object no longer exists," the melancholic must somehow manage to eject it, by "disparaging it, denigrating it, and even as it were killing it," in order to obtain relief (255, 257).

Freud's discomfort with this explanation manifests itself in the abruptness with which he brings his essay to a close. Immediately after invoking the wound metaphor, he admits: "But here once again, it will be well to call a halt. . . . As we already know, the interdependence of the complicated problems of the mind forces us to break off every enquiry before it is completed—till the outcome of some other enquiry can come to its assistance" (258). The effect of these concluding remarks is to hold the wound metaphor in suspension, as if melancholia itself were an interminable illness.

Freud's investigation into the dynamics of melancholia at least a year and a half before his father's death suggests that more than so-called normal mourning is at issue. Since he (as well as his patients) suffered from depression at this time, it seems likely that his theoretical labor was autobiographically informed from the beginning. Taking these suppositions together with the memories of early childhood loss that emerged in the aftermath of Jacob Freud's death and the specifically oral nature of Freud's description of melancholia in the 1917 essay, one might easily speculate that the "open wound" metaphor he uses to convey the psychic affect of melancholia also gives expression to his feelings about the ruptures and losses of his early life.

What is most striking about the wound metaphor, of course, is its resemblance to Freud's later language about castration, a condition that he attributes literally only to females. While the boy may act to repress his desire for his mother under the *threat* of castration, only the girl *experiences* it through her awareness of phallic lack. Whereas the sight of the little girl's genitals arouses a "terrible storm of emotion" in the boy, who feels a "horror of the mutilated creature," as Freud states in "Some Psychical Consequences of the Anatomical Distinction between the Sexes" (1925), the girl incurs a "wound to her narcissism" and "develops, like a scar, a sense of inferiority" (252–53). Melancholia, in contrast, is not gender marked. Both boys and girls, men and women, may be subject to its wounding, internal hemorrhaging, and psychic scars.

Whereas Freud's concept of the castration complex acts to displace and defer the threat of wounding for the boy, his representation of melancholia as a painful hole in the psyche suggests otherwise. For the melancholic, struggling to preserve his (or her) love objects, castration has always already taken place. Such a construction of lack—as primary loss—not only obviates the gender imbalance of Freud's oedipal construct, but it also avoids the problem of positing separation, or the inception of the Symbolic stage, as a function of the father.[24] Only if one imagines an originary state of blissful mother-infant union, moreover, does such a step become necessary.[25]

When Freud looked back to his early childhood, what he remembered was not a paradisal condition of oneness with his mother, but rather multiple contexts of pain, disappointment, and loss. Although he invented psychoanalysis under the sign of mourning—for his father Jacob Freud and for the child he once was—he chose to theorize from a text that offered him more consoling images. Out of the tragic material of *Oedipus Rex,* Freud forged a hopeful, if sober, psychic construct. Perhaps more importantly, he fashioned a family he could live with—one that revolved around a vigorous and commanding father, an ideally loving mother, and a lively, upstart son. Having taken this momentous step, he rarely looked back. As if in response to the dream request to close the eyes, Freud appears to have averted his gaze from the scene of mourning, effectively deferring the question of his own grief.

Yet Freud's image of pathological mourning as an open wound attests to the hold of this issue over his imagination, in addition to its status as an ongoing theoretical problem. Given Freud's own depression both before and after Jacob Freud's death, one might say that psychoanalysis, insofar as it originates in his self-analysis, begins, not with Oedipus, but with the wound. One might even say that for Freud, being *in* psychoanalysis (founding it, laboring within it) was like being *in* mourning.[26]

For Freud, loss is not a foundational concept. Being in mourning, like being "uprooted," was perhaps too painful a position for him to contemplate as a basis for psychoanalytic theory as a whole. From the perspective of feminism, however, it may offer a more useful starting point than the Oedipus construct, which decides one's sexual and cultural destiny with a single phallic stroke.

Notes

1. J. J. Bachofen, in *Mother-Right* (1861), postulates an early matriarchal stage of the family in which women exercised power. At the same time, he considers the emergence of the patriarchal family as a definite advance in human civilization. Many other nineteenth-century theorists accept the idea of a matrilineal phase in human history, while rejecting Bachofen's concept of matriarchy per se. Freud, while reluctant to posit an *initial* matriarchal phase, nevertheless tried to incorporate the notion of matriarchy as a transitional moment in the evolution from an original father-dominated primal horde to the modern form of the patriarchal family. His discomfort with the very idea of matriarchy, however, manifests itself in the confused accounts he gives of this process in *Totem and Taboo* (1913) and in *Moses and Monotheism* (1939). I treat this subject (including the complicating factor of Freud's rivalry with Jung) at greater length in *The Spectral Mother* (1990, 86–119).

2. Juliet Mitchell, in *Psychoanalysis and Feminism* (1974), makes a case for reading Freud in a descriptive, rather than a prescriptive sense. In this way, she argues, we may better comprehend the unconscious structure of patriarchy—as a necessary first step in dismantling it. While Mitchell reads Freud through the lens of Lacanian theory, Nancy Chodorow offers an object relations approach. In her enormously influential book *The Reproduction of Mothering* (1978), she analyzes the development of masculinity and femininity within the confines of the patriarchal nuclear family. Paradoxically, however, the very success of her exposition has proved an obstacle to envisioning social change, as many feminists have found her description of feminine development within patriarchy more attractive than otherwise.

3. Stephen Mitchell, in *Hope and Dread in Psychoanalysis* (1993), gives a lucid account of the developments in psychoanalytic theory since Freud that have combined to displace his drive theory model of interpretation in favor of a more interactive approach, one that recognizes the subjective situation of both analyst and analysand in the construction of meaning. Psychoanalysis, he believes, participates in the shift toward perspectivist explanation that characterizes contemporary philosophy and science. "For Freud," he observes, "psychoanalysis was embedded in the broad, invigorating, reassuring, scaffolding of the scientific worldview. . . . That scaffolding does not sustain us in the same way it did for Freud and his contemporaries, cannot sustain us; this fact has, in some sense, stranded psychoanalysis, unmoored it from the context that gave it its original meaning. Those who think of analysis in ways similar to our analytic ancestors seem to most of us today more like cultists than scientists" (21).

4. Feminists who take psychoanalysis seriously, at one point or another, come up against the Oedipus complex. For a while during the 1970s, it seemed that an emphasis on the preoedipal period might offer a theoretical avenue of escape from the imposition of oedipal authority. The *a priori* definition of this phase as standing somewhere outside of the Symbolic order, however, limits the possibilities for the liberation of female (and maternal) subjectivity. More recently, feminists have focused either on locating the mother-infant relationship *within* the Symbolic order or on redefining the Oedipus complex in such a way as to soften its patriarchal implications. Kaja Silverman offers an example of the former strategy in *The Acoustic Mirror* (1988), where she proposes a new reading of the mother-daughter relationship. "To situate the daughter's passion for the mother within the Oedipus complex," she argues, "is to make it an effect of language and loss, and so to contextualize both it and the sexuality it implies firmly within the symbolic" (123). Jessica Benjamin (1988), rather than accepting the presymbolic/symbolic dichotomy (and hence the location of men and women on opposite sides of the cultural divide), offers a redefinition of the Oedipus complex from the standpoint of intersubjective theory. "The three pillars of oedipal theory," she concludes, "the primacy of the wish for oneness, the mother's embodiment of this regressive force, and the necessity of paternal

intervention—all combine to create the paradox that the only liberation is paternal domination. . . . By going beyond Oedipus we can envisage a direct struggle for recognition between man and woman, free of the shadow of the father that falls between them" (181). While I am in sympathy with these (and other) efforts to reposition women in relation to the Oedipus complex, I prefer to interrogate the process by which Freud arrived at this problematic construct.

5. Ernest Jones, until recently Freud's most eminent biographer, considers Freud's self-analysis as "his most heroic feat." Far from questioning Freud's (or anyone's) capacity to carry out such a task, he valorizes its achievement. "It is hard for us nowadays," he states, "to imagine how momentous this achievement was, that difficulty being the fate of most pioneering exploits. Yet the uniqueness of the feat remains. Once done it is done forever. For no one again can be the first to explore those depths" (1953, 319). Peter Gay, who brings Jones' work up to date, admits that "self-analysis would seem to be a contradiction in terms," yet he excuses Freud on the grounds that he had "no teachers but had to invent the rules for it as he went along" and he does not question its results (1988, 96, 98).

6. See, for instance, Liz Stanley's *The Auto/biographical I* (1992), which summarizes the developments in Foucaultian and poststructuralist theory that give rise to these assumptions. See also William Epstein's *Contesting the Subject* (1991) for reflections on how contemporary views of the self affect the writing of biography.

7. Mark Edmundson, whose argument parallels mine in certain respects, sees Freud's invention of the Oedipus complex as an act of self-creation. "Freud's textual practice," he states, "suggests . . . that the Oedipal complex is the negative term in a symbolic drama of private self-recreation, the fruit of which is a new discourse, a new terminological field" (1990, 41). Edmundson regards Freud's oedipal narrative as confining and recommends a skeptical stance toward this aspect of his achievement.

8. I am indebted to Peter Rudnytsky's *Freud and Oedipus* (1987) for this account.

9. This behavior recurred, in a more extreme form, at Freud's mother's death in 1930. Freud not only did not attend her funeral, but he also seems to have experienced more relief than grief. Given that Amalie died at the age of ninety-five and that her son was himself seventy-four at the time, it may not be surprising that Freud felt no active pain. Yet the parallel with his earlier avoidance behavior around his father's funeral suggests otherwise. Herbert Lehmann (1983) speculates that Freud's very identification with his mother from an early age made it difficult for him to acknowledge the reality of her loss. Harry Hardin, who sees Freud's relationship with his mother as profoundly ambivalent, offers the explanation that he sent his daughter Anna as a "mourner by proxy," because she "could grieve without the constraints her father experienced because of his lifelong alienation from her grandmother" (1988a, 85). Peter Homans observes that in Freud's "unconscious his anxiety about his own death and his anxiety

about his mother's death were probably linked, condensed, maybe even inter-changeable." He connects Freud's "psychological sense of his own death" in later life with this profound identification (1989, 98).

10. Marianne Krüll makes this point in a different way. She reads the dream injunction "to close the eyes" as Freud's warning to himself against exploring his father's tendencies toward perversity, among which she includes his (presumed) habit of masturbation. She concludes that "the two central threads running through Freud's entire theoretical and therapeutic work—the subject of sex-uality, which was to become the pivot of his theory of human behavior, and the subject of guilt of the sons toward the father . . . were the very areas in which Jacob Freud himself felt beset with guilt" (1986, 101). Jeffrey Masson (1984) emphasizes Freud's conflict of allegiance between his patient Emma Eckstein and his friend Wilhelm Fliess (over the matter of Fliess' bungled operation on her nose), arguing that Freud chose to side with Fliess rather than with Eckstein when he abandoned the seduction theory. For Samuel Slipp, the most important factor in Freud's repudiation of the seduction theory is his problematic relationship with his mother. He speculates that "Freud abandoned the Seduction theory as an attempt to deny the traumatic impact of others, since he could not deal with a pre-Oedipal conflict with his mother" (Slipp 1988, 155). Larry Wolff (1988) locates the discussion of Freud's seduction theory in the context of several well-publicized trials involving child abuse at the turn of the century in Vienna, making the point that Freud would have had deliberately to ignore the questions raised by these scandals in order to relinquish his own theory.

11. Marianne Krüll believes that Jacob Freud conveyed an unspoken mandate to his son, that he "was expected to turn his back on tradition but not on one of its most central tenets, that of filial piety on which, ultimately, the entire Jewish tradition is based" (1986, 178). In the face of his father's death, Freud was unable to resist this mandate, and hence, "dutiful son that he was, took the guilt upon his own shoulders with the help of his Oedipus theory" (179). Although I do not agree with every point of Krüll's argument concerning Jacob Freud's transgres-sions, I believe that her reading of Freud's inability to point the finger of blame at his father after his death is accurate.

12. In one of Shakespeare's sources, Geruth (Gertrude) betrays her husband *before* his death with his brother Fengon (Claudius), thus raising the suspicion "that she had been the causer of the murther, thereby to live in her adultery without controle" (Belleforest 1992, 136). See Janet Adelman's *Suffocating Mothers* (1992, 25–26) for a lucid exposition of the fantasy content of the Player Queen's lines.

13. In a series of essays on Freud's early mothering, Harry Hardin (1987, 1988a, 1988b) argues that a child's loss of a surrogate mother is fully as traumatic as the loss of a biological mother. He believes that Freud experienced some alienation from his actual mother as a result of his having had a nanny, but that he could not admit to these feelings.

14. Samuel Slipp provides this information. He believes that Amalie Freud's unhappiness made it difficult for her to respond fully to the needs of her first-born son. After listing the multiple disappointments of her early marriage, he concludes that by the time the family left Freiberg, "not only may she have felt disillusioned and trapped in her marriage, but in all likelihood she was in mourning for her dead brother and son" (1988, 158).

15. There is general agreement that Freud's father was mild-tempered and nonauthoritarian in manner, and that his easy-going nature stood in contrast to that of his wife. Robert Holt (1992) and Estelle Roith (1987) explore the reversal of conventional gender roles in Freud's family as it affected his construction of theory. William McGrath (1986) believes that Jacob Freud's lack of resistance to anti-Semitic insult meant that he could not provide a masculine model for his son, while Samuel Slipp (1988) sees Jacob's failure in business as possibly contributing to Amalie Freud's disappointment with him as a husband.

16. Freud himself makes the connection between the sight of the gas jets and his travel phobia (Masson 1985, 285).

17. Freud's word for uprooted is "*entwurzelt.*" Mark Edmundson notes: "To be uprooted is to be naked, vulnerable, exposed, but also to take up a new position, unburied and unblinded, in a fresh relation to experience" (1990, 43). I am inclined to lay the emphasis on Freud's sense of vulnerability and exposure.

18. Kathleen Woodward comments astutely: "*The Interpretation of Dreams* may be read as a son's book of mourning for his father, albeit a strange one. But I also want to insist that to the extent the figure of the dead father dominates the book in the abstract, the figure of the infirm and aged father haunts it. It is aging, not death, which castrates the father. . . . The infirm father is all too literally present as painfully weak" (1991, 33).

19. Didier Anzieu's treatment of Freud's articulation of the Oedipus complex, though somewhat hyperbolical, is typical of the way most readers approach this subject. He writes: "In the course of his discovery of the Oedipus myth, Freud completes the threefold process—at once subjective, objective, and self-representing—which began to get under way at the start of his self-analysis. It is the discovery of a universal truth; the discovery of himself; and the discovery of itself, by which I mean the correlative discovery of the very process through which the main discovery is made" (1986, 244).

20. One might argue that reformulating the Oedipus complex in such a way as to dissolve its primary impact constitutes an effort to abolish it, yet those whose work might be construed in this way do not make this claim. Shoshana Felman, for instance, so thoroughly rewrites the Oedipus complex in her essay "Beyond Oedipus" (1987, 99–159) that one might wonder how much of Freud's concept remains. At the same time, she does not propose changing Freud's nomenclature.

21. A case could be made that Melanie Klein's (1935) concept of the depressive position works a transformation of this sort. Yet she herself does not make this

claim, and her allegiance to the Oedipus complex, however reworked in her system of thought, stands in the way of a full break from Freud. Julia Kristeva's *Black Sun* (1989) comes close to such a break by emphasizing loss as the point of departure for the subject's entry into language. However, Kristeva adheres to Lacan's assumption of the necessity of third-party intervention (the function of the father) in order for this development to take place, hence invoking the phallus as a privileged signifier. Peter Homans (1989) sees the invention of psychoanalysis as a work of personal and cultural mourning, but he does not critique the outcome of this process.

22. Kathleen Woodward comments on the inadequacy of Freud's account of "normal mourning." "In this unequivocal distinction [between mourning and melancholia]," she observes, "I find a peculiar kind of piety, an almost ethical injunction to kill the dead and to adjust ourselves to 'reality.' In 'Mourning and Melancholia' Freud leaves us no theoretical room for another place, one between a crippling melancholia and the end of mourning" (1991, 116). I am very much indebted to this insight.

23. Freud later abandoned the attempt to blend psychology with neurology. For a full discussion of the impact of Freud's neurological training on his psycho-analytic constructs, see Frank Sulloway's *Freud: Biologist of the Mind* (1979).

24. I have argued this position more extensively in *The Spectral Mother* (1990), where I make a case for regarding the ego as an "elegiac construct."

25. According to Daniel Stern, contemporary observations of mother-infant interactions reveal that there is no such thing as a period of mother-infant sym-biosis. He states: "Infants begin to experience a sense of self from birth. They are predesigned to be aware of self-organizing processes. They never experience a period of total self/other undifferentiation. There is no confusion between self and other in the beginning or at any point during infancy" (1985, 10).

26. Peter Homans (1989), who regards psychoanalysis as the result of Freud's *ability* to mourn, emphasizes the success of this process. My focus, in contrast, is on the inhibited or failed aspects of Freud's mourning and his consequent *in-ability* to acknowledge the full impact of loss.

References

Adelman, J. 1992. *Suffocating Mothers: Fantasies of Maternal Origin in Shakespeare's Plays, "Hamlet" to "The Tempest."* New York: Routledge.

Anzieu, D. 1975. *Freud's Self-Analysis.* Trans. P. Graham. London: Hogarth, 1986.

Bachofen, J. J. 1926. *Myth, Religion, and Mother-Right.* Trans. R. Manheim. Prince-ton, N.J.: Princeton Univ. Press, 1967.

Belleforest, F. de. 1992. *The Hystorie of Hamblet, Prince of Denmarke.* In William Shakespeare, Hamlet, ed. C. Hoy. New York: Norton, pp. 134–43.

Benjamin, J. 1988. *The Bonds of Love: Psychoanalysis, Feminism, and the Problem of Domination.* New York: Pantheon.

Chodorow, N. 1978. *The Reproduction of Mothering: Psychoanalysis and the Sociology of Gender.* Berkeley: Univ. of California Press.

Edmundson, M. 1990. *Towards Reading Freud: Self-Creation in Milton, Wordsworth, Emerson, and Sigmund Freud.* Princeton, N.J.: Princeton Univ. Press.

Epstein, W., ed. 1991. *Contesting the Subject: Essays in the Postmodern Theory and Practice of Biography and Biographical Criticism.* West Lafayette, Ind.: Purdue Univ. Press.

Felman, S. 1987. *Jacques Lacan and the Adventure of Insight: Psychoanalysis in Contemporary Culture.* Cambridge: Harvard Univ. Press.

Freud, E., ed. 1975. *The Letters of Sigmund Freud.* Trans. T. and J. Stern. New York: Basic Books.

Freud, S. 1900. *The Interpretation of Dreams.* In *The Standard Edition of the Complete Psychological Works,* ed. and trans. J. Strachey et al. 24 vols. (hereafter S.E.). London: Hogarth, 1953–74, vols. 4 and 5.

———. 1901. *The Psychopathology of Everyday Life. S.E.,* vol. 6.

———. 1910. A Special Type of Choice of Object Made by Men. *S.E.,* 11:163–75.

———. 1913. *Totem and Taboo. S.E.,* 13:1–161.

———. 1917. Mourning and Melancholia. *S.E.,* 14:237–58.

———. 1925. Some Psychical Consequences of the Anatomical Distinction between the Sexes. *S.E.,* 19:241–58.

———. 1939. *Moses and Monotheism. S.E.,* 23:1–137.

Gay, P. 1988. *Freud: A Life for Our Time.* New York: Norton.

Hardin, H. 1987. On the Vicissitudes of Freud's Early Mothering: Early Environment and Loss. *Psychoanal. Q.* 56:628–44.

———. 1988a. On the Vicissitudes of Freud's Early Mothering: Alienation from His Biological Mother. *Psychoanal. Q.* 57:72–86.

———. 1988b. On the Vicissitudes of Freud's Early Mothering: Freiberg, Screen Memories, and Loss. *Psychoanal. Q.* 57:209–23.

Holt, R. 1992. Freud's Paternal Identifications as a Source of Some Contradictions within Psychoanalysis. In T. Gelfand and J. Kerr, eds., *Freud and the History of Psychoanalysis.* Hillsdale, N.J.: Analytic Press, pp. 1–28.

Homans P. 1989. *The Ability to Mourn: Disillusionment and the Social Origins of Psychoanalysis.* Chicago: Univ. of Chicago Press.

Jones, E. 1953. *The Life and Work of Sigmund Freud,* 3 vols., 1953, 1955, 1957. New York: Basic.

Jung, C. G. 1912. *Psychology of the Unconscious (Transformations and Symbols of the Libido).* Trans. B. Hinkle. New York: Moffat, 1916.

Klein, M. 1935. A Contribution to the Psychogenesis of Manic-Depressive States. In *The Selected Melanie Klein,* ed. J. Mitchell. New York: Free Press, 1987, pp. 115–45.

Kristeva, J. 1989. *Black Sun: Depression and Melancholia.* Trans. L. Roudiez. New York: Columbia Univ. Press.

Krüll, M. 1979. *Freud and His Father.* Trans. A. J. Pomerans. New York: Norton, 1986.

Lehmann, H. 1983. Reflections on Freud's Reaction to the Death of His Mother. *Psychoanal. Q.* 52:237–49.

McGrath, W. J. 1985. *Freud's Discovery of Psychoanalysis: The Politics of Hysteria.* Ithaca, N.Y.: Cornell Univ. Press.

Masson, J. 1984. *The Assault on Truth: Freud's Suppression of the Seduction Theory.* New York: Farrar, Strauss & Giroux.

———., trans. and ed. 1985. *The Complete Letters of Sigmund Freud to Wilhelm Fliess, 1887–1904.* Cambridge: Harvard Univ. Press.

Mitchell, J. 1974. *Psychoanalysis and Feminism.* New York: Pantheon.

Mitchell, S. 1993. *Hope and Dread in Psychoanalysis.* New York: Basic Books.

Roith, E. 1987. *The Riddle of Freud: Jewish Influences on His Theory of Female Sexuality.* London: Tavistock.

Rudnytsky, P. 1987. *Freud and Oedipus.* New York: Columbia Univ. Press.

Shakespeare, W. 1992. *Hamlet,* ed. C. Hoy. New York: Norton.

Silverman, K. 1988. *The Acoustic Mirror: The Female Voice in Psychoanalysis and Cinema.* Bloomington: Indiana Univ. Press.

Slipp, S. 1988. Freud's Mother, Ferenczi, and the Seduction Theory. *J. Am. Acad. Psychoanal.* 16:155–65.

Sprengnether, M. 1990. *The Spectral Mother: Freud, Feminism, and Psychoanalysis.* Ithaca, N.Y.: Cornell Univ. Press.

Stanley, L. 1992. *The Auto/biographical I: The Theory and Practice of Feminist Auto/biography.* Manchester: Manchester Univ. Press.

Stern, D. 1985. *The Interpersonal World of the Infant: A View from Psychoanalysis and Developmental Psychology.* New York: Basic Books.

Sulloway, F. 1979. *Freud: Biologist of the Mind.* New York: Basic Books.

Wolff, L. 1988. *Postcards from the End of the World: Child Abuse in Freud's Vienna.* New York: Atheneum.

Woodward, K. 1991. *Aging and Its Discontents: Freud and Other Fictions.* Bloomington: Indiana Univ. Press.

Chapter Two

"Mother, Do You Have a Wiwimaker, Too?": Freud's Representation of Female Sexuality in the Case of Little Hans

Peter L. Rudnytsky

It is by now commonplace to observe that Freud's case histories are themselves great works of literature that demand to be read with the sophisticated techniques of literary criticism.[1] Whatever one may think of Freud's ideas, there can be no doubt of his brilliance as a writer. Indeed, it is a testimony to Freud's genius that his works continue to be sources of instruction and inspiration for each new generation of readers, however much one finds in them to dispute.

The case of Little Hans, otherwise known as *Analysis of a Phobia in a Five-Year-Old Boy* (1909), has a special place in the annals of psychoanalysis because it is the first recorded instance of a child analysis. Part of the distinctiveness of the case, moreover, is that the child in question, whose real name was Herbert Graf, was not analyzed by Freud himself (though he did see the child for a single consultation) but by his own father, the musicologist Max Graf, who belonged to the small group of Freud's adherents that in 1908 became known as the Vienna Psychoanalytic Society. The complex narrative structure inherent in any case history, which must strive to capture the dynamics both of the treatment process and of the patient's life, is thus compounded by the way that Freud's text contains extensive extracts of dialogue and other material reported by the father, punctuated by Freud's editorial comments. The effect is to create a multilayered text, much like a work of modernist fiction, in which Hans plays the part of the hero, the father of the unreliable narrator, and Freud of the omniscient narrator.[2] Underlying these formal intricacies is what by today's standards would be deemed the highly irregular transferential situation, in which the father combined the roles of parent and analyst and had in addition his own deeply invested relationship to Freud.[3] Hans's mother, moreover, had herself been a patient of Freud's, and it was thanks to her that her husband had been introduced first to Freud's work and then to the man himself in 1900 (Graf 1942, 467). Rather than the therapy of an individual child, therefore, the case of Little Hans is better understood as an instance of family therapy, a precursor of Freud's own even more dubious experiment in commingling parental and professional roles in his prolonged analysis of his daughter Anna (Mahony 1992).[4]

In what follows, I shall approach the case of Little Hans from a feminist standpoint. Precisely because it constitutes Freud's quintessential depiction of the crystallization of masculine sexuality and identity, I shall argue, this text likewise shows the genesis of his views on sexual difference and *female* sexuality, which are codified in his notorious later papers. It thus calls for a critique along the lines laid down by Luce Irigaray (1974) in her brilliant dissection of Freud's chapter on "Femininity" in his *New Introductory Lectures on Psycho-Analysis* (1933).[5] Accordingly, I shall examine Freud's confused and misogynistic attitudes toward female sexuality in Little Hans and show their connection to his phallocentric perspective; in a brief coda, I shall contend that the case also reveals a heterosexist bias.

The first words of Little Hans, spoken before the age of three and two years before the outbreak of his phobia, to be reported by his father and quoted by Freud in his case history, are the question: "'Mother, do you have a wiwimaker [*Wiwimacher*], too?'" (*G.W.*, 7:245; *S.E.*, 10:7).[6] Like the first communication by a patient entering analysis, these words acquire an ever-increasing resonance and can by the end of the process be seen to have held the key to the entire mystery. Strictly speaking, Hans's "analysis"—if we deign to refer to the didactic interest taken by his father in Hans's condition by this term—has not yet commenced; but insofar as Hans's analysis now exists only in the form of Freud's written record, everything that is contained therein may be said to belong to it.

The question of whether or not women possess a penis is no less urgent for Freudian theory as a whole than it is for Little Hans's analysis. Indeed, if we regard all of Freud's writings as fragments of his interminable self-analysis, it is not difficult to surmise that the introduction of this issue as a leitmotif is determined chiefly by Freud's own preoccupations. When, fifteen years later, Freud in "The Infantile Genital Organization" codifies his conviction that initially "for both sexes, only one genital, namely the male one, comes into account" by the interpolation of the phallic phase into his libido theory (1923, 142), he does so with reference to the case of Little Hans.[7] Pursuing the same line of thought, he explains fetishism (1927) exclusively in phallic terms (ignoring its potential, for example, to serve as a defense against unduly abrupt separation from the maternal breast) as a means of repressing castration anxiety, triggered by the boy's glimpse of the female genitals, a substitute for the disavowed missing penis of the mother.

In probing the way that sexual difference is presented in the case of Little Hans, we find confusion perpetrated at every turn by adults—by Little Hans's parents and above all by Freud—and the child doing his best to sort things out for himself. To Hans's repeated queries about whether she has a wiwimaker, his mother answers "'of course'" and "'naturally'" (*G.W.*, 7:245, 247; *S.E.*, 10:7, 10).[8] Like his parents' promulgation of the fable that the stork is responsible for bringing his baby sister Hanna, this misleading account of the female genitalia deserves to be called a lie. Linked to sexual difference is the distinction between what is animate and inanimate, and here too the wiwimaker comes into play. At three and three quarters, Hans sees a locomotive from which water is being released and says it is "'making wiwi.'" He wonders where its wiwimaker is located. He adds on reflection: "'A dog and a horse have a wiwimaker; a table and a chair don't.'" On this Freud comments: "So he has gained an essential characteristic for differentiating between the animate and the inanimate" (*G.W.*, 7:246–47; *S.E.*, 10:9).

The confusion into which Hans is led by those who should know better is not only anatomical but also semantic. Indeed, in the interplay between biological and linguistic frames of reference in the term "wiwimaker," we can observe the penis in the process of becoming the phallus or transcendental signifier in the strict Lacanian sense of this term. Although by "wiwimaker" Hans most obviously means "penis," the word itself refers to an organ for urination, which women of course do possess. Thus, in one sense Hans's mother is correct to say that she does have a wiwimaker, though not in the disingenuous way that she implies. That Hans is concerned not simply with whether women have a penis but with how they urinate is made clear when he asks his father: "'But how do girls make wiwi if they don't have a wiwimaker?'" His father gives him an evasive answer: "'They don't have a wiwimaker like yours. Haven't you seen when Hanna has been given a bath?'" Moments earlier, however, Hans's father had told him that "girls and women don't have a wiwimaker" (*G.W.*, 7:267; *S.E.*, 10:31). These statements do not cohere. The father uses "wiwimaker" ambiguously to say both that women possess an anatomy unlike Hans's and that they do not have a penis. He thus simultaneously defines women in terms of a lack when measured against a male norm and adumbrates the possibility of regarding the two sexes as different but equal (though the word "wiwimaker" retains an androcentric bias that forever precludes this possibility from being realized).

Freud, as I have indicated, far from mitigating Little Hans's bewilderment, actually exacerbates it. His ready acceptance of the equation between the female and the inanimate is especially disturbing. (As one of my students at the University of Florida exclaimed, "I guess I'm a table!"). In the final section of his narrative, "Epicrisis,"[9] Freud reiterates that Hans "discovers that on the basis of the readiness-to-hand [*Vorhanden-seins*] or absence of the wiwimaker one can differentiate between what is living and lifeless" (*G.W.*, 7:341; *S.E.*, 10:106). By treating this hypothesis as a "discovery" on Hans's part, instead of as a childish error, Freud remakes Hans in his own image as a phallocrat. Of course, Hans uses his own body as a basis for comparison and wonders how his mother and other females are different. But the point of his questions is precisely to clarify how they are different, not to assume that they must be identical. That is *Freud's* mistake, not Hans's. He writes of Hans's displays of affection toward boy as well as girl playmates: "Hans is homosexual, as all children may well be, completely in accordance with the not to be over-looked fact that he only *knows one kind of genital*, a genital like his own" (*G.W.*, 7:344–45; *S.E.*, 10:110; Freud's italics). By employing the collective noun "children" (*Kinder*) instead of the gender-specific "boys" (*Knaben*), Freud elides the situation of girls, who presumably also take their own bodies as a point of reference even though, according to his theory, they too only know one kind of genital—that belonging to males.[10] (How girls, who supposedly know only genitals *unlike* their own, could ever become homosexual remains mysterious in Freud's account.)

Freud's insistence on the primacy of the phallus is allied to his conviction of the centrality of the castration complex to the discovery of sexual difference. The case of Little Hans provides the prototype upon which he bases this claim; not coincidentally, the term "castration complex" is introduced with reference to it.[11] In a pattern that Freud does not hesitate to call "typical for the sexual development of the child" (*G.W.*, 7:245; *S.E.*, 10:7), Hans is first threatened by his mother with castration as a punishment for masturbation and later catches sight of the genitalia of his baby sister, which brings home to him the reality of this threat. The structure of retrospective signification linking these two events exemplifies a distinctively psychoanalytic mode of temporality. As Freud remarks, "it would be entirely the typical procedure if the threat of castration now came to effect through *deferred action [nachträglich]*" (*G.W.*, 7:271; *S.E.*, 10:35).

In order to realize how deep an impression the case of Little Hans left on Freud's thinking, it suffices to quote the following passage from "Femininity" in the *New Introductory Lectures:*

> In [boys] the castration complex arises after they have learnt from the sight of the female genitals that the organ which they value so highly need not necessarily accompany the body. At this the boy recalls to mind the threats

he brought on himself by his doings with that organ, he begins to give credence to them and falls under the influence of fear of castration, which will be the most powerful motive force in his subsequent development. (1933, 124–25)

Freud does not cite the analysis of Little Hans as corroboration, but he has clearly relied on it as a precedent. Not only is there an identical sequence of events—a verbal threat followed by a visual glimpse—but Freud's emphasis on the gaze that defines the female genitalia in terms of absence is crucial to the case. The primacy of the phallus thus has as its corollary the primacy of the gaze, and both define female sexuality simply as the negative of the male. The above-quoted passage from "Femininity" continues: "The castration complex of girls is also started by the sight of the other sex" (22:125).[12]

Hans's father's equivocal pronouncements about the female genitalia are efforts to implement the advice of Freud. In order to rid Hans of his desire to see his mother's genitals and set him on the "way to sexual enlightenment," Freud counsels, his father should inform him at a propitious moment that "his mama and all other female beings—as indeed he could know from Hanna—do not possess a wiwimaker at all" (*G.W.*, 7:264; *S.E.*, 10:28). The problem here again is that of defining women solely in terms of privation. As Jules Glenn has observed, "Hans was to be told that a girl has no penis, thus indicating that she is deficient," and not that a girl "has a vulva (including the clitoris), vagina, and uterus" (1980, 125).[13] Although it might not have been necessary to enter with Little Hans into encyclopedic detail concerning the female anatomy, it surely ought to have been possible to present the facts of life to him in a less distorted way. When Freud writes that "the enlightenment . . . that women truly do not have a wiwimaker can only have shattered his self-confidence and awakened his castration complex" (*G.W.*, 7:271; *S.E.*, 10:36), he is right in his assessment of the traumatic effects on Little Hans of his father's lessons, but wrong to dignify misinformation by calling it "enlightenment."

Despite Freud's recommendation that Hans be told that women do not have a wiwimaker, moreover, Hans's father persists in using this word. "'You know, don't you, how Hanna's wiwimaker looks?'" (*G.W.*, 7:297; *S.E.*, 10:62), he asks later in the analysis; and he doggedly insinuates (notwithstanding his son's denials) that Hans has seen his mother's genital area: "'Perhaps black hair by the wiwimaker, when you were curious and looked'" (*G.W.*, 7:302; *S.E.*, 10:67). Thus, just as Hans's mother leads him into confusion by her affirmative answers to his question about whether she has a wiwimaker, so his father undercuts such accurate information as he does impart about the difference between the sexes by continuing to speak of girls and women as possessing wiwimakers.

In keeping with its function as a transcendental signifier, the word "wiwimaker" is used by Hans's parents with a range of connotations— penis, urinary organ, genital organ, and genital area—and their failure to disentangle these multiple meanings exacerbates his dilemmas. Because the primary definition of "penis" cannot be escaped even when the metonymic reference is more general, however, the word, as I have already indicated, inevitably carries a sexist overtone.[14] Freud's semantics prove even slipperier than those of Hans's parents. In a lengthy footnote near the beginning of the narrative, which expatiates on Hans's alleged inability to credit his perception that his baby sister does not have a wiwimaker, Freud adds that "behind the error a piece of correct recognition is hidden. The little girl to be sure also possesses a little wiwimaker, which we call the clitoris, even though it doesn't grow, but remains stunted" (*G.W.,* 7:249n1; *S.E.,* 10:12n3). In this version, his contention is not that women don't have penises, but that they have vestigial ones. To the other meanings of wiwimaker, therefore, we must add that of the clitoris. The best retort to Freud's demeaning view of this organ is provided by Jodi Bray, one of my students at the University of Florida, who has remarked that the clitoris "grows to the size necessary to perform its very useful functions" (1992, 8). Indeed, the clitoris grows larger as the child matures and undergoes tumescence during sexual activity. Little Hans seems to have grasped this truth more securely than Freud, for to his father's statement that when Hanna grows up her wiwimaker will not look like his, he replies: " 'I know that. It will be the way it is, only bigger' " (*G.W.,* 7:297; *S.E.,* 10:62).

In view of Freud's own obfuscation of the complexities of the female genitals, it is ironic that he should remark: "The child naturally lacks an essential piece in the understanding of sexual relations as long as the female genital is undiscovered" (*G.W.,* 7:323; *S.E.,* 10:87). That children of both sexes lack a knowledge of the vagina is an integral component of Freud's phallocentric perspective. What makes this contention most outrageous in context is its complete irrelevance to the foregoing conversation between Hans and his father, which has to do not with the female body but with Hans's doubts about the father's role in procreation and how he can "belong" to the latter when it is his mother who has brought him into the world.[15]

Just as Freud insists on children's ignorance of the vagina, so he refuses to believe that it is possible for boys to envy women their procreative capacity. Notwithstanding Freud's denials, however, Hans on numerous occasions voices a desire to give birth to children as his mother has done. To his father's assertion, "'You would like to be the Daddy and be married to Mommy, would like to be as big as I am and have a moustache, and would like Mommy to have a child,'" Hans replies: "'Daddy, and until I'm married I'll only have one when I want to, when I'll be married to Mommy, and if I don't want to have a child, God doesn't want it either, when I've gotten married'" (*G.W.*, 7:328; *S.E.*, 10:92). The confused syntax captures the child's primary process thinking, but what comes through unmistakably is that Hans, despite his father's Freudian promptings, desires not simply to marry but to *be* Mommy. The child's identifications are multiple, maternal as well as paternal. Most strikingly, Hans shows that he has introjected his mother's ambivalent attitude toward becoming pregnant, since his declaration, "'if I don't want to have a child, God doesn't want it either,'" is a direct allusion to his mother's words in an earlier quarrel with his father (*G.W.*, 7:327; *S.E.*, 10:91). Ignoring all this empirical evidence, Freud protests in a footnote: "There is no necessity here to ascribe to Hans a feminine trait of longing to have children" (*G.W.*, 7:328; *S.E.*, 10:93).[16]

Further proof of Hans's awareness of the female anatomy is his mockery of the hypothesis that his sister Hanna was brought by the stork. When Hans tells his father that until the preceding year, when the newly born Hanna accompanied the family by train on their summer holiday to Gmunden, "'*But always before that she travelled with us in the box,*'" the "box," as Freud interprets in a footnote, "is naturally the womb" of the mother (*G.W.*, 7:304; *S.E.*, 10:69–70; Freud's italics).[17] Freud continues: "What can the assertion that the preceding summer Hanna already travelled to Gmunden 'in the box' mean other than his knowledge of the pregnancy of his mother?" (*G.W.*, 7:305; *S.E.*, 10:71). Just as absurdity in dreams, according to Freud, often heralds mockery in the latent dream thoughts, so Hans's seemingly nonsensical replies to his father's questions are a way of saying, in Freud's paraphrase: "*If you can expect me to believe that the stork brought Hanna in October, when I already noticed mother's big body in the summer when we travelled to Gmunden, then I can require you to believe my lies*" (*G.W.*, 7:305; *S.E.*, 10:70–71; Freud's italics). Hans likewise indicates a grasp of the concept of a fetus when he tells his father: "'She was already in the world a long time, even when she wasn't there yet'" (*G.W.*, 7:308; *S.E.*, 10:73).

In addition to noticing his mother's pregnancy, Hans conveys a comprehension of sexual intercourse through two fantasies involving himself and his father. In the first, as he says, "'I was with you in Schönbrunn near the sheep, and then we crawled under the cord, and we told the guard at the entrance of the garden about it, and he packed us up'" (*G.W.*, 7:275; *S.E.*, 10:40). In the second, "'I was travelling with

you on the train, and we smashed a window, and the guard took us away' "
(*G.W.*, 7:276; *S.E.*, 10:41). Freud sums up Hans's conception of sexual
intercourse near the conclusion of the case history:

> it must have to do with an act of violence, which one carried out on the
> Mama, with a smashing, a creating of an opening, a forcing into an en-
> closed space, the impulse to which the child could feel in himself. But
> although he was on the way, aided by the sensations in his penis, to postulat-
> ing the existence of the vagina, he still could not solve the riddle [*das Rätsel
> nicht lösen*], because to his knowledge no such thing existed as his wiwi-
> maker needed; much rather did the conviction that his Mama possessed a
> wiwimaker like his own stand in the way of the solution [*Lösung*]. (*G.W.*,
> 7:366; *S.E.*, 134–35]

As so often, Freud is at once incontrovertibly right and alarmingly
wrong—right in his interpretation of Hans's fantasies and wrong in his
assertion that Hans is ignorant of the existence of the vagina. For what is
the "enclosed space" into which Hans imagines forcing himself, that
opening he longs to penetrate, if not his mother's vagina, the reality of
which he is more than dimly aware, just as he intuits her possession of the
womb in which she carries his baby sister?

What is mysterious in all this is not the mentation of Little Hans but
how Freud could persist so resolutely in not seeing what lay before him in
plain sight. Time after time, Freud introduces evidence that demonstrates womb envy or an accurate picture of the female sexual organs on
the part of Little Hans, yet disregards it and insists on his own bizarre
theories of the maternal penis and female castration.[18] Although a biographical examination of the origins of Freud's phallocentrism is beyond
my scope here, scholars have convincingly traced Freud's phallocentrism
to his conflicted relationship with his preoedipal mother (Roith 1987;
Hardin 1987, 1988a, 1988b; Sprengnether 1990). But I hope to have
made it clear that a feminist perspective is no less relevant to reading the
case history of the male Little Hans than that of the more celebrated
heroine Dora. With the benefit of hindsight, it is salutary to contrast the
obsolescence of Freud's views on gender with the percipience of Karen
Horney, the first and still one of the most incisive of his feminist critics.
She writes:

> On the one hand, of course, a boy will automatically conclude that every-
> one else is made like himself; but on the other hand his phallic impulses
> surely bid him instinctively to search for the appropriate opening in the
> female body—an opening, moreover, that he himself lacks, for the one sex
> always seeks in the other that which is complementary to it or of a nature
> different from its own. (1932, 140)

Although not referring to Little Hans, Horney's remarks are a far more adequate interpretation of his sexual fantasies than Freud's claim that "to his knowledge no such thing existed as his wiwimaker needed." Equally pertinently, though again without appealing to Little Hans for confirmation, Horney challenges Freud's exclusive preoccupation with penis envy by observing that "in boys of the same age, we meet with parallel expressions in the form of wishes to possess breasts or to have a child" (1933, 151).[19] Without indicting Freud by name, Horney intimates the personal origins of his theoretical blindness: "If the grown man continues to regard woman as the great mystery, in whom is a secret he cannot divine, this feeling of his can only relate ultimately to one thing in her: the mystery of motherhood. Everything else is merely a residue of his dread of this" (1932, 141).

As a coda to this discussion, it cannot be overlooked that Freud evinces an attitude toward homosexuality no less prejudiced than that toward female sexuality. Recent work in gay and lesbian studies has extended the intellectual revolution wrought by feminism, while at the same time providing a salutary reminder that the dynamics of gender and sexuality need to be analyzed separately.[20] In their preoccupation with issues of *gender* difference, in other words, feminists are in danger of eliding equally important issues of *sexual* difference.

I cite three instances of Freud's heterosexist bias in Little Hans, all from the first section of the case. Right at the outset, after introducing Hans's question to his mother about whether she has a wiwimaker, Freud reports that Hans saw a cow being milked and said that milk was coming out of its wiwimaker. Then, invoking his own earlier data in the Dora case, Freud assures the reader that "one does not need to be unduly shocked if one finds in a female being the idea of sucking at the male member," since it has an innocent origin in the experience of sucking at the mother's breast, and the cow's udder provides a ready visual link between the breast and the penis (*G.W.*, 7:245; *S.E.*, 10:7). But why does Freud limit his exculpation to women, since fellatio is an act performed also by men? The answer can only be that he is thinking exclusively in heterosexual terms. Several pages later, Freud describes the four-year-old Hans's verbal and physical displays of affection toward a male cousin of five and exclaims: "Our little Hans seems to be truly a paragon of depravities!" (*G.W.*, 7:252; *S.E.*, 10:15). Yet again, Freud lauds Hans for refusing to renounce his desire to sleep with the fourteen-year-old Mariedl despite his mother's threat that he would have to leave the house: "Our little Hans conducted himself like a real man in the face of his mother's challenge, in spite of his homosexual proclivities" (*G.W.*, 7:254; *S.E.*, 10:17). Homosexuals, therefore, must not be real men. These remarks are all admittedly lighthearted, but it is precisely their casual nature that allows us to catch Freud offguard, as it were, and to glimpse the bourgeois prejudices that are veiled in his more circumspect theoretical pronouncements. That Freud's disparagement of homosexuality, no less than of female sexuality, is seriously disturbing cannot, I think, be doubted; and it should be censured by all those who are drawn to psychoanalysis as a means not of oppressing but of emancipating the human spirit.

Notes

1. See Marcus (1974) for an early and exemplary demonstration of this claim with respect to the Dora case.

2. On the thematics of writing in Freud's text, see Mahony (1993). Unlike Mahony, however, who holds that "Freud's treatise is almost wholly based on the notetaking by Max Graf" (1245), I read Freud's narrative as a largely independent fiction.

3. That this relationship was a conflicted one is attested by Max Graf's invaluable memoir, where he qualifies his admiration for Freud's "creative imagination and real genius" by recalling that when Freud in 1910 issued the ultimatum compelling his followers to choose between attending his group or Adler's, Graf refused "to submit to Freud's 'do' or 'don't' . . . and nothing was left for me but to withdraw from his circle" (1942, 475; see Silverman 1980, 115).

4. Apparently, the experiments in unconventional analysis continued in the Graf household. In a February 2, 1910 letter to Jung, Freud writes: "I should have thought it impossible to analyze one's own wife. Little Hans's father has proved to me that it can be done. In such analysis, however, it just seems too difficult to observe the technical rule whose importance I have lately begun to suspect: 'surmount counter-transference'" (McGuire 1974, 291). One wonders what Freud thought of this "technical rule" when it came to his own analysis of Anna. On the case of Little Hans as family therapy, see Strean (1967).

5. For other powerful readings of Freud in the French feminist tradition, see Cixous and Clément (1975) and Kofman (1980). None of these writers, however, deals with Little Hans. A direct riposte to Freud's views on female sexuality in this case history is, however, furnished by Chasseguet-Smirgel (1975), whose reading anticipates my own in both its line of argument and illustrative examples. See also Meltzer, who from a Kleinian standpoint likewise indicts Freud's tendency to "diminish the significance of the boy's femininity in favour of the role of his masculine castration complex in the formation of his oedipus conflict" as the "chief weakness in his interpretative work" (1978, 47). Meltzer nonetheless hails Freud's exposition of Hans's multilayered treatment as "undoubtedly the most delightful piece of writing in the whole of psycho-analytic literature" (48), a judgment with which I am tempted to agree.

6. Because this paper is based on a reading of Little Hans in the original German, all passages from this case history are my own translation. For ease of

reference, volume and page citations will be provided to both the *Gesammelte Werke* and the *Standard Edition*. Strachey's translation of Wiwimacher as "widdler" is an inspired one, but in order to preserve the derivation from the verb form "to make wiwi" I prefer a more literal rendering. Other works by Freud will be cited from the *Standard Edition*.

7. In his notes to this paper in the *Standard Edition*, James Strachey draws attention to Freud's allusions to the case of Little Hans in his twofold claim that boys look for a penis not only in all living creatures but also in inanimate objects and that they ward off threats of castration by convincing themselves that girls do possess a penis, but a small one, which will soon grow bigger (1923, 142n1, 144n1).

8. As Mahony observes (1993, 1245–46), when Freud adduces Little Hans as an exemplar of sexual curiosity in young children in "The Sexual Enlightenment of Children" (1908a), the only passage of dialogue reported by his father that diverges materially from the version found in the case history concerns Hans's question about the female wiwimaker. In place of the "'Of course. How come?'" (*"Selbstverständlich. Weshalb?"*) in the case (*G.W.*, 7:245; *S.E.*, 10:7), Hans's mother is quoted in the paper as having replied, "'Naturally, so what did you think?'" (*"Natürlich, so was hast du denn gedacht?"*) (*G.W.*, 7:23; *S.E.*, 9:134). Her "naturally" echoes the occurrence of this word two pages later in the case history, but the latter part of her answer has no counterpart in Freud's narrative. "The Sexual Enlightenment of Children" was written by Freud when Little Hans was still four years of age and prior to the outbreak of his phobia.

9. The German word *"Epikrise"* is defined as a "concluding critical judgment of a course of illness from the side of the doctor" (Duden). Strachey's translation of "Discussion" in the *Standard Edition* is lackluster.

10. In 1923 Freud appended a footnote to this passage in which he directs the reader to "The Infantile Genital Organization," and asserts that Hans finds himself at the period of sexual development that "is quite generally characterized through its acquaintance with only one genital—the masculine. In contrast to the later period of maturity, it consists not in genital primacy, but in the primacy of the phallus" (*G.W.*, 7:345; *S.E.*, 10:110). Hans himself commits a linguistic error comparable to Freud's when he declares, "'And all men have wiwimakers'" (*G.W.*, 7:269; *S.E.*, 10:34), using the generic word for people (*Menschen*) in place of the restricted word for males (*Männer*). This universalization of the masculine perspective finds its consummate expression in Freud's invocation of the Oedipus myth in *The Interpretation of Dreams*: "It is the fate of all of us, perhaps, to direct our first sexual impulse toward our mother and our first hatred and our first murderous wish against our father" (1900, 262), where, again, the subject-position of girls is elided. On the consequences of Freud's reliance on a masculine and oedipal-centered paradigm, see Madelon Sprengnether's essay in this volume.

11. Although in a note to the case of Little Hans in the *Standard Edition* Strachey identified what he believed to be the first appearance of the term

(10:8n1), he later corrected himself and acknowledged that Freud had used it in print earlier in "On the Sexual Theories of Children" (1908b, 217n1). But here, too, Freud is summarizing material from Hans's analysis, so the castration complex retains its connection with this case. Strachey's self-correction is pointed out by Lindon (1992, 377–78). See also the entry "Castration Complex" in Laplanche and Pontalis (1967, 56–60).

12. *"The gaze is at stake from the outset.* Don't forget what 'castration,' or the knowledge of castration, owes to the gaze, at least for Freud" (Irigaray 1974, 47). "It is the boy who looks and is horrified first, and . . . the little girl merely doubles and confirms by reduplication what he is supposed to have seen. Or not seen" (49).

13. "The pleasure gained from touching, caressing, parting the lips and vulva simply does not exist for Freud. . . . Just as he will never refer to the pleasure associated with the sensitivity of the posterior wall of the vagina, the breasts, or the neck of the womb" (Irigaray 1974, 29).

14. Although Freud says nothing about it in this case, the male genitals consist of a scrotum and testicles as well as a penis. In "The Infantile Genital Organization," however, in a footnote to the passage about the penis as a criterion for distinguishing between the animate and inanimate that refers to Little Hans, Freud remarks on "what a small degree of attention the other part of the male genitals, the little sac with its contents, attracts in children. From all one hears in analyses, one would not guess that the male genitals consisted of anything more than the penis" (19:142). But given the belief of many children that the scrotal sac functions as a container for urine, and the emphasis on "making wiwi" in the case of Little Hans, it may be Freud himself, and not his young patient, who is guilty of forgetting about the testicles in this analysis (Silverman 1980, 114–15).

15. The German text of this dialogue indicates a slippage in Hans's mind between the awareness that "'a boy gets [*kriegt*] a girl and a girl gets a boy'" and his father's reply that "'A boy doesn't get [*bekommt*] children. Only women, mommies get children.'" Hans is struggling with the connection—and the distinction—between having sex and having children and obtaining no help from his father. Similarly, just as "wiwimaker" can be used equivocally to refer either to the urinary or genital organs possessed by members of both sexes or to the exclusively masculine penis, so Hans asks how he can "belong" (*gehören*) to his father when his mother has given him birth. The concept of "belonging" is no less ambiguous than that of the wiwimaker, only here the model is female rather than male since the father both is and is not a parent like the mother. Hans's father, again, makes matters not less but more obscure by successively telling Hans: (a) that Hans "belongs" both to him and Hans's mother; (b) that Hanna "belongs" only to Mommy and not to Hans; and (c) that Hanna belongs at once to him, Mommy, and Hans. The concept of "belonging" has been attenuated to encompass being not simply a parent but any family member, and Hans is left to sort out

how being a sibling differs from being a mother or a father (*G.W.*, 7:322–23; *S.E.*, 10:87).

16. What is more, the theory, expounded to Hans by both his parents, that "children grow in the Mommy and then, when great pains come, are brought into the world by being pressed out like a 'lumpf,'" not only contributes to his anal fixation but reinforces his fantasy that pregnancy is something of which he too is capable (*G.W.*, 7:323; *S.E.*, 10:87).

17. Just before this he says in another footnote that both the box and the bathtub are for Hans "representations of the space in which babies are found" (*G.W.*, 7:304; *S.E.*, 10:69)

18. When Hans laughs at the sight of Hanna's wiwimaker, Freud claims that this is "the first time that he acknowledges the difference between the male and female genital in this way, instead of denying it," but earlier he had quoted Hans's declaration, after his mother had given birth to Hanna, "'But out of my wiwimaker there comes no blood'" (*G.W.*, 7:257, 248; *S.E.*, 10:21, 10). Hans pinpoints a crucial difference between the male and female genitalia, but Freud is unable to give him his due. On the allied theme of menstruation in psychoanalysis, see Lupton (1993).

19. "Why not *also* analyze the 'envy' for the vagina? Or the uterus? Or the vulva? Etc. The 'desire' felt by each pole of sexual difference 'to have something like it too'?" (Irigaray 1974, 52).

20. For an outstanding synthesis of gay and lesbian scholarship in Shakespeare studies, see Traub (1992). Traub defines "sex" as "those anatomical, biological distinctions by which cultures differentiate between males and females"; "gender" as "the culturally prescribed roles and behaviors available to the two 'sexes'"; and "sexuality" as "erotic desires and practices, including but not limited to the direction and scope of erotic preference (i.e., object choice)" (21).

References

Bray, J. 1992. Young Lover or Reluctant Oedipus: The Identified Patient in the Case of Little Hans. Unpublished manuscript.

Chasseguet-Smirgel, J. 1975. Freud and Female Sexuality: The Consideration of Some Blind Spots in the Exploration of the "Dark Continent." In *Sexuality and Mind: The Role of the Father and the Mother in the Psyche*. New York: New York Univ. Press, 1986, pp. 9–28.

Cixous, H., and C. Clément. 1975. *The Newly Born Woman*. Trans. B. Wing. Minneapolis: Univ. of Minnesota Press, 1988.

Freud, S. 1900. *The Interpretation of Dreams*. In *The Standard Edition of the Complete Psychological Works*, ed. and trans. J. Strachey et al. 24 vols. London: Hogarth Press, 1953–74, (hereafter S.E.), vols. 4 and 5.

————. 1908a. The Sexual Enlightenment of Children. *S.E.,* 9: 131–39. Zur sexuellen Aufklärung der Kinder. In *Gesammelte Werke,* ed. A. Freud et al. 18 vols. (London: Imago, 1940–68), (hereafter G.W.), 7:19–27.

————. 1908b. On the Sexual Theories of Children. *S.E.,* 9:209–26. Über infantile Sexualtheorien. *G.W.,* 7:171–88.

————. 1909. *Analysis of a Phobia in a Five-Year-Old-Boy. S.E.,* 10: 5–149. *Analyse der Phobia eines fünfjährigen Knaben. G.W.,* 7:243–377.

————. 1923. The Infantile Genital Organization. *S.E.,* 19:141–45.

————. 1927. Fetishism. *S.E.,* 22:152–57.

————. 1933. *New Introductory Lectures on Psycho-Analysis. S.E.,* 22:5–182.

Glenn, J. 1980. Freud's Advice to Hans's Father. The First Supervisory Sessions. In Kanzer and Glenn 1980, pp. 121–27.

Graf, M. 1942. Reminiscences of Professor Sigmund Freud. *Psychoanal. Q.* 11:465–76.

Hardin, H. 1987. On the Vicissitudes of Freud's Early Mothering: Early Environment and Loss. *Psychoanal. Q.* 56:628–44.

————. 1988a. On the Vicissitudes of Freud's Early Mothering: Alienation from His Biological Mother. *Psychoanal. Q.* 57:72–86.

————. 1988b. On the Vicissitudes of Freud's Early Mothering: Freiberg, Screen Memories, and Loss. *Psychoanal. Q.* 57:209–23.

Horney, K. 1932. The Dread of Woman: Observations on a Specific Difference in the Dread Felt by Men and by Women Respectively for the Opposite Sex. In Horney 1967, pp. 133–46.

————. 1933. The Denial of the Vagina: A Contribution to the Problem of the Genital Anxieties Specific to Women. In Horney 1967, pp. 147–61.

————. 1967. *Feminine Psychology.* Ed. H. Kellman. New York: Norton, 1973.

Irigaray, L. 1974. *Speculum of the Other Woman.* Trans. G. C. Gill. Ithaca, N.Y.: Cornell Univ. Press, 1987.

Kanzer, M., and J. Glenn, eds. 1980. *Freud and His Patients.* New York: Aronson.

Kofman, S. 1980. *The Enigma of Woman: Woman in Freud's Writings.* Trans. C. Porter. Ithaca, N.Y.: Cornell Univ. Press, 1985.

Laplanche, J., and J. B. Pontalis. 1967. *The Language of Psycho-Analysis.* Trans. D. Nicholson-Smith. New York: Norton, 1973.

Lindon J. A. 1992. A Reassessment of Little Hans, His Parents, and His Castration Complex. *J. Am. Acad. Psychoanal.* 20:375–94.

Lupton, M. J. 1993. *Menstruation and Psychoanalysis.* Urbana: Univ. of Illinois Press.

Mahony, P. J. 1992. Freud as Family Therapist: Reflections. In T. Gelfand and J. Kerr, eds., *Freud and the History of Psychoanalysis.* Hillsdale, N.J.: Analytic Press.

————. 1993. The Dictator and His Cure. Int. J. Psycho-Anal. 74:1245–51.

Marcus, S. 1974. Freud and Dora: Story, History, Case History. In *Freud and the Culture of Psychoanalysis: Studies in the Transition from Victorian Humanism to Modernity.* Boston: Allen and Unwin, 1984, pp. 42–86.

McGuire, W., ed. 1974. *The Freud/Jung Letters: The Correspondence between Sigmund Freud and C. G. Jung.* Trans. R. Manheim and R. F. C. Hull. Princeton, N.J.: Princeton Univ. Press.

Meltzer, D. 1978. *The Kleinian Development. Part I. Freud's Clinical Development.* Reading: Clunie Press, 1985.

Roith, E. 1987. *The Riddle of Freud: Jewish Influences on His Theory of Female Sexuality.* London: Tavistock.

Silverman, M. A. 1980. A Fresh Look at the Case of Little Hans. In Kanzer and Glenn 1980, pp. 95–127.

Sprengnether, M. 1990. *The Spectral Mother: Freud, Feminism, and Psychoanalysis.* Ithaca, N.Y.: Cornell Univ. Press.

Strean, H. S. 1967. A Family Therapist Looks at "Little Hans." *Family Process* 6:227–33.

Traub, V. 1992. *Desire and Anxiety: Circulations of Sexuality in Shakespearean Drama.* New York: Routledge.

Chapter Three
Of Footnotes and Fathers:
Reading Irigaray with Kofman

Ranita Chatterjee

In the first discursive footnote to *The Enigma of Woman* (1980c), Sarah Kofman curiously discredits the work of another French feminist philosopher, Luce Irigaray. Comparing Freud's original German texts to the existing French translation, Kofman concludes that the latter "is quite dreadful" and "omits many passages" (14n6). She goes on to attack Irigaray for relying on this same translation, charging that she therefore lacks "minimal intellectual honesty." Although Kofman's project in *The Enigma of Woman* is very similar to Irigaray's in *Speculum of the Other Woman* (1974b), Kofman criticizes Irigaray's understanding of Freud. Both deconstruct Freud's seminal essays on femininity and female sexuality: Kofman in the chapter "Freud Investigates," and Irigaray in "The Blind Spot of an Old Dream of Symmetry." Why is Kofman so antagonistic to Irigaray? What is the relationship between these two female theorists who quibble over the de(con)struction of the father of psychoanalysis? I will argue that although both Kofman and Irigaray successfully subvert Freud's speculations about women, they do so using different strategies. My reading thus seeks not only to distinguish between two feminists who are often paired, but also to examine their methods of challenging a dominant discourse.

I thank Elizabeth Harvey for her enabling criticism in the early stages of this essay and the editors of this volume for helping me refine the arguments. Its preparation was assisted by funds from the Social Sciences and Humanities Research Council of Canada.

UNTANGLING IRIGARAY

Before turning to their texts, it is worth discussing the reception accorded to Kofman and Irigaray. Of the two, Kofman remains much less well known in North America. Although several of her books have been translated into English, only *The Enigma of Woman* has attracted widespread critical attention. Apart from Elizabeth Berg's review in *Diacritics* (1982) and Elizabeth Harvey's discussion in *Ventriloquized Voices* (1992), there is virtually no substantive discussion in English of Kofman's work.[1] I suspect that Kofman has been a victim of what Kelly Oliver describes as "the aversion to French feminism on the American scene . . . due to a certain importation of Kristeva, Irigaray, and Cixous" (1993, 163). Kofman, therefore, may have reason to resent both Irigaray's prominence and the neglect of her own work, particularly by Anglo-American feminists.

Since their diffusion both severally and through Elaine Marks and Isabelle de Courtivon's anthology *New French Feminisms* (1980), Irigaray's obscure and elliptical texts have been greeted by an ambivalent mixture of admiration and disparagement. Because Irigaray, like Julia Kristeva and Hélène Cixous, has focused on articulating the experience of the female body, Anglo-American feminists have tended to regard them as a triad and to mute the radical differences between their projects. Toril Moi, for example, concludes that "Irigaray's vision of femininity and of feminine language remains indistinguishable from Cixous's" (1985, 143). Most disconcertingly, this judgment reflects the prevailing response to French feminist theory despite the growing number of studies that discuss each figure individually.[2] In this climate, Kofman's work continues to be slighted, while Irigaray's is frequently misunderstood by being lumped with those of Cixous and Kristeva. This association has led to two widely held false assumptions: that Irigaray's methodology is problematic for feminist politics because of its affinity with Derridean deconstruction; and that her theories are essentialist because they rely on a correspondence between women's bodies and their ontology.

As to the first criticism, Elizabeth Grosz points out that "few contemporary French intellectuals are untouched by or indifferent to Derrida's interrogations of key texts from the history of philosophy" (1989, 103), and Irigaray is no exception. For Irigaray, Derrida's concept of *différance* is indispensable "to refer to the differences *between* one sex and another" (Grosz 1989, 104). Moreover, it undergirds Irigaray's critique of what she terms "the Law of the Self-same" in psychoanalysis (1974b, 32–34). Notwithstanding her overt challenge to Freud and Lacan, some detractors contend that Irigaray's theories remain "under the influence of patriarchal ideology" (Moi 1985, 146). Irigaray's defenders, on the other hand, counter that to employ deconstruction as a critical technique does not imply an adherence to patriarchy.

In my view, Irigaray's mimicry and subversion of the discourse of psychoanalysis from within does carry with it the risk of identification, but this risk is unavoidable if change is to be effected. As Irigaray has remarked:

> We do not escape, in particular, by thinking we can dispense with a rigorous interpretation of phallogocentrism. There is no simple manageable way to leap to the outside of phallogocentrism, *nor any possible way to situate oneself there, that would result from the simple fact of being a woman.* (1977, 162)

To reject Irigaray's work on the grounds that it is parasitic on patriarchy presupposes that being a feminist somehow guarantees one immunity from phallogocentrism. But the most effective way to subvert phallocentrism is not to reject it globally, for any such act of defiance will be recuperated by the hegemonic discourse. Irigaray's deliberate presentation of herself as feminine according to patriarchal norms is a necessary preliminary to deconstructing their pretensions to universality. Thus, Whitford proposes that "Irigaray's project [should be seen] as 'philosophy in the feminine,' that is to say, philosophy which does not regard the social situation and struggles of women as something external or irrelevant to its discourse" (1991a, 7).[3]

Irigaray's desire to bring sex into her feminist project of subverting patriarchal texts has led to the tiresome critique that her theories are essentialist. Ann Rosalind Jones (1985, 364–65, 371–72) and Toril Moi (1985, 143–47) both argued that Irigaray's equation of women with the "two lips" of the vulva affirms the patriarchal reduction of women to their sexual organs. But Jones and Moi take Irigaray too literally. When Irigaray celebrates the two lips, she is not referring to the female body as a biological entity, but rather introducing *différance* into the Symbolic order. Irigaray answers Lacan's phallus with her two lips since the former is no more the embodiment of a masculine essence than the latter is of a feminine. The lips at once give women an ideal with which to identify in the Imaginary order and complicate sexual difference in the Symbolic order through a strategic displacement and doubling of the hitherto transcendental phallic signifier. When Moi warns that "to define 'woman' is necessarily to essentialize her" (1985, 139), she fails to consider that women lack positive representations in the received Imaginary order. As Whitford counters, "biology (or nature) must receive a symbolic mediation which is more adequate for women" (1991a, 173). Far from being essentialist, Irigaray's trope of the two lips fittingly accomplishes a bifold purpose: it exposes the arbitrariness of privileging the phallus as the guarantor of authentic speech in the Symbolic order, and it augments the possibilities of the Imaginary order by furnishing an affirmative metonymy for the female body.

THE COMPETING SISTERS

In *This Sex Which Is Not One* (1977), Irigaray devotes a chapter to the reception of *Speculum of the Other Woman*. Although I do not mean to privilege the theorist's perception of her own work, Irigaray's verdict corroborates my assessment of her project. She portrays "The Blind Spot of an Old Dream of Symmetry" as an attempt "to move back through the 'masculine' imaginary, that is, our cultural imaginary" (1977, 162) through a feminist Lacanian reading of Freud's writings on female sexuality and femininity.[4] Kofman's exegesis of the same Freudian texts in "Freud Investigates" appears at first glance to be very similar to Irigaray's, but upon closer inspection a basic difference emerges: Kofman purges her Derridean deconstructive technique of any trace of Lacanian psychoanalysis. Far from being simply an acerbic dismissal of Irigaray's project, however, Kofman's confrontation with her predecessor—which occurs primarily in footnotes—is a dialectical encounter.

First published in 1980, six years after Irigaray's *Speculum of the Other Woman*, *The Enigma of Woman* is uncomfortably aware of the legacy of Irigaray's exposure of the gaps in Freud's writings on female sexuality. In fact, Kofman's text begins with an onslaught against Irigaray, as if to mark its difference from *Speculum of the Other Woman*. The second paragraph of *The Enigma of Woman* contains a parenthetical remark that is clearly a criticism of Irigaray's interpretative skills: "In his lecture 'Femininity' ('Die Weiblichkeit'), a text recently denigrated—to put it mildly—by a woman psychoanalyst" (1980c, 12). This "woman psychoanalyst" who is unnamed in the text is named in a footnote. The chapter, aptly (if ambiguously) titled "The Battle of the Sexes," concludes with a lengthy footnote attacking Irigaray for using the French translation of Freud, "a translation that she knows is faulty" (1980c, 14n6). In Irigaray's first footnote, however, she clearly states that she has had "occasion to modify the translation somewhat, to complete it in certain cases where fragments of statements in the original have been omitted" (1974b, 13n1). Thus, although Kofman, too, takes pride in having retranslated Freud's German, her censure of Irigaray's reliance on a French translation is unwarranted and an indication of her own carelessness in reading Irigaray's text.[5] Furthermore, while Kofman accuses Irigaray of not "manifesting the minimal intellectual honesty that consists in criticizing an author in terms of what he has said rather than what someone has managed to have him say" (1980c, 14n6), she too becomes Freud's ventriloquist in *The Enigma of Woman*. What is ultimately at stake is not the status of the existing French translation of Freud, but Irigaray's idiosyncratic rendering of Freud's German as opposed to Kofman's.

Later in the opening pages of "Freud Investigates," Kofman argues that "nothing in [Freud's] text justifies Luce Irigaray's reading (according to which Freud, like Aristotle, deprives women of the right to the logos and to the phallus alike)" (104). In stating that "nothing in the text" can support Irigaray's reading, Kofman assumes that Freud's text possesses a univocal meaning that Irigaray has missed. Kofman deprives Irigaray of "the right to the logos and to the phallus alike" by claiming to possess the truth herself. Paradoxically, while Kofman professes fidelity to Freud's "original" German text, she too acknowledges the fragmented nature of Freud's corpus. By exposing Freud's many theoretical contradictions, Kofman reveals a palimpsestic Freud, a Freud who has no fixed or final meaning; yet Kofman continues to wage a guerilla war against Irigaray's readings. The issue at hand is why Kofman in her own feminist deconstructive text relegates Luce Irigaray to the margins, the position generally occupied by women in our society, both inside and outside the academy. For both Kofman and Irigaray realize that the Freudian discourse needs to be analyzed from the standpoint of one of the pathological conditions that Freud identifies as inevitable for woman.[6]

PENETRATING FREUD

Kofman's rereading of Freud's "Femininity" (1933) pays close attention to textual details. Hers is a patient reading that subtly exposes the numerous gaps, absences, and contradictions in Freud's writing. Irigaray's reading, on the other hand, is by turns a rhapsodic celebration and an ironic assault on Freud. But Kofman's philological scrupulousness seems overly serious. In *This Sex Which Is Not One* Irigaray explains that "to escape from a pure and simple reversal of the masculine position means in any case not to forget to laugh" (1977, 163). For Irigaray, laughing is the first step in undermining the self-importance of Freud's postulates about the *normal* path to femininity and a crucial strategy for deflating the significance of the phallus/penis.[7] To hear the feminine laugh within the masculine discourse is already to subvert that discourse. Kofman produces a convincing argument against Freud's use of penis envy to explain all of woman's behavior. But she does not laugh at Freud, and denies Irigaray her pleasure.

Irigaray, with her seemingly "careless" reading of Freud's words, her disrespect for the seriousness of the Freudian enterprise, and her lack of patience with Freudian assumptions, weaves fluidly in and out of Freud's text. Moreover, the masterful Freudian discourse appears alongside Irigaray's critique both in her own voice and in the ironically ventriloquized voice of Freud. As Carolyn Burke has noted, in Irigaray's works the feminist theorist directly addresses her antagonist, rather than just talk about him: "Irigaray adopts several disorienting textual strategies: her own words and those of her interlocutor are intermingled, and she deliberately dispenses with the usual scholarly conventions governing citations and other textual references" (1989, 238n18). Irigaray's refusal to acknowledge ownership—to indicate whose words are whose—is part of her critique of ideas of property. According to Irigaray, because her "organ which has nothing to show for itself also lacks a form of its own" (1977, 26), woman strictly speaking has no place in the Symbolic order. Woman has no "morphologically designatable organ" (26) equivalent to the penis to assure a unified identity of the self-same. "She is neither one nor two": woman has "no 'proper' name" (26). Therefore, she cannot assume mastery or ownership of signification—of her own or another's discourse—except through mimesis. In other words, Irigaray's sometimes tacit ventriloquism of Freud is a far more self-conscious act of subversion than Kofman's, who conscientiously documents her sources.

Furthermore, Irigaray's rhetorical strategy of dispensing with proper citation or pronominal markers such as Kofman's "I, Freud" enables her to expose the limits and weaknesses of Freud's authoritative pronouncements on female sexuality. Irigaray's ventriloquism, like Kofman's, enables woman to occupy the place of Freud's words, but it differs from Kofman's in that it "call[s] into question the exclusionary rules of proprietariness that govern the use of that discourse" (Butler 1993, 36). Irigaray uses her mimicry to subvert the phallocentric "hom(m)osexual" Freudian discourse. As Irigaray herself puts it, "to play with mimesis is thus, for a woman, to try to recover the place of her exploitation by discourse, without allowing herself to be simply reduced to it" (1977, 76). Because Irigaray mimics Freud's voice but not his strategies of linearity and logical progression—mastery/ownership/propriety—she deflects the thrust of his statements.[8] That which cannot be thematized, articulated, or theorized within the confines of Freud's lecture on femininity is necessarily exterior to that discourse and must, therefore, remain incoherent in order to "define" what is conceivable within Freud's theories.[9] Irigaray's mimicry of the Freudian text, then, is a self-reflexive strategy intended to expose the exclusion of the feminine from Freud's analysis of femininity.

Indeed, Irigaray's reading of Freud is not a simple deconstruction that seeks to reveal the gaps and ambiguities of a discourse. Through all of her "play," Irigaray emphasizes both the prohibition against and the passion for women embracing one another: women "need to constitute a place to be among themselves, in order to learn to formulate their desires, in the absence of overly immediate pressures and oppressions" (1977, 127). Additionally, Irigaray suggests that women's neuroses, their "depressions and chronic somatizations" as well as their general lack of "social interest," are all indicators of the "lack of an auto-erotic, homosexual economy" (1974b, 102). If one provisionally accepts this description, Irigaray's reading of Freud's text may be described—in the Freudian sense—as that of a neurotic woman who refuses to be bound by the strict confines of masculine discourse. Since woman remains the material base of the patriarchal signifying system, she does not have the capacity to articulate her desires:

> It is not that she lacks some "master signifier" or that none is imposed upon her, but rather that access to a signifying economy, to the coming of signifiers, is difficult or even impossible for her because she remains an outsider, herself (a) subject to their norms. She borrows signifiers but cannot make her mark, or re-mark upon them. Which all surely keeps her deficient, empty, lacking, in a way that could be labelled "psychotic": a *latent* but not actual psychosis, for want of a practical signifying system. (1974b, 71)

Ultimately, Irigaray concludes that the only recourse for woman "to save her sexuality from total repression and destruction" is "hysterical miming" (72).

Kofman, however, follows in Freud's footsteps as he progresses on an apparently straight path. And yet Kofman manages to ambush Freud along the way. "Freud Investigates," like "This Blind Spot of an Old Dream of Symmetry," is a chorus of many voices, the clearest one being Kofman's own critique of Freud's text. Along with the German and translated French passages of Freud's writings, Kofman occasionally assumes Freud's voice. By using Freud's own theories against him, Kofman exposes his inconsistencies. A particularly important site for Kofman's feminist deconstruction and subsequent exposure of Freud's duplicitous argumentation is his theory of bisexuality.

Kofman exposes Freud's inability to accept his own femininity while proclaiming the right to subsume female sexuality under the rubric of a universal human bisexuality. In her reading of Freud's account of bisexuality, Kofman makes him into a hysteric:

> By using the thesis of bisexuality as a double-edged sword (it allows him both to break down the metaphysical opposition of "pure" masculinity and femininity and to continue to keep masculinity in its traditionally priv-

ileged position), in his theory Freud "mimics" the hysteric, whose symptoms serve precisely to confirm his thesis of bisexuality. (1980c, 123)

Thus, Kofman argues that "Freud makes himself an accomplice of the hysteric, the criminal, by dissimulating in his turn, by keeping the (professional) secret, but on condition that the woman first agree to be *his* accomplice" (45). Hysteria, as Kofman tells us, is structurally similar to bisexuality in that the hysteric participates in both the masculine and feminine libidinal economies. She cites the example of a patient of Freud's who simultaneously "holds her dress against her body with one hand (as a woman) while with the other hand she tries to pull it away (as a man)" (123).[10] The repression of primary bisexuality with the concomitant inability to become a "normal" Freudian woman causes bisexuality to surface again in a hysterical way, "like an accident along the 'woman's' path in the process that is to lead from her bisexuality to her femininity" (125).[11]

Freud's concealment of his own femininity even as he uses the theory of bisexuality becomes a type of linguistic hysteria. By his contrast at the end of "Femininity" of the visibility and promise radiated by a man of thirty with a "woman of the same age [who] . . . often frightens us by her psychical rigidity and unchangeability" (1933, 134), Freud contains the potential bisexuality of woman in his ossification of her. He therefore limits the power of bisexuality itself, transforming it into a handicap for women. By remaining both within and without the Freudian discourse, Kofman reactivates this bisexuality in both "woman" and Freud, making it a positive attribute for the woman but negative for Freud (in the sense that it exposes Freud's masculine bias). As a result, Kofman comes to occupy the position of the hysteric whose bisexuality enables her to be both the female hysterical patient and the male psychoanalyst because of her simultaneous ability to participate in and subvert a masculine discourse. Like Dora, who came to occupy Freud's position as analyst by deciding when her treatment would end, Kofman deconstructs the gendered analyst/analysand relationship.

In her discussion of Kofman, Elizabeth Harvey points out·that if Freud's role is complicit with the hysteric to the extent that he mimics her, so is Kofman's in that she assumes a "hysterical voice, a bisexual voice . . . to represent Freud's insight about the speculative, provisional nature of the masculine/feminine opposition" (1992, 53). In other words, if Freud is the hysteric's accomplice who has been exposed as a hysteric himself, Kofman is in the role of both the hysteric and the accomplice since her careful reading of Freud mimics his precise analysis of the hysteric. However ironic Kofman's miming of the hysterical voice may be, she nevertheless proceeds through the Freudian text, deconstructing it point by point in a meticulous fashion without considering her own transferential relationship to what she reads. As Jane Gallop observes, "without transference, psychoanalysis is simply literary criticism, by an unimplicated, discriminating reader, lacking either affect or effect" (1982, 73). Kofman states at the beginning of *The Enigma of Woman* that her reading of Freud is intended to "verify" that his

> thesis of bisexuality, declared valid in principle for all humans, is in the last analysis used only as a strategic weapon in connection with women . . . [a]nd it is as though Freud were loudly proclaiming the universality of bisexuality in order better to disguise his silent disavowal of his own femininity, his paranoia. (1980c, 15)

In the process of deconstructing the master psychoanalyst, Kofman, however, conceals her own "silent disavowal," her "paranoia," which concerns the psychoanalytic model itself. In assuming the hysterical voice from outside the psychoanalytic discourse, Kofman repeats the mimetic gesture of the hysteric.

This, then, is her greatest difference from Irigaray, who recovers the repressed feminine within the psychoanalytic discourse. Since Kofman still privileges the logical argumentative strategies of the masculine discourse, she mimics Freud mimicking the hysteric, and thus places herself in the position of the hysteric's accomplice. What is radical about Irigaray's reading is that she not only mimics but literally becomes the hysteric through her disregard for the rules of citation and intellectual property. In the process, Irigaray is able to subject psychoanalysis to its own logic of hysteria and to subject Freud to her laughter.

Although both Irigaray and Kofman enter the Freudian discourse through a double-voiced position, only one escapes being the hysteric's accomplice. Irigaray does not tie herself to Freud's exact words, preferring instead to laugh at his theories. She repeats Lacan's gesture of claiming that "Freud, the very name's a laugh" (Lacan 1975, 157). While Kofman undermines Freud, she does so by ignoring the discourse of psychoanalysis—its unconscious, its repressed feminine. As Moi argues:

> The book [*The Enigma of Woman*] as a whole may be taken as a sustained attempt to refute Irigaray's reading of Freud in *Speculum*. Influenced by Derridean deconstruction, Kofman pays painstaking attention to the letter of the texts in question, frequently accusing Irigaray of mistranslating Freud. . . . Pursuing the question of why Freud never really returned to the theme of the powerful, self-sufficient woman, Kofman reads his lecture on femininity as an attempt to maintain a defence against his vital, but devastating, insight that *man* cannot ever solve the enigma of woman. (1987, 11)

But Kofman does not solve the enigma either. Irigaray laughs away the enigma, but Kofman cannot laugh. Perhaps it is Kofman's anger at Irigaray's laughter that causes her both to incorporate (for one cannot deny the influence of Irigaray's work on Kofman) and to dismiss Irigaray. Irigaray is on one level the elder sister with whom Kofman must fight in order to receive the love of Freud, the father. But at a deeper level Irigaray is the mother, visualized as phallic, who knows the secret but will not tell. She is the mother from whom Kofman is desperately trying to separate, but this hatred of the mother is part of the masculine economy. Elizabeth Berg's discussion of competition among women aptly delineates this scenario:

> Women are in general much more willing to concede the superiority of men than they are to entertain the possibility that another woman might know something that they do not. There seems always to remain a fear that the mother may in fact possess her phallus intact, and that possibility would be far more disturbing than simply accepting one's own castration, knowing that all women are subject to the same deprivation. (1982, 15)

This is precisely the situation Irigaray attempts to transform through a call to laughter and a release of pleasure among women. Kofman's repetition of the hatred for the mother is no more than a symptom of the lack of a female imaginary and symbolic. Kofman's attack on Irigaray is the only choice left for a daughter who desires to distinguish herself from her mother in a masculine economy. But if Kofman had truly listened to Irigaray, instead of judging her, she might have joined her in laughing at Freud.

One is reminded here of Gallop's insightful discussion of the "quarrel" (1982, 92) between Eugénie Lemoine-Luccioni and Irigaray. A project not unlike mine, Gallop's considers Lemoine-Luccioni's 1975 review of Irigaray's *Speculum of the Other Woman*, and Irigaray's 1977 response. As with Kofman and Irigaray, an analysis of the footnotes is crucial in Gallop's juxtaposition of the two "Lacanian-trained women psychoanalysts interested in working on and writing about women" (93). Gallop suggests that Irigaray in her response to Lemoine-Luccioni "cannot listen to the erratic, erotic letter" of the latter's book (101). "Irigaray's adversary position traps her into repeating the fault of which she accuses the other woman—not listening to the '*particulier* of the subject's desire,' but only using it as 'proof' for an argument" (101). Indeed, this is what Kofman does to Irigaray—she cannot hear the pleasure in Irigaray's erratic, erotic encounter with Freud's writings. She accuses Irigaray, as Irigaray has accused Lemoine-Luccioni. And yet, Kofman's attack on Irigaray signals her simultaneous desire to be seduced by and to resist

Irigaray's pleasure. Kofman can see through Irigaray's desire to deflate Freud but cannot completely disregard her; hence Kofman's criticisms remain marginal and parenthetical. Freud suggests that "by making our enemy small, inferior, despicable or comic, we achieve in a roundabout way the enjoyment of overcoming him—to which the third person, who has made no efforts, bears witness by his laughter" (1905c, 103). But Kofman has made an effort and, like Irigaray, bears witness by taking up the challenge of reading Freud anew.

Notes

1. For a brief discussion of *The Enigma of Woman*, see Culler (1982, 169–74). Like Kofman, Culler argues that rather than "reject Freud" (which they both wrongly suggest Irigaray does), one should take Freud's writings "seriously and see how his theory, which so clearly privileges male sexuality and defines woman as an incomplete man, deconstructs itself" (169).

2. See Shiach (1991), Oliver (1993), and Whitford, whose lucid critical study (1991a) and editing of *The Irigaray Reader* (1991b) have greatly contributed to Irigaray scholarship.

3. While agreeing with Whitford that Irigaray's work is philosophical, Moi charges that Irigaray's "failure to consider the historical and economic specificity of patriarchal power, along with its ideological and material contradictions, forces her into providing exactly the kind of metaphysical definition of woman she declaredly wants to avoid. She thus comes to analyse 'woman' in idealist categories, just like the male philosophers she is denouncing" (1985, 148).

4. Although Irigaray nowhere employs the terms "feminist" or "Lacanian," it is clear that they furnish the coordinates for "The Blind Spot of an Old Dream of Symmetry."

5. Interestingly, in her discussion of fetishism Kofman herself incorrectly renders the German title of Freud's famous essay on the uncanny as "Die Unheimlichkeit," instead of "Das Unheimliche." She thus feminizes Freud's neuter term (1980b, 98; 1980c, 82). I thank Peter Rudnytsky for bringing Kofman's error to my attention.

6. Freud states that from the moment of the little girl's discovery of her castration, there are "three possible lines of development . . . one leads to sexual inhibition or to neurosis, the second to change of character in the sense of a masculinity complex, the third, finally, to normal femininity" (1933, 126). For Freud, hysteria and bisexuality are two of the conditions that may arise if the girl cannot successfully complete the path "to normal femininity" (1931, 226–227; 1933, 131).

7. Cixous too invokes the power of feminine laughter to subvert masculine discourses. She transforms the horror of the mythic Medusa into an empowering

figure for women writers in "The Laugh of the Medusa" (1975), and compares the male threat of castration with the female suppression of laughter in "Castration or Decapitation?" (1976).

8. I am not suggesting that Irigaray's strategy is in any way illogical. Because she fragments the Freudian discourse and inserts her own often lengthy discussion of each passage, her discourse subverts Freud's logical sequence of ideas. While Irigaray's argumentative strategies are fluid and nonlinear, they still follow a deliberate progression, albeit one that is not readily visible.

9. Judith Butler's (1993) discussion of Irigaray and Plato has helped me to think through the notions of exclusions, borders, and limits as they relate to Irigaray's use of mimicry.

10. Freud mentions this case twice. See "Hysterical Phantasies and Their Relation to Bisexuality" (1908, 166) and "Some General Remarks on Hysterical Attacks" (1909, 230).

11. For Freud, the "final normal female attitude [is that stage] in which she takes her father as her object and so finds her way to the feminine form of the Oedipus complex" (1931, 230). He further states that the normal "feminine situation is only established, however, if the wish for a penis is replaced by one for a baby" (1933, 128).

References

Berg, E. L. 1982. The Third Woman. *Diacritics* 12:11–20.

Burke, C. 1989. Romancing the Philosophers: Luce Irigaray. In D. Hunter, ed., *Seduction and Theory: Readings of Gender, Representation, and Rhetoric.* Urbana: Univ. of Illinois Press, pp. 226–40.

Butler, J. 1993. *Bodies That Matter: On the Discursive Limits of "Sex."* London: Routledge.

Cixous, H. 1975. The Laugh of the Medusa. Trans. K. Cohen and P. Cohen. In Marks 1980, pp. 245–64.

———. 1976. Castration or Decapitation? Trans. A. Kuhn. Signs 7.11 (1981–82): 41–55.

Culler, J. 1982. *On Deconstruction: Theory and Criticism after Structuralism.* Ithaca, N.Y.: Cornell Univ. Press.

Derrida, J. 1967. *Of Grammatology.* Trans. G. C. Spivak. Baltimore: Johns Hopkins Univ. Press, 1976.

———. 1987. Interview. In *Criticism in Society,* ed. I. Salusinszky. New York: Methuen, pp. 8–24.

Freud, S. 1905a. *Fragment of an Analysis of a Case of Hysteria. The Standard Edition of the Complete Psychological Works,* ed. and trans. J. Strachey et al. 24 vols. London: Hogarth Press, 1953–74 (hereafter *S.E.*), 7:7–122.

———. 1905b. *Jokes and Their Relation to the Unconscious. S.E.,* Vol. 8.

————. 1905c. *Three Essays on the Theory of Sexuality. S.E.,* 7:125–245.

————. 1908. Hysterical Phantasies and Their Relation to Bisexuality. *S.E.,* 9:155–66.

————. 1909. Some General Remarks on Hysterical Attacks. *S.E.,* 9:227–34.

————. 1931. Female Sexuality. *S.E.,* 21:223–43.

————. 1933. Femininity. *S.E.,* 22:112–35.

Gallop, J. 1982. *The Daughter's Seduction: Feminism and Psychoanalysis.* Ithaca, N.Y.: Cornell Univ. Press.

Grosz, E. 1989. *Sexual Subversions: Three French Feminists.* Sydney: Allen and Unwin Press.

Harvey, E. D. 1992. *Ventriloquized Voices: Feminist Theory and English Renaissance Texts.* London: Routledge.

Irigaray, L. 1974a. *Speculum de l'autre femme.* Paris: Les Editions de Minuit.

————. 1974b. *Speculum of the Other Woman.* Trans. G. C. Gill. Ithaca, N.Y.: Cornell Univ. Press, 1985.

————. 1977. *This Sex Which Is Not One.* Trans. C. Porter and C. Burke. Ithaca, N.Y.: Cornell Univ. Press, 1985.

————. 1991. Interview. In *French Philosophers in Conversation,* ed. R. Mortley. London: Routledge, pp. 62–78.

Jones, A. R. 1985. Writing the Body: Toward an Understanding of l'Écriture féminine. In E. Showalter, ed., *The New Feminist Criticism: Essays on Women, Literature, and Theory.* New York: Pantheon, pp. 361–77.

Kofman, S. 1970. *The Childhood of Art: An Interpretation of Freud's Aesthetics.* Trans. W. Woodhill. New York: Columbia Univ. Press, 1988.

————. 1974. *Freud and Fiction.* Trans. S. Wykes. Cambridge: Polity Press, 1991.

————. 1980a. The Narcissistic Woman: Freud and Girard. *Diacritics* 10.3 (Fall 1980):36–45.

————. 1980b. *L'Enigme de la Femme: la Femme dans les textes de Freud.* Paris: Editions Galilée.

————. 1980c. *The Enigma of Woman: Woman in Freud's Writings.* Trans. C. Porter. Ithaca, N.Y.: Cornell Univ. Press, 1985.

————. 1982. The Economy of Respect: Kant and Respect for Women. Trans. N. Fisher. *Social Research* 49.2:383–404. (Excerpted from 1982 *Le Respect des femmes* [Paris: Editions Galilée].

————. 1983. Autobiographical Writings. Trans. F. Bartkowski. *Sub-Stance* 49 (1986): 6–13.

————. 1988. Rousseau's Phallocratic Ends. Trans. M. Dukats. *Hypatia* 3.3 (Winter 1989): 122–36.

Lacan, J. 1975. A Love Letter. In *Feminine Sexuality: Jacques Lacan and the école freudienne,* ed. J. Mitchell and J. Rose, trans. J. Rose. New York: Pantheon, 1985, pp. 149–61.

Marks, E., and I. de Courtivron., eds. 1980. *New French Feminisms: An Anthology.* Amherst: Univ. of Massachusetts Press.

Moi, T. 1985. *Sexual/Textual Politics*. London: Methuen.

———. 1987. Introduction. In *French Feminist Thought: A Reader*, ed. Moi. Oxford: Basil Blackwell, pp. 1–13.

Oliver, K. 1993. *Reading Kristeva: Unraveling the Double-bind*. Bloomington: Indiana Univ. Press.

Ragland-Sullivan, E. 1986. *Jacques Lacan and the Philosophy of Psychoanalysis*. London: Croon Helm.

Shiach, M. 1991. *Hélène Cixous: A Politics of Writing*. London: Routledge.

Spivak, G. C. 1993. Feminism and Deconstruction Again: Negotiations. In *Outside in the Teaching Machine*. New York: Routledge, pp. 121–40.

Whitford, M. 1991a. *Luce Irigaray: Philosophy in the Feminine*. London: Routledge.

———., ed. 1991b. *The Irigaray Reader*. Oxford: Blackwell.

Part II
Fashioning Femininity

Chapter Four

Marlene, Maggie Thatcher, and the Emperor of Morocco: The Psychic Structure of Caryl Churchill's *Top Girls*

Patricia Reid Eldredge

During several years of contemplating the subject of this discussion—Caryl Churchill's play, *Top Girls* (1982)—I have found myself turning once again to the psychology of Karen Horney for my interpretative model. There are two special reasons, in this case, for my preference. The first is the applicability of Horney's theory, based as it is on interpersonal conflict, to the dramatic genre with its concern for "illuminating through its fictive variations the actuality of mimetic relationships between persons" (Wilshire, 1982, 16). The second is the potential I believe Horney has for contributing to our understanding of the gender issues this play addresses, issues of "feminine" dependency and "masculine" dominance. In hopes of demonstrating both these advantages of the model, I want to share a reading of *Top Girls* that focuses on the interpersonal and intrapsychic conflicts of the central character, Marlene, and to consider its implications for Churchill's politics of gender.

The Horneyan method of literary criticism has been developed by Bernard Paris and applied extensively in his writing, including his studies of Shakespeare, (1991a, 1991b), which exhibit its usefulness for the exploration of dramatic characterization. In using his approach, I will engage in the controversial process of discussing a mimetic character "as if" she were an actual person "whose behavior makes sense in motivational terms" (1991b, 15), while not forgetting that she is an imaginative creation of metaphorical significance. For theater, such analysis is of particular value because an actor must so often work with psychic motivation in order to give a character life on stage, and I have found it helpful here to stay close to the theater through imagining how I would want to see Marlene performed in my ideal production of the play.

The basis for my approach to gender, which is a departure from the gender neutrality of classic Horneyan theory, is Marcia Westkott's *The Feminist Legacy of Karen Horney* (1986). Westkott re-visions Horney's work as a critical theory of female psychology that has contemporary relevance because it enables us to "deconstruct" dependency as the core problem in women's personality development. It is a theory that critiques the competitiveness of our culture (71), the therapeutic deconstruction of which is put forward as a condition of social change (13). Although I am convinced that Horney's work is also relevant for men—and must, in fact, be equally applied to male dominance if we want to take full advantage of its implications for gender—Westkott's analysis of a prevalent cultural pattern in female development has so far proved sound in my literary experiments. Above all, I am indebted to her for enabling me to hear a revolutionary voice in Horney's work that can be a valid response to Churchill's cry for change.

In *Feminist Theatre* (1984), Helene Keyssar aptly describes my experience of *Top Girls* when she writes of Churchill, "In her plays, inner 'psychological' conflicts and outer 'social' conflicts walk together, and equally, on stage" (94); and an increasing appreciation of this double effect has come with my repeated readings of the script. Structurally, *Top Girls* is an odd play, nonlinear in plan and disjunctive in effect: it opens with a scene in which Marlene celebrates a job promotion by having dinner with five ghostly women from history and legend, moves on to the everyday reality of the Top Girls employment agency where she works, and then, in the final scene, shifts to her visit at her sister Joyce's home, a year before the dramatic "present." Disconcerting at first, the pattern began to make sense to me as I realized that a conflict in the present, intensified when the professionally successful Marlene is visited by a daughter doomed to failure, is framed by a fantasy and a memory, each an exploration of the roots of the conflict: the fantasy dramatizes the inner conflict as a social event, while the memory of a bitter personal and political argument between two sisters gradually reveals the causes of inner conflict. It is these opening and closing scenes, in particular, that I want to look at through the lenses of Horney's psychology, which, since it may be unfamiliar to readers, I will introduce with some initial examples from Churchill's text.

If I had to state in one phrase what *Top Girls* is "about," I would say that it is about the absence of what Judith Jordan calls a "we identity" (1991, 68), and Horney's theory begins with that absence in the life of a child. Her premise is that individual development must take place in an environment created by other persons and that its most profound disruption is the "basic anxiety"—the opposite of Erik Erikson's "basic trust"—that results when an unloved child "does not develop a feeling of belonging, of 'we,' " but instead feels isolated, helpless, and deeply insecure (Horney 1950, 18). In *Top Girls*, Churchill gives Marlene and Joyce parents they remember as being too absorbed in their own pain to create a loving environment—poor, overworked, the father alcoholic and the mother abused, "their lives were rubbish" (2.2). Since this background is not known to the audience until the last scene, Marlene's underlying anxiety is one of the final revelations, expressed in her incoherent account of how she once crept down at night and saw her mother beaten: "I had to get out, I knew when I was thirteen, out of their house, out of them, never let that happen to me, never let him, make my own way, out" (2.2).

Marlene's frantic impulse to escape, acted on after she has an illegitimate child at seventeen, illustrates what Horney saw as one of the basic strategies of an anxious child: one can move toward other people, against them, or away from them. Inherently desirable, such moves, when used defensively, become "compulsive, rigid, indiscriminate, and mutually exclusive" (1945, 89), providing the rudiments of later conflicts. In Marlene's case, the move "away from" family is a violent solution that ruptures her ties to parents she pities, an older sister who provided her closest childhood bond, and her "niece" Angie, the daughter she gave to Joyce. Although London is a few hours from home, she now visits only once every few years and almost never writes. Her adult existence is a precarious balance of "away from" and "against": she has made her own way by becoming aggressively successful in business while apparently having only transitory relationships with men and strictly professional contacts with fellow employees.

In her mature theory, Horney's basic strategies are seen to function as dynamic complexes, "solutions" to anxiety that ironically generate more conflict than they resolve. Displacing healthy desires for agency (independent activity) and community (participation with others) are the expansive solution—moving against others to achieve mastery at any price—and the self-effacing solution—moving toward others with a longing to merge with them and be loved totally. A third solution, detachment, moves so far away from others, emotionally, that a healthy desire for personal freedom becomes a quest for a "magic circle" that others cannot penetrate (1945, 91). Because many persons choose one of these three solutions as a predominant strategy, the theory may look like a simple typology when, in fact, it is identifying something far more complicated, as even the "inner life" of a mimetic character demonstrates. At great cost, Marlene has constructed a "combination solution" of expansiveness for her work life and detachment for her personal life. What she fears most is the compliance that has traditionally been the preferred strategy of women in our culture, and what she has lost in defending against that fear is her sense of community.

Westkott finds it most likely that for women "domination and detachment emerge . . . as a protest against powerlessness, only after the core dependent character is formed" (1986, 87), and this would seem true of Marlene: if her first solution (the core) was a submissive move that she experienced as a failed solution, this explains her frantic flight from home and her terror of self-effacing behavior. From the perspective of gender, moreover, it is essential to realize that what she has done is to turn to a solution experienced as masculine, since mastery and detachment are typically encouraged in men (Westkott 1986, 185; Symonds 1978, 196). Both of these observations will be supported by the content of her fantasy.

Finally, to complete this initial sketch of Marlene's conflict, we need to recognize one other defensive move, her attempt to place herself *above* others—in Churchill's wonderfully appropriate metaphor, to become a "top girl." Such an effort, which Horney saw as the ultimate defensive strategy of persons living in a competitive society, is accomplished by forming, from cultural stereotypes, an idealized image of self and identifying with it, so that the real self—all the potential for what one *could* be—is replaced by a glorified concept of what one *should* be. For the typically compliant woman, the idealized self is "the internalization of culturally prescribed femininity" (Westkott 1986, 146); but when a woman like Marlene sets out to trade solutions, she creates "a new idealized self—the Independent Woman—who contemptuously denies the deeply rooted dependency that remains" (208–09) and strives to become "the triumphant exception to the constraints endured by all others" (182). What results is an intensified conflict: among the competing tendencies of compliance, expansiveness, and detachment; between the idealized and the despised selves; and between the real self and this entire false-self system.

The opening scene of *Top Girls* is one of the best literary representations of this complex inner conflict that I have ever found, and were I directing it, I would want my audience first to experience it as Marlene's fantasy. This is an interpretative decision because Churchill has refused to provide any realistic justification for the scene, stating simply, "In the theatre anything's possible" (Fitzsimmons 1989, 62). Yet there is much to invite my psychological reading. Marlene's ghostly guests quite obviously share many experiences with her, particularly the struggle over whether to stay home or go away and the agony of parting with their babies. More importantly, however, they all share Marlene's conflict, in five variations, so that their interactions on stage dramatize the complex inner process that I have described above.

Thus we may imagine an offstage Marlene alone in front of the "telly," getting slowly drunk while she has the waking dream she acts out on the stage. Her five guests are Isabella Bird, a Victorian traveler from Edinburgh; Lady Nijo, a medieval Japanese courtesan who became a wandering Buddhist nun; Joan, the apocryphal female Pope of the ninth century; Patient Griselda from Chaucer's "The Clerk's Tale"; and Dull Gret, a peasant women who leads a charge through hell in a Brueghel painting. Over dinner at a restaurant, these women narrate their stories. Because the playwright has included special instructions for overlapping dialogue, the conversation is a cacophony of voices, which John Simon hears as the "discontinuity of communication" that "makes for loss of community" (1983, 78). The emotional movement of the scene involves an unexpected twist, beginning with an "anticipation of a unique celebration of women's potential" and ending on "a single chord of misery and anger" (Kritzer 1991, 143). Psychologically, these effects suggest to me an unintegrated psyche, in which the various parts of the self are out of touch, with a progressive movement toward less conscious levels of conflict as the fantasy releases repressed emotions and produces increasingly enigmatic images.

Isabella and Nijo, actual historical figures, begin the storytelling and dominate the early part of the scene. As the unrelenting voice for mastery and freedom, Isabella best represents Marlene's present solution. Like Marlene, she began her travels by leaving behind a sister, Hennie, a "sweet soul" who was a stereotypically dependent Victorian woman. Unlike Marlene, however, she eventually let family responsibilities draw her home, where she nursed her dying sister and married her sister's doctor, John, another compliant figure. She thus tests out Marlene's fear of returning, and the results are not encouraging. Hennie and John were "so good" that Isabella felt guilty for not being like them, so she became an aggressive do-gooder, but discovered that such detested activity made her physically ill: "The very presence of people exhausted my emotional reserves. . . . It is dangerous to put oneself in depressing circumstances." Only another journey, after her husband died, released her from suffering—a confirmation of Marlene's belief that her own escape was a matter of life and death.

But if the wanderer can never return to the past, neither can she let go of it. In the juxtaposed narrative, Lady Nijo rarely speaks of her adventures as an itinerant nun but is preoccupied with memories of her early life that include her various pleasures and humiliations as a royal concubine, the death of her father (Marlene's father has also died), and the loss of several babies. Nijo is a fitting symbol of Westkott's sexualized, devalued, and dependent feminine type (Westkott, chs. 4–6). Born to be a courtesan, she was expected to be totally submissive; her father gave her to the emperor when she was fourteen. Since she had no value apart from her service to men, she became an outcast when she lost royal favor after her father's death, and by the end of the scene her anger at all of this has surfaced. Yet she cannot forget the satisfactions of being the special object of powerful others—saintly father, kingly husband—and so a more independent life later simply leaves her feeling homesick and empty, "dead already." Hers is the persona masking pain: to the suggestion that traveling cheered her, she replies curtly, "I'm not a cheerful person, Marlene. I just laugh a lot."

With these two narrators creating between them the dramatic tension of expansive "moving out" and submissive "staying home," Pope Joan, as she becomes more vocal in the middle of the scene, initially tips the scale for expansiveness. Disguised as a boy, Joan left home at twelve in a tenacious pursuit of scholarly truth and eventually, still disguised, succeeded to the papacy. At this triumphant point in the narrative, Marlene rises to acknowledge her own promotion—"Well, it's not Pope but it is managing director"—and toast them all: "To our courage and the way we changed our lives and our extraordinary achievements. We chose the masculine way, and it worked!" But then the tone changes abruptly, from celebration to commiseration, with the account of how Joan delivered a child in the middle of a procession and was stoned to death—betrayed, at the pinnacle of success, by her female body. Terror of the dangers that accompany a rise to power is now aroused, preparing the way for self-effacement to take the floor when Griselda makes her belated entrance.

The legend of Patient Griselda, the submissive wife who allowed her aristocratic husband to deprive her of her children until he chose to reward her by returning them, is the cultural epitome of idealized compliance. Griselda appeals to Marlene, I suggest, because her single-minded commitment to her solution eliminates conflict and because, paradoxically, she masters through compliance and lives happily ever after. Yet her entrance into the fantasy at this point simply makes things worse: Marlene protests against her attitude all through the narrative, exclaims "I can't stand this" and leaves for the restroom when told how the first child is taken away, and orders a double round of brandies to help them all endure the climax of the tale. For the other guests, too, the idea of perfect submission seems intolerable, and as tears and anger erupt around her, even Griselda is forced to wonder whether "it would have been nicer if Walter hadn't had to."

Toward the end of the scene, Joan begins to recite, drunkenly and in Latin, a passage from Lucretius' *On the Nature of the Universe:* It is a joy, says the speaker, to watch a disaster at sea from the safety of the shore or a battle from the sidelines, but an even greater joy to stand in a quiet citadel, fortified by wisdom, and look down on the aimless wanderings of others (2. 1–19). Obliquely, Joan is now revealed to embody Marlene's unconscious impulses to resolve the conflict by withdrawing to the position of onlooker. The detached person, Horney says, "lives as if he were sitting in the orchestra and observing a drama acted on the stage" (1950, 261); so Joan wants to join the audience—but only if she can have the king's box! For Marlene/Pope Joan, detachment is not a safe alternative unless one can reach the citadel, that is, fully become the idealized self who is above conflict. But Joan, being a woman, couldn't reach that point even as Pope; and Marlene, the new executive, may be presumed to have a glass ceiling between her and an equivalent achievement. Although the detached position is longed for intensely, it cannot resolve the dilemma.

Instead, the fantasy concludes with a reaffirmation of expansiveness that leaves the dreamer pretty much where she began. First, while Joan's Latin chant continues in the background, Dull Gret, who otherwise speaks in monosyllables, brings the scene to a climax with her account of how she led a crowd of women in a charge through hell. Jane Thomas identifies Gret as the "violent rebellion" that is the antithesis of Griselda's obedience (1992, 180), and I suggest a similar polarization: at the unconscious core of her conflict, Marlene is "the conflicted female psyche who sweetly complies with her devaluation" (Griselda) and "rages to triumph over it" (Gret) (Westkott 1986, 1). Since it is largely a description of Brueghel's painting, Gret's narrative has the static, appropriately hellish quality of repressed rage. Whatever the constructive possibilities of this internal subversive may be, for Marlene she only refuels the effort to triumph through the idealized expansive self, represented by Isabella's closing description of her final journey: "I was the only European woman ever to have seen the Emperor of Morocco." The masterful traveler gets the last word, but her victory at the feet of a masculine ideal is a dubious one at best.

The one hopeful note in all this is the fact that, for all the babble, the fantasy is not without signs of sympathy and sharing that might indicate some self-empathy on the part of the dreamer. When the pain starts, the ghosts move to comfort each other: Gret, who has been stealing the wine, begins to share it; Joan tries to comfort a weeping Nijo; Griselda, in turn, cares for a vomiting Joan. As for Marlene, she plays the good hostess to her psychic guests; with the exception of her moments of resistance to Griselda, she is the one who listens, devoting nearly all her lines to the encouragement of the narratives, so that she really does seem to attempt to understand her inner people.

In light of this possibility, it is discouraging to move from the Saturday night dream to the Monday morning "reality" of the employment agency. Asked why scene 2, a brief agency scene that seems to belong to act 2, is sandwiched into the middle of act 1, one of my students convincingly defended the playwright's choice. He was shocked, he said, after watching Marlene interact with the imaginary women, to see her so unsympathetic with her client Jeanine, and he decided that was just the point. Whatever capacity for empathy Marlene has, it does not carry over into her professional life: in her fantasy she appears caring but powerless, out of control, whereas in her outer world she is powerful but generally uncaring.

Churchill's presentation of the agency scenes clearly indicates that Marlene's work environment, ruled by a competitive ethic, fosters her expansiveness at every turn, with the fact that actors from scene 1 double for the agency roles also helping to keep the psychological and the social juxtaposed. Clients and other agents have conflicts similar to Marlene's: Jeanine, for instance, a role doubled with Patient Griselda's in the original British production, is a timid woman torn between her longings for change and travel and her desire for marriage. But such personal problems are briskly dismissed: Marlene simply warns Jeanine against mentioning marriage in interviews, slots her into a couple of commonplace secretarial openings because she doesn't fit "something glossier," and holds out the lure that "you'll be at the top with new girls coming in underneath you" (1.2). The business of creating top girls and topping them all in the process offers Marlene immense satisfaction, allowing her to shut out other impulses as inappropriate for the workplace. There is, at most, only a fleeting awareness that she might use her problems to understand someone else's.

I say "fleeting awareness" because I think I would direct the main actress in my production to be a little closer than usual to her emotions on this particular Monday. In act 2, scene 1, in the midst of several episodes depicting the empty, restless lives of other agents and their clients, two incidents give her chances to be aware. The first begins with the arrival of Mrs. Kidd, wife of Howard, the man who competed with Marlene for promotion and is now responding to his failure by falling ill. Typically self-sacrificing—"I put him first every inch of the way"—Mrs. Kidd confronts Marlene, suggesting that she step aside for Howard's sake, which, needless to say, Marlene is not about to do. In all likelihood the audience will applaud when Mrs. Kidd's "You're one of those ballbreakers" is countered by Marlene's "Could you please piss off?"—and yet there is a ring of truth in the wife's accusation that "You don't care." At the end of the scene, news comes that Howard has had a heart attack, and the agents don't care, beyond the gesture of sending flowers: "Lucky he didn't get the job if that's what his health's like," is Nell's opinion.

Whether Marlene is touched has to be determined by how she says her two words, "Poor sod," which I would be inclined to make more reflective pause than careless dismissal. Either way, however, the episode serves to remind the audience that a system fostering a driven expansiveness creates an uncaring environment for men as well as women.

The exchange between Marlene and Mrs. Kidd has had an unambivalent onstage audience in the person of Angie, the "niece," who, having just arrived in London hoping to be part of her aunt's world, gapes in admiration at the "piss-off" putdown. Actually Marlene's daughter, as she herself has come to suspect (1.3), she is an awkward, overweight, maladjusted adolescent, motivated by anger at her "mother," Joyce, and blind admiration for her "aunt." She is a most unpromising candidate for a top girl, and when Win calls Marlene's attention to her desire to be one, Marlene pronounces judgment on her dozing child, "Packer in Tesco more like. . . . She's not going to make it." Since these are chronologically the last lines of the play, the tone in which they are uttered matters considerably. Is this a rejection, not only of Angie's future but of Angie herself? I think it is, and yet I imagine Marlene speaking, not harshly, but thoughtfully, as she remembers the event that we now see in the final scene.

A year ago, in response to a secret invitation from Angie, she visited Joyce's home for the first time in six years, and the sisters quarreled. Their recollected argument is the climax of the play, and, like the opening scene, it is a marvelous dramatization of conflict as Marlene contends with the sister who is her opposite. Again, as in the fantasy scene, overlapping dialogue is used to create the effect of two persons who fail to listen to each other. Though occasional critics have tried to make Joyce, the working-class woman, the voice of a truth Marlene cannot hear, most recognize, as Amelia Kritzer does, that Churchill is offering us "two unacceptable others" (1991, 148)—for me, the expansive woman and the self-effacing woman.

Growing up in the same family as Marlene, Joyce has just as much conflict as she does, only in a way that corresponds much more closely to the Westkott type with her sweet compliance and submerged anger. Joyce is the one who stayed when Marlene went, and, having agreed fifteen years ago to raise her sister's child, she now regards that sister with jealousy and resentment; she has separated from her husband and is earning her living with cleaning jobs, and she feels, not without some justification, that Marlene has been liberated at her expense. Moreover, when Marlene does return, she still reaches out to Joyce for maternal support, little sister to elder. Their relationship is one indication that Marlene has not resolved her dependency conflicts, which is why she stays away. As for Joyce, she is what Westkott aptly names the "undernurtured nurturer" (1986, 139), trying to give to others from emotional supplies she does not have.

What this visit gives Joyce is a chance to cash in all her chips in an effort to make Marlene feel as guilty as possible, and Marlene, long a fighter, is quick to rise in her own defense. Throughout the scene each woman uses every device she can think of to "get at" the other. Joyce, for instance, reveals that she had a miscarriage "because I was so tired looking after your fucking baby." As she fumes, "That's the only chance I ever had," Marlene interrupts with "I've had two abortions, are you interested?" Joyce accuses Marlene of trying to take Angie away from her; Marlene threatens to remove that danger by staying away another six years; Joyce says fine, and Marlene starts to cry—and wins the first round by getting Joyce to comfort her.

A particularly good example of their two defensive solutions in action is their exchange over their aging, senile mother, who they agree has lived a wasted life in poverty and abuse. Joyce visits her every week because "Somebody has to" and "How would I feel if I didn't go?" whereas Marlene, having just called on her for the first time in years, defends that as her choice, twice declaring, "It's up to me." Like so many self-effacing women, Joyce is compulsively dutiful, and it would not be surprising if her needy mother were foremost among those she has tried to nurture (Westkott 1986, 31–34). Marlene, on the other hand, deludes herself with this illusion of choice, since it is fear of the same web that traps Joyce that is keeping her away.

At the height of the quarrel, with both women now drinking as freely as the ghosts did in act 1, we reach the point in the play where the political and the psychological come together most overtly. The political beliefs of the sisters are inseparable from their conflicts, as Churchill herself confirms: "The argument is a drunken one between two angry sisters, not a considered political assessment, and is exaggerated and oversimplified on both sides" (Fitzsimmons 1989, 64). So Marlene's "I hate the working class" is uttered amid agonizing recollections of her parents, and her "I don't believe in class" is a denial of anything that could keep her from rising to the top. Predictably, she admires the "tough lady," Margaret Thatcher, England's current top girl, whose style and policies fit so well the values of expansiveness. And just as predictably, Joyce, seeing Thatcher as a symbol of evil, "Hitlerina," plunges into a vengeful fantasy of a revolution that will "get" the Maggies and Marlenes: "So don't come around here when it happens because if someone's kicking you I'll just laugh." In what proves to be her winning move, she begins to argue in terms of "us and them," claiming her right as the good girl who stayed home to be "us" with family and community, and successfully making Marlene feel her exclusion as "them." Marlene tries to make up, but this time Joyce refuses her bid for affection, so that the action concludes without a closing of the rift between them.

The play ends on a single note of anxiety—Angie's basic anxiety. As Marlene prepares for sleep, her daughter—how much of the quarrel has she overheard?—stumbles in mumbling, "Frightening," the last word of the script. Moments before, Marlene proclaims that she will not help people find jobs "if they're stupid or lazy or frightened," and Joyce replies, "What about Angie? . . . She's stupid, lazy and frightened, so what about her?" Frightened, yes, but lazy and stupid? Probably not naturally so, anyway, because there is plenty of textual evidence for the psychological causes of Angie's ineptitude, allowing us to see her as the most unhealthy child of all in this destructive family cycle. Joyce's resentment makes her an ambivalent mother, whose language can swing in an instant from "Want a choccy biccy, Angie?" to "Fucking rotten little cunt" (1.3), while her ex-husband "was never that fond" of a child that wasn't his (2.2). In a singularly ironic moment, she sums up the atmosphere of her home when she tries to comfort a teary Marlene with "Everyone's always crying in this house. Nobody takes any notice." There is considerable irony also in the scene Churchill devotes to Angie and her friend Kit (1.3): "squashed together" in "a shelter made of junk," the two share their fears of the adult world and show their emotional dependence on each other, much as we would imagine Joyce and Marlene doing in their childhood.

The tragedy of *Top Girls* is that Marlene, in the play's hypothetical future, probably will do nothing for Angie; it is most likely that, seeing in her "the least attractive face of dependency" (Kritzer 1991, 148), she will send her back home and continue to stay far from mother, sister, and daughter because she so clearly sees in them dependent defenses she fears in herself. As Marlene's director, then, although I would have her remember "What about Angie?" and not without pain, I would do nothing to suggest that she is about to help. As her audience, without judging what she did at seventeen with her baby, I *want* her to help now, even as I understand why she can't. To defend against helplessness, Angie has developed a pathological need for control: when Marlene, during the visit, goes to her room to say goodnight, she learns that the "lazy" child devotes her energies to constructing a secret society from such materials as black magic and politics, which, she quips to Joyce, must be "a plot to take over the world." For Angie, Auntie Marlene, seemingly in wonderful control of her life, embodies the idealized self, a self Angie will never be. What she might actualize, in the worst scenario, is the violent self who wants to kill her mother with a brick (1.3); her double on stage is Dull

Gret, who, in Irving Wardle's words, shares her "hopeless yearning and suppressed anger" (Fitzsimmons 1989, 59). As a metaphor for young women enmeshed in dependency conflicts, Angie *is* the future, and the future is frightening.

I believe Churchill has written a compassionate play in which, as Robert Cushman observes, "sympathy is withheld from no one" (Fitzsimmons 1989, 58). She has not, however, written a hopeful one, at least in the sense of giving us an answer to the dramatic conflict through anyone on stage, and she recognizes this. "I quite deliberately left a hole in the play," she has said, "rather than give people a model of what they could be like. I meant the thing that is absent to have a presence in the play" (Fitzsimmons 1989, 61). What she has in mind quite evidently has to do with the values of feminist socialism, but I think what she has done most importantly is to create a sense of "absent presence" that may perhaps be named differently for each interpretation, and I want to conclude by naming it for mine.

Actually, this script is full of absent persons whose presence is felt on the stage, most notably all the men—Howard, Marlene's dead father, Angie's unmentioned father—and Marlene's mother. But there is also, oddly, a sense of absent protagonist, because Marlene can strike the audience as so unsympathetic and untranscendent that she becomes the antagonist, an embodiment of the misuses of power. I have explained in psychological terms why I think this happens, but this doesn't entirely address the problem of an antagonistic protagonist; and so I will hazard the suggestion, fully aware of all the questions it raises, that the central absent presence is what Horneyan theory would call Marlene's "real self."

I use the term "real self" to mean the self of genuine potential that will be actualized if the false-self system is therapeutically deconstructed, leaving a person free to fulfill her own combination of individual and communal potentialities without rigid oppositions and defensive ideals. In a way that fits nicely my search for the missing protagonist, Westkott makes the woman who engages in this deconstructive process the true female hero, whose goal is the real self as an existential "locus of choice" (1986, 199). Yet caution is necessary here because of the risk of creating new idealizations: Westkott has argued that Jean Baker Miller's "self-in-relation" is really an "idealized empathetic self" (1989, 248), but, perhaps because she deemphasizes the dangers of expansiveness in women, she herself is less cautious about the heroic autonomous self, a concept precariously close to the masculine ideal Marlene idolizes. Though therapy takes great personal courage, its most basic assumption is that one cannot go it alone but will become conscious of the real self as "a structure of coherent separateness and meaningful connection" (Jordon 1991, 79) only within the context of a relationship. Agency and community are found together, and Marlene remains a telling example of the woman who needs both.

In my experience, the real self of actual persons is most likely to be a kind of absent presence, so that even when it is deeply repressed, one glimpses it in those moments when defenses relax. I have tried to imagine Marlene being acted in that way: we, the audience, come to the end of my hypothetical production knowing what she could be or, even more importantly, since she has no life beyond performance, what we desire for her. On the one hand, then, we want her to become a person capable of genuine choice. We may recognize even in her defensive "choices" a measure of heroic achievement, since she has saved herself from a worse life than the one she has, while at the same time we understand that only liberation from the entire false-self system, with its idealized heroic self and its despised dependent self—Isabella and Nijo, Joan and Griselda— could give her free choices, particularly in human relationships, where she personally needs them most. We may imagine, for instance, that she would return home more than once in a decade if she could really have a choice.

Kritzer believes that "the vision animating *Top Girls* is a fusion of power and nurturing" (1991, 142), and Westkott has that same vision for her female hero: "She practices an empowered caring that risks conflict to change the world so that women and the socially necessary need to care for one another are no longer devalued" (1986, 203). "Empowered caring" seems to me the most precise phrase for naming abstractly the missing presence in the play, which then may be made more concrete by continuing to imagine what a conflict-free Marlene might do. She might do those things that she is so well positioned to do at the end of the script. She might, after having established a better relationship with Joyce and Angie, be capable of acts of caring empowerment that would help to turn their lives in better directions. Learning to care more for other women, she might either change the practices of the Top Girls agency or start a new one with policies better designed to meet the needs of working women. And to restore the presence of men to her life, she might even find a social circle including someone other than "fellas who like to be seen with a high-flying lady" (2.2).

By leaving a hole in a play that addresses so honestly the entanglement of women in their conflicts, the socially conscious Churchill risked a black hole of despair; and quite possibly, given the arduous therapeutic task of untangling even one person's conflicts to get from what is to what might be, psychological explanations such as mine leave readers who want social change with the black hole effect. But I hope not. Her analysis as mimetic character concluded, Marlene returns to being a metaphor, who will never reach "might be." Change is a matter for us, the living audience of the play or readers of its interpretations—a matter of what we do with our explorations of the psyche and with our vision of what it is desirable to change in the lives of women and men.

References

Churchill, C. 1982. *Top Girls.* London: Samuel French.

Fitzsimmons L., ed. 1989. *File on Churchill.* London: Methuen,

Horney, K. 1945. *Our Inner Conflicts.* New York: Norton.

———. 1950. *Neurosis and Human Growth.* New York: Norton.

Jordon, J. V. 1991. Empathy and Self Boundaries. In J. V. Jordon et al., *Women's Growth in Connection.* New York: Guilford, pp. 67–80.

Keyssar, H. 1984. *Feminist Theatre.* New York: St. Martin's.

Kritzer, A. H. 1991. *The Plays of Caryl Churchill.* New York: St. Martin's.

Lucretius. 1951. *On the Nature of the Universe.* Trans. R. E. Latham. New York: Penguin.

Paris, B. J. 1991a. *Bargains with Fate: Psychological Crises and Conflicts in Shakespeare and His Plays.* London: Associated Univ. Press.

———. 1991b. *Character as a Subversive Force in Shakespeare.* London: Associated Univ. Press.

Simon, J. 1983. Crime, Women, and Song. *New York,* March 28:76–78.

Symonds, A. 1978. The Psychodynamics of Expansiveness in the Success-Oriented Woman. *Am. J. Psychoanal.* 38:195–205.

Thomas, J. 1992. The Plays of Caryl Churchill: Essays in Refusal. In A. Page, ed., *The Death of the Playwright: Modern British Drama and Literary Theory.* New York: St. Martin's, pp. 160–84.

Westkott, M. 1986. *The Feminist Legacy of Karen Horney.* New Haven, Conn.: Yale Univ. Press.

———. 1989. Female Relationality and the Idealized Self. *Am. J. Psychoanal.* 49:239–50.

Wilshire, B. 1982. *Role Playing and Identity: The Limits of Theatre as Metaphor.* Bloomington: Indiana Univ. Press.

Chapter Five
Dishing It Out:
Patterns of Women's Sadism in Literature

David Galef

Over half a century ago, Helene Deutsch wrote: "In some corner of her heart, every woman has a masochistic need to experience the torments of longing and the suffering that deep love can bring" (1944, 190). The topic of women's masochism has received much attention since then, largely from critics interested in debunking this Freudian stereotype.[1] Much passive or masochistic behavior, runs the counterargument, is not a function of biology or psychological predisposition but rather a social construct. This line of reasoning is egalitarian insofar as it proposes gender as a set of possibilities. In the flurry of discussion over masochism, however, few have broached the complementary issue of women's sadism.

Some feminist critics have dismissed the issue, claiming that sadism is patriarchal in origin and hence almost exclusively the province of men.[2] This assumption seems ingenuous at best. On the other hand, the Sadeian woman in leather and brandishing a whip appears to be more a product of the male imagination than a real female preference.[3] Gilles Deleuze notes: "In our opinion the woman torturer belongs entirely to masochism" (1989, 42). In *The Sadeian Woman,* Angela Carter amplifies this idea: "her cruelty is only the manifestation of the victim or patient's guilt before the fact of his own sexuality, of which he is ashamed. She is not cruel for her own sake, or for her own gratification. She is most truly subservient when most apparently dominant" (1979, 21). This analysis leaves open the question of what forms actual sadism in women might take.

If writers such as Nancy Chodorow (1978) are right in asserting universal psychological gender differences, a claim for which modern studies of brain physiology are showing more and more support, then perhaps the entire concept of sadism should be redefined to include a feminine version.[4] Everyone experiences *Schadenfreude* from time to time, but not everyone gives vent to it physically. When women act sadistically, they tend to employ subtler modes: inflicting guilt, withholding emotion, or subverting seemingly innocuous situations through latent hostility. Inaction and silence, for example, often read as socially enforced passivity, may also function on another level as socially acceptable aggression. As in Freud's "The Economic Problem of Masochism" (1924), such a decision is often economic or pragmatic, using the only means available. Men may certainly act in these ways, but for largely social and some biological reasons—as Konrad Lorenz (1963) documented—their sadism is usually a more blatant affair. Finding the more oblique forms of women's social aggression is relevant not just for psychoanalysis, but also as a guide to reading texts by both male and female authors that have traditionally seemed dull and intractable (the patriarchal interpretation) or simply repressed (a standard feminist interpretation). In short, a subtler behavioral etiology suggests a new mode of reading between the lines.

Definitions of sadism vary somewhat but tend to converge on a few basic principles. Erich Fromm divides sadism into three categories:

> One is to make others dependent on oneself and to have absolute and unrestricted power over them, so as to make of them nothing but instruments, "clay in the potter's hand." Another consists of the impulse not only to rule over others in this absolute fashion, but to exploit them, to use them, to steal from them, to disembowel them, and, so to speak, to incorporate anything eatable in them. This desire can refer to material things as well as to immaterial ones, such as the emotional or intellectual qualities a person has to offer. A third kind of sadistic tendency is the wish to make others suffer or to see them suffer. This suffering can be physical, but more often it is mental suffering. Its aim is to hurt actively, to humiliate, embarrass others, or to see them in embarrassing and humiliating positions. (1941, 144)

Fromm's elegant divisions notwithstanding, the three modes tend to merge. In fact, the third type of sadism, "the wish to abuse others," seems to subsume the other two. As for the behavioral etiology, Melanie Klein traces it to the child's instinctive desire for nourishment that leads to biting the mother's breast: such "phantasies and feelings of an aggressive and of a gratifying, erotic nature, which are to a large extent fused together (a fusion which is called sadism), play a dominant part in the child's early life" (1936, 293). Susanne P. Schad-Somers relies on a far more social model, observing that sadomasochism is often thought to stem from maternal aloofness or parental narcissism in general, adding,

"It is my own conviction that *persecution* coupled with *humiliation* and *shame* are the *key variables* in the formation of the sadomasochistic character formation" (1982, 39). Such psychological abuse may be inflicted on both girls and boys, but society permits boys to react in a more physical way. Since the repression in girls is greater, the resulting behavior is likely to be more indirect and subtle, even seemingly passive. In *Female Perversions,* Louise J. Kaplan describes such conduct as "a mental strategy that uses one or another social stereotype of masculinity or femininity in a way that deceives the onlooker about the unconscious meanings of the behaviors she or he is observing" (1991, 9). For women in particular, seeming to stay within gender stereotypes may be as important as the accompanying deception that covers one's divergence.

What kind of action resembles inaction and uses the oppressor's force against him? The closest fitting term for this kind of behavior is *passive-aggressive,* which Benjamin Wolman defines as a "behavior syndrome characterized by passivity and aggressiveness with the aggressiveness often expressed by obstructionism, stubbornness, pouting, etc. This pattern usually reflects hostility and resentment at the individual's inability to establish a satisfactory relationship with a person or institution upon which he is overdependent" (1973, 276). The behavioral implications of this description are often noted by both sexes but too rarely scrutinized. What does it mean for someone to act in these ways, to the point where the actions become an independent system in the personality rather than merely a product of frustration?

For one thing, overt aggression will be muffled and diverted, the seemingly innocuous turned vicious. Textual evidence of this behavior is not uncommon; engaged interpretation is. In some ways, a more apt title for this chapter might be "Reading for the Gaps: Patterns of Passive-Aggression," stressing that passive-aggressive behavior is by no means only a female trait, and that in any event this analysis is restricted to textual description (dangerous territory, for art works can be interrogated, but they cannot answer back). In another sense, however, this chapter is meant to push boundaries aside; hence, the extension of sadism to the female sphere. The definition enabling this recognition is based on a conflation of Fromm's three types of sadism: pleasure in control, in exploitation, or in another's pain.

This paradigm is an expansion insofar as it defines pleasure to include satisfaction or a release of tension. It does not ignore etiology, but takes as a given that the sadist is enacting a form of revenge on an oppressive figure, whether actual or symbolic. Thus, a boy tearing the wings off a fly may seem the essence of a sadist, whereas a woman schoolteacher whipping boys because the patriarchy has denied her an identity may be termed a victim, but the truth is far murkier: that any act of sadism is traceable to earlier oppression (witness the link between sex offenders and their abusive parents). This study does not in the least exculpate (or applaud) domination but does observe its wide scope, choosing to concentrate on the gender often thought to be comparatively free of it. The levels of metaphor and displacement that form equivalencies in a text are quite a different matter in the real world, where to attack an innocent man is entirely different from attacking an abusive husband—even when one man may stand for millennia of patriarchal tyranny. This reading, confined to a psychoanalytic treatment of literary texts, is meant to fill in a symbolic gap.

As Nancy Henley and Jo Freeman observe in "The Sexual Politics of Interpersonal Behavior": "Social interaction is the battlefield where the daily war between the sexes is fought" (1981, 179). Poets such as Sylvia Plath, Adrienne Rich, Anne Sexton, and Marge Piercy expose these covert hostilities. In "What's That Smell in the Kitchen?", for example, Piercy claims: "All over America women are burning dinners" (1983, 20). The meaning is easy to read because Piercy emphasizes the message in both metaphor and social reality: "Anger sputters in her brainpan, confined / but spewing out missiles of hot fat." "Burning dinner," she concludes, "is not incompetence but war." The insistence at the end of the poem is necessary, however, precisely because the behavior does resemble culinary sloppiness, the purposeful masquerading as the accidental. Also, paired with the rage and hostility is the opposite and equal impulse to avoid confrontation. As Piercy writes in "Ragged Ending": "Silently / I scream my head off" (18). Or, as a patient reflects on her husband in Estela V. Welldon's *Mother, Madonna, Whore*, "I hate him, but I don't want to show it" (1992, 22).

The reason that this seeming passivity covers naked aggression is multiply determined. The primary one may stem from Lorenz's psychobiology: in a situation where the aggressor possesses a stronger body, a physical confrontation would be folly. Moreover, if the opponent is lacking in subtlety, a hard-to-read strategy may succeed in getting around him. On a more complex level, however, the ego may deflect one's desires. Thus, an unacceptable impulse may be sublimated or displaced through metaphoric substitution: the urge to murder one's mate eventuates in burning his dinner. These acts, resembling the tropes of metonymy and synecdoche, may in fact be read as such on the page. Similarly, in *A Map of Misreading* (1975), Harold Bloom links poetic images with rhetorical tropes, which are in turn tied to psychic defenses: high and low images are part of hyperbole and litotes, for example, which are functions of repression. This broadened definition of sadistic behavior parallels Andrea Dworkin's (1985) expanded definition of pornography as almost any form of objectification. Admittedly, this is one of the potential pitfalls of reading reality as a text or vice versa: though both may be multiply determined, reality has a base and interpretative consequences that texts do not have. On the other hand, T. S. Eliot's objective correlative (1919) can pair specific audience responses with particular scenarios in part because characters within the works also act as guides to behavior, simulacra of real life and its psychological paradigms.

Piercy's "What's That Smell" stresses the desire to get even, to sabotage the complacent patriarchal order. Passive-aggressive behavior can also be used as a sadistic means of control. Distinguishing between the two impulses, however, is not easy. One can try to classify cruelty according to its etiology: retaliating for received hurt, for example, versus getting pleasure from even an innocent stranger's pain. But in any systematic or repeated infliction of harm, it becomes extremely difficult to separate out the competitive or corrective impulses from the satisfaction of seeing another suffer. Lynn S. Chancer describes their common root: "Sadomasochism is fueled and motivated by a restless desire to somehow, in some way, procure recognition from an other" (1992, 69). This echoes Jessica Benjamin's point about human development and its need for recognition, more complexly the "conflict between assertion of self and the need for the other" (1988, 31).[5] As Faulkner's Addie Bundren thinks about her pupils in *As I Lay Dying:* "I would hate my father for ever having planted me. I would look forward to the times when they faulted, so I could whip them. . . . I would think with each blow of the switch: Now you are aware of me!" (1930, 162). In a Skinnerian paradigm (1957, 154), such behavior becomes its own reinforcer, the means and the results conflated in an endless chain of signifiers, and the question of who first antagonized whom is almost beside the point.

Passive-aggressive sadism runs the gamut from overt antagonism to covert withdrawal. To list several manifestations: nagging, gossip, guilt-infliction, sexual teasing, and removal of emotional affect. Sadeian control of the body is replaced by the manipulation of behavior, or simply psychic force. These coercions are particularly well masked, however, because they correspond so precisely to stereotypical images of female behavior. They are, in that sense, a double revenge upon patriarchal strictures—discipline handed out by the overly disciplined. Whether the sadism is unconscious is more or less irrelevant, in the same way that an author's intentions are not the arbiter of his or her work.

One of the most blatant forms of passive-aggressive control is nagging, often stereotyped as a wifely or maternal trait. The wife in James Thurber's classic "The Secret Life of Walter Mitty" (1942), for instance, is a model of the type, constantly reminding her husband of his failings, from his poor driving to his need for overshoes. Masked as uxorial solicitude, her domestic control is such that Walter Mitty can find refuge only in daydreaming, which she also attacks. When Walter protests, "Does it ever occur to you that I am sometimes thinking?", she responds, "I'm going to take your temperature when I get you home" (80). Resistance is interpreted as sickness, and even Mrs. Mitty's diction, "get you home," shows her authority. Walter's last daydream, appropriately, is about facing a firing squad.[6] One could argue that Mrs. Mitty's behavior is a species of moral sadism, just as Freud distinguishes between erotogenic and moral masochism (1924, 161), but the two species often combine. One may use humility or moral righteousness as weapons, as the schoolmistresses Miss Miller and Miss Scatcherd do in *Jane Eyre,* or employ a drive for perfection to subdue all those who fail to meet one's own exacting standards.

Closely allied with nagging is the stratagem of inducing guilt, which often works through paradox. That is, the guilt-inducer controls another through self-claims of inferiority and inadequacy. This, too, is conventionally associated with the province of the mother or wife. In Philip Roth's *Portnoy's Complaint,* for example, the main reason that Alex lands on the psychoanalytic couch is to come to terms with the tremendous guilt he feels. Though his mother may be a master at dishing it out, far eclipsing her is a neighboring woman, Mrs. Nimkin, who shames her son to suicide and then exclaims, "Why? Why? Why did he do this to us?" As Alex cannily points out: "Hear? Not what might we have done to him, oh no, never that—why did he do this *to us?* To us! Who would have given our arms and legs to make him happy and a famous concert pianist into the bargain!" (1969, 97). As Karen Horney remarks of this pattern: "A dominating mother feeling resentment about a child's disobedience will believe, and declare, that the child does not love her" (1937, 170). The paradigm works with uncannily precise effects: by making the subject aware of both his inadequacy and privileged position, one can induce shame and torment, control the subject's very thoughts.

As Henley and Freeman point out, "In fact, the sheer use of verbalization is a form of dominance because it can quite literally render someone speechless by preventing one from 'getting a word in edgewise'" (1981, 186). This is the kind of strategy employed by Mme X in Strindberg's *The Stronger* (1889), in which she triumphs over her husband's mistress Mme Y by explaining the situation at length, rescripting it in her own terms. Controlling all the words, Mme X manipulates her rival, inverting the whole dramatic situation: "And why are you always silent, silent, silent? I used to think it was because you were strong; but perhaps it was just that you had nothing to say. Because your head was empty" (234). Significantly, though now with an altered significance, Mme Y says nothing. This exchange, if it can be called that, shows two further features of sadistic revenge through passive-aggressive means: first, silence is one of its strategies, though it tends to be a weaker form. Sarcasm, after all, one of the verbal means of aggression, comes from the Greek *sarkasmos,* the tearing of flesh. Second, these tactics are by no means directed exclusively against men, but are often deployed among groups of women or girls.

In Margaret Atwood's *Cat's Eye* (1989), for instance, the protagonist Elaine's childhood is scarred by three so-called friends who police her every action. As she recounts, from the vantage of age but with the memory of fear: "They comment on the kind of lunch I have, how I hold my sandwich, how I chew" (126). The merest incident, such as a phone call from one of her friends, Grace, becomes a control-game, though no game for the victim: "'You want to come out and play?' she says, in her neutral tone that is at the same time blank and soft, like glazed paper. I know Cordelia is standing beside her. If I say no, I will be accused of something. If I say yes, I will have to do it. I say yes" (144). The words "neutral," "blank," and "soft" provide the kind of cover that prevents detection from outside the enclosed relation.

The difference between this kind of coercion and typically male sadism is keenly observed by Elaine herself, who wishes her brother would intervene: "Cordelia does nothing physical. If it was boys, chasing or teasing, he would know what to do, but I don't suffer from boys in this way. Against girls and their indirectness, their whisperings, he would be helpless" (166). The situation is strikingly similar to Michel Foucault's description of control in *Discipline and Punish:* "The agent of punishment must exercise a total power, which no third party can disturb; the individual to be corrected must be entirely enveloped in the power that is being exercised over him" (1977, 129). The near-hypnotic spell is broken only after Elaine follows a last cruel order to enter a frozen ravine and nearly dies—the physical pain of exposure refuting the subtler pain of psychological manipulation. Later, Elaine will have troubled relations with the dominant feminist sisterhood that judges her art. Her awkward withdrawals signify what Kaplan characterizes as "a collaboration between a woman's personal solution to the traumas of childhood and a social gender stereotype of femininity" (1991, 513). Women learn how to cope; women learn what will accomplish their aims in their given situation.

As women mature, sexual rivalry can bring out an aggressive instinct quite similar to that in men, as in Fay Weldon's *The Life and Loves of a She-Devil* (1983). The point of female sadism is not so much eroticism, however, as controlling the sexual bond, or avenging its loss, a tradition extending back beyond Medea. Tactics range from reining in the loved one to destroying her rival for his affections. Ruth in *The Life and Loves of a She-Devil* does both on a grand scale, reducing her errant husband to an incarcerated wreck and her rival to a cancer ward. Weldon's novel is a sadistic tale of revenge, as immensely satisfying as it is fantastic. John

Updike's *The Witches of Eastwick* (1984) is another such instance, where three modern suburban witches vent their spleen mostly on other women. Both novels are grimly humorous, suggesting that for women reversals of empowerment are funny, but also that blatant sadism for them is generally possible only in the realm of fantasy.

On a more realistic level, more prosaic forms of manipulation occur. In an earlier Weldon work, *The Fat Woman's Joke* (1967), the rival woman who has seduced the protagonist's husband explains: "He was so grey and middle-aged and clever and superior and in control, and his flies were so tightly buttoned"; she talks of "the excitement of dissolving him and stripping away the veneer and turning him into a naked little boy again" (59). Regression is key here, as it is in so many instances of female domination, undermining the authority of the patriarchy in order to reassert one of the more primal forms of power, that of the mother over the infant.[7] The image of woman as nurturer is so ingrained in our species that it is almost unquestioned and may therefore function as a covert means of control. In the poem "Making Breakfast" (1990), for example, Mary Stewart Hammond describes cooking an elaborate breakfast after lovemaking. But the marriage has worn thin in places, and the ritual is more than a labor of love:

> the act smacks of Massa, looks shuffly as
> all getout, adds to his belly, which is bad
> for his back, and will probably give him
> cancer, cardiac arrest, and a stroke. So,
> you do have to wonder these days as you
> get out the fatback, knead the dough,
> adjust the flame for a slow boil,
> flick water on the cast-iron skillet
> to check if it's ready and the kitchen
> gets steamy and close and smelling
> to high heaven, if this isn't an act
> of aggressive hostility and/or a symptom
> of regressed tractability. (40)

What begins as an act of thanks is revealed as half-unconscious manipulation; or rather, more accurately, it is both simultaneously, the way a Sadeian controller adores seeing his victim respond appropriately. Hammond continues:

> I look at his face,
> that weak-kneed, that buffalo-eyed,
> Samson-after-his-haircut face, all of him

burnished with grits and sausage and my
power. . . . (40)

In a sense, this reaction formation is the opposite of Piercy's barely restrained fury and Plath's "Viciousness in the kitchen!" in "Lesbos" (1966, 30); that is, it lovingly immobilizes the victim instead of lashing out at him. The action has the further dividend of rendering the subject unfit for others to prey upon.

Clearly, more is at stake here than calories. If Benjamin is correct that domination is a matter of self-assertion taking precedence over the need for another, sadism nonetheless requires both: the need to be recognized, along with another person to acknowledge one's power. This pull is particularly seductive when one is both an independent self and a caregiver, though it obviously affects some women more than others. Feeding is a way of establishing a sense of mastery, a relationship between the nurturer and the feeder. It is what Lacan might call a re-bonding with the Other, as the infant turns away from the mirror and back to the maternal breast. The woman who longs for this kind of control is a typical Anita Brookner heroine, as in *Providence* (1982), where Kitty Maule feeds the man she covets her portion of tomato salad and bread at a restaurant: "she could only concentrate on what she had in front of her: Maurice, captive, his mouth limpid with oil" (116). Or, as Blanche Vernon in *The Misalliance* (1986) tells her separated husband on one of his occasional visits, "You are putting on a good deal of weight, I see. Have some more cake" (35). Similarly, in *Family and Friends* (1985), the slim, dashing Frederick Dorn is so lavishly entertained by his female admirers that he becomes violin-shaped.

Where overnurturing proves unsuccessful in manipulating the subject, the opposite strategy often prevails. Withholding and withdrawal are often undertaken as a corrective. Increased frustration may be brought about by leading the other person on, then stopping short: in sexual terms, flirting without consummation, though the promise can be anything from coitus to simple empathy to the divulging of information. Typical of this forestalling behavior is sexual teasing, as in Keats' *"La Belle Dame sans Merci"* (1820), where the knight is seduced, only to be told by previous victims: "'La belle Dame sans Mercy / Hath thee in Thrall!'" (202).

The woman's emotional withdrawal may be necessary to cut off her nurturing instinct. It may also help establish a position of superiority over the object. In fact, the passive-aggressive figure who betrays too much passion in the proceedings is doing herself a disservice: the rage that impels the sadist to cathect the object can back up and paralyze the manipulator. Miss Kilman in Virginia Woolf's *Mrs. Dalloway* (1925) is such a figure, revealed for what she is:

> Turning her large, gooseberry-coloured eyes upon Clarissa, observing her small pink face, her delicate body, her air of freshness and fashion, Miss Kilman felt, Fool! Simpleton! You who have known neither sorrow nor pleasure; who have trifled your life away! And there rose in her an over-mastering desire to overcome her; to unmask her. If she could have felled her it would have eased her. But it was not the body; it was the soul and its mockery that she wished to subdue; make feel her mastery. If only she could make her weep; could ruin her; humiliate her; bring her to her knees crying, You are right! (125)

The anxiety is transformed into hostility, but discharged only through fantasy and covert behavior since outright confrontation is impossible. This is precisely what Horney means when she writes, "To put it categorically, the normal striving for power is born of strength, the neu-rotic of weakness" (1937, 163). Miss Kilman's disingenuous disclaimer that she "did not hate Mrs. Dalloway" (125) is transparent, an unsuccess-ful attempt to rise above pettiness. Unable to harm Mrs. Dalloway as much as she would like, she goes after Mrs. Dalloway's daughter Eliz-abeth. The flood of affect is nonetheless so strong that Miss Kilman remains awash in her own bile, unable to shield herself from her own destructive impulses.

A similar pattern emerges in Toni Cade Bambara's "The Lesson," in which the narrator Sylvia expresses hatred of her mentor Miss Moore in a voice of sullen hostility. Sylvia's environment is the slums, her dominant mood irritation. Miss Moore's aim is to break through the apathy of ghetto children by exposing them to the socioeconomic disparities around them: the main event of the story is a visit to F.A.O. Schwartz. Because the power relation runs so obviously against Sylvia—she has neither the age, the education, nor the comparative wealth of Miss Moore—all she can do is withhold her response when Miss Moore clearly wants a reaction: "I never talk to her, I wouldn't give the bitch that satisfaction" (1972, 93). This is not to say that Sylvia has a passive person-ality, rather that she has chosen withdrawal, since arousal is exactly what Miss Moore wants. When an equal or lesser individual challenges Sylvia, for example, she can be quite confrontational—and physical: "And Sugar kept givin me the elbow. Then later teased me so bad I tied her up in the shower and turned it on and locked her in" (93). In the company of Miss Moore, Sylvia displaces her sadistic impulse toward Sugar: "And I'm jealous and want to hit her. Maybe not her, but I sure want to punch somebody in the mouth." Since showing even this level of emotion will appease Miss Moore, she immediately engages in a type of reaction formation: "I'm mad, but I won't give her that satisfaction. So I slouch around the store bein very bored and say, 'Let's go' " (94).

The situation is intriguing in part because the usual terms of sadistic infliction are reversed: angry words are good (and therefore to be avoided); silence is hurtful. As an averbal form of behavior, silence is quite open to interpretation—and misinterpretation. In "Power, Sex, and Nonverbal Communication," Nancy Henley discusses eye-contact, space, touching, demeanor, and other factors as establishing dominance and submission in a relationship (1975, 191ff.). Such aspects of social space, however, can be construed differently depending on their context: touching as a form of intimacy, for example, versus touching as a form of aggression, and the two may even merge in one gesture.

Of course, many of these behaviors seem to be protective reactions rather than initiating actions, and as such may be less malevolent than traditionally masculine sadism, though to put the matter in moral or judgmental terms is to miss the point: here is a clinical syndrome transcribed into literature. As such, it cannot be interrogated. Occasionally, however, an author's or character's view of passive-aggression may strip away any protective ambiguity in the very act of describing the covert hostility.

In *One Flew over the Cuckoo's Nest* (1962), Ken Kesey provides a vicious instance of a near-omnipotent sadist in the Big Nurse. Nurse Ratched, whose name resembles *ratchet*, a device that twists ever-tighter without turning back, is, in popular parlance, a control freak. She even teaches one of her assistants "not to show his hate and to be calm and wait, wait for a little advantage, a little slack, then twist the rope and keep the pressure steady" (32). The psychiatric ward is her province, and she rules it less with an iron hand, as a male martinet might, than with one sheathed in velvet through emotional manipulation, indirect force, and suggestion. As the patient known as Chief observes: "She walks around with that same doll smile crimped between her chin and her nose and that same calm whir coming from her eyes, but down inside of her she's tense as steel. I know, I can feel it. And she don't relax a hair till she gets the nuisance attended to—what she calls 'adjusted to surroundings' " (30).

The connection between sadism and masculinity is so much the social norm that Nurse Ratched comes across as male at times. Instead of a purse, she carries a bag the shape of a toolbox, filled with pills and needles, forceps and wire. The Chief sometimes compares her to a machine, a Sadeian defense against unruly nature. At other times, the Chief sees her as an androgyne: she has flattened her womanly breasts beneath her starched nurse's uniform, and she plunges her phallic needles into the male patients she wants to subdue. Her first appearance in the novel, in fact, is heralded by her key in the lock, her fingertips an odd orange: "Like the tip of a soldering iron. Color so hot or cold if she touches you with it you can't tell which" (10). When she grows angry at her subordinates, she appears to grow larger, acquiring an almost mythical destructive force: "swells till her back's splitting out the white uniform and she's let her arms section out long enough to wrap around the three of them five, six times" (11), an image reminiscent of the sea serpents strangling Laocoön and his two sons. At the same time, she is quite clearly the Big Mother, who treats her adult charges like unruly children.

As in so much passive-aggressive sadism, concealment is part of Nurse Ratched's method. The patient Harding notes sourly: "'She doesn't need to accuse. She has a genius for insinuation'" (60). Only the seemingly shameless McMurphy can evade her guilt-inducing, though he finally cannot bear how she destroys the will of the others. When she drives Billy Bibbit to suicide by threatening him with mortal embarrassment, McMurphy cannot stand it any longer and physically attacks the nurse, an act resulting in a lobotomy for him. In a war of nerves, physical action is weakness. Passive-aggressive strategy, in a system where taking direct action is damaging, thus exposes and preys upon typical male aggressive behavior. That the Chief ends up smothering McMurphy in a mercy-killing is ironic since this is what Nurse Ratched was doing to McMurphy on a symbolic level.

Sadistic pleasures and their related strategies are as varied as the individuals who practice them. Some avenues of female sadism are explicitly sexual, as in the poetry of Sylvia Plath or in the physical actions of Samois, the feminist-lesbian-sadist group. Others are more abstract, cloaked in the enforced passivity that hides the urge to control. One may use one's own weakness to pull down and subdue others. Herein lies the intersection of sadism and masochism; as Freud states: "A sadist is always at the same time a masochist" (1905, 159). Horney explains further: "Most of us know of relationships between marriage partners, siblings, friends, in which the neurotic person acts like a slave driver, using his helplessness as a whip in order to compel the other to serve his will" (1937, 176).

This helplessness may be partly a ruse, as in Sacher-Masoch's famous *Venus in Furs* (1870), where the effeminate Severin coerces his mistress to act out his masochistic fantasies. At times, the helplessness may be purely a pose, as in Julian Barnes' *Before She Met Me* (1982). As the protagonist Graham Hendrick describes his ex-wife: "While I was asleep she used to pull out the sheets and blankets from her side of the bed and push them over to mine, and then give me all the eiderdown as well, and then pretend to wake up and bollock me for stealing all the bedclothes"

(100). This sadistic imposition of guilt stops abruptly when Graham, lying awake in bed one night, catches her at it. This unmasking, or successful interpretative act, renders the pattern unrepeatable, save with another subject or reader.

Sadistic behavior thus entails a paradox common to all neuroses. On the one hand, it is often hard to spot, camouflaged among behaviors so various as to include its opposite, masochism. On the other hand, it involves certain recurrent patterns, including the wish to possess, control, or subjugate others. Moreover, far from being a clinical aberration, sadomasochism is a distressingly common pattern of behavior.[8] As Natalie Shainess points out, a classic pattern is sadistically to harm another and then masochistically to feel guilt for it (1984, 103). One cannot have a psychology of victimization or oppression without noting the internalization of both impulses.

The word *passive* comes from the Latin deponent verb *patior,* to suffer. The capacity to suffer aggressively, or use meekness as a weapon, is older than the New Testament, which employs just such a strategy. Yet passivity is typically a female trait—or so Freud believes, though he adds an important qualification: "One might consider characterizing femininity psychologically as giving preference to passive aims. This is not, of course, the same thing as passivity; to achieve a passive aim may call for a large amount of activity" (1933, 115). The Freudian framework has been difficult to shake, since its explanatory power is intertwined with its sexist orientation. Perhaps for this reason, Juliet Mitchell (1992) notes sarcastically: "Men are perverse, women neurotic" (iii). The related question is harder to resolve: Do the social manifestations emanate from the individual, or does the individual take her cue from society? As Sandra Lee Bartky concludes in *Femininity and Domination,* "Clearly, then, economic and political oppression are themselves psychologically oppressive. But there are unique modes of psychological oppression that can be distinguished from the usual forms of economic and political domination" (1990, 23). Or perhaps, as Henry James observes: "What is character but the determination of incident? What is incident but the illustration of character?" (1888, 15). Literature reflects the difficulty of such questions, yet spurs our perpetual curiosity as readers and interpreters. In the end, the best form of power is knowledge.

Notes

1. See, for example, Shainess (1984), Marcus (1974), or Caplan (1985). Of crucial interest to many critics is the debate between social versus biological origins of masochism (see Walsh 1987, 59ff.). As Sue Cox notes, however: "Of

course, we may never know what psychological sex differences are in fact innate since we can never hold constant the social and cultural conditioning each sex group receives" (1981, 18).

2. See, for instance, Gilligan (1982), who posits a woman's ethic of care and responsibility in place of the masculine power structure. As Tavris (1992) shows, though, not only is Gilligan's data-pool rather limited, but her conclusions rest on shaky psychosexual assumptions largely borrowed from Chodorow (1978). See also Pollitt (1992).

3. The realm of fantasy is large, however, and some female examples of stereotypically male behavior do exist, most notably in the feminist-lesbian-sadist group Samois. The group states: "We believe that S/M can and should be consistent with the principles of feminism," and defines *sadism* as "Sexual pleasure derived from inflicting pain or wielding power over a sexual partner in a safe, consensual situation" (1979, 2, 7). Whether this is true sadism or mere game-playing is moot since much of sadomasochism tests exactly that boundary.

4. See Tavris (1992) for an overview of gender differences ranging from testosterone studies to observations on child-rearing. Kaplan (1991) argues that some of these differences are socially induced, but not all. For cross-cultural comparisons, see Friedl (1975) and Bodine (1975).

5. Benjamin's intersubjective approach ends with a plea for a society based on mutual recognition (1988, 224). This is certainly an admirable goal, but as sociobiologists including Edward O. Wilson (1975) have contended, domination and hierarchy may be ingrained in the species.

6. Thurber in his fiction and cartoons presents a pantheon of such women, in part inspired by his first wife Althea. As his brother Robert noted, "She was the domineering type, bossy and pushy, always wanting her own way." At one point in Thurber's writing career, Althea set him a limit of forty-five minutes per piece (Bernstein 1975, 116, 158).

7. Child-rearing is another potential arena of female competition. In Eva Figes' *The Seven Ages,* the witch-woman Moruiw casts a long shadow: "But it was also rumored that it was not so much her cunning which kept her own child alive as evil words and deeds which caused the babes of other women to sicken and die" (1986, 3).

8. "The 'normal' and the 'perverse' have in common the sexualization of domination and submission, albeit to different degrees" (Bartky 1990, 50–51).

References

Atwood, M. 1989. *Cat's Eye.* New York: Doubleday.

Bambara, T. C. 1972. The Lesson. In *Gorilla, My Love.* New York: Random House. pp. 85–96.

Barnes, J. 1982. *Before She Met Me.* New York: McGraw-Hill.

Bartky, S. L. 1990. *Femininity and Domination: Studies in the Phenomenology of Oppression.* New York: Routledge.

Benjamin, J. 1988. *The Bonds of Love: Psychoanalysis, Feminism, and the Problem of Domination.* New York: Pantheon.

Bernstein, B. 1975. *Thurber: A Biography.* New York: Dodd, Mead.

Bloom, H. 1975. *A Map of Misreading.* New York: Oxford Univ. Press.

Bodine, A. 1975. Sex Differentiation in Language. In *Language and Sex: Difference and Dominance,* ed. B. Thorne and N. Henley. Rowley, Mass.: Newbury House, pp. 130–51.

Brookner, A. 1982. *Providence.* New York: Dutton, 1985.

———. 1985. *Family and Friends.* New York: Pantheon.

———. 1986. *The Misalliance.* New York: Harper & Row, 1988.

Caplan, P. J. 1985. *The Myth of Women's Masochism.* New York: Signet-NAL.

Carter, A. 1979. *The Sadeian Woman: An Exercise in Cultural History.* London: Virago.

Chancer, L. S. 1992. *Sadomasochism in Everyday Life: The Dynamics of Power and Powerlessness.* New Brunswick: Rutgers Univ. Press.

Chodorow, N. 1978. *The Reproduction of Mothering: Psychoanalysis and the Sociology of Gender.* Berkeley: Univ. of California Press.

Cox, S. 1981. Introduction to *Female Psychology: The Emerging Self.* 2nd ed. S. Cox, ed. New York: St. Martin's Press, pp. 1–22.

Deleuze, G. 1989. *Masochism: Coldness and Cruelty.* Trans. J. McNeil, with *Venus in Furs,* by L. von Sacher-Masoch, trans. A. Willm. New York: Zone Books.

Deutsch, H. 1944. *The Psychology of Women: A Psychoanalytic Interpretation.* Vol. 1. New York: Grune & Stratton.

Dworkin, A. 1985. *Pornography: Men Possessing Women.* New York: Putnam.

Eliot, T. S. 1919. Hamlet and His Problems. In *Selected Essays.* New York: Harcourt, Brace and World, 1964, pp. 121–26.

Faulkner, W. 1930. *As I Lay Dying.* New York: Random House, 1964.

Figes, E. 1986. *The Seven Ages.* New York: Pantheon.

Foucault, M. 1975. *Discipline and Punish: The Birth of the Prison.* Trans. A. Sheridan. New York: Pantheon, 1977.

Freud, S. 1905. *Three Essays on the Theory of Sexuality.* In *The Standard Edition of the Complete Psychological Works of Sigmund Freud.* Trans. and ed. J. Strachey et al. 24 vols. London: Hogarth Press, 1953–74 (hereafter *S.E.*), 7:123–245.

———. 1924. The Economic Problem of Masochism. *S.E.,* 19:155–70.

———. 1933. *New Introductory Lectures on Psycho-analysis. S.E.,* 22:1–182.

Friedl, E. 1975. *Women and Men: An Anthropologist's View.* New York: Holt, Rinehart and Winston.

Fromm, E. 1941. *Escape from Freedom.* New York: Holt, Rinehart and Winston, 1976.

Gilligan, C. 1982. *In a Different Voice: Psychological Theory and Women's Development.* Cambridge: Harvard Univ. Press.

Hammond, M. S. 1990. Making Breakfast. *The New Yorker,* April 23, p. 40.

Henley, N. 1975. Power, Sex, and Nonverbal Communication. In B. Thorne and N. Henley, eds., *Language and Sex: Difference and Dominance*. Rowley, Mass.: Newberry House, 184–203

Henley, N., and J. Freeman. 1981. The Sexual Politics of Interpersonal Behavior. In Cox 1981, pp. 179–89.

Horney, K. 1937. *The Neurotic Personality of Our Time*. In *The Collected Works of Karen Horney*. Vol. 1. New York: Norton, 1964.

James, H. 1888. *The Art of Fiction and Other Essays*. New York: Oxford Univ. Press, 1948, pp. 3–23.

Kaplan, L. J. 1991. *Female Perversions: The Temptations of Madame Bovary*. New York: Doubleday.

Keats, J. 1820. *Selected Poems and Letters*. Ed. D. Bush. Boston: Houghton Mifflin, 1959.

Kesey, K. 1962. *One Flew over the Cuckoo's Nest*. New York: Signet-NAL.

Klein, M. 1936. Weaning. In *Love, Guilt and Reparation and Other Works*. New York: Delacorte, 1975, pp. 290–305.

Lorenz, K. 1963. *On Aggression*. Trans. M. K. Wilson. New York: Bantam, 1967.

Marcus, M. 1974. *A Taste for Pain: On Masochism and Female Sexuality*. Trans. J. Tate. New York: St. Martin's Press, 1981.

Mitchell, J. 1991. Foreword to Welldon 1992, pp. iii–iv.

Piercy, M. 1983. *Stone, Paper, Knife*. New York: Knopf.

Plath, S. 1966. *Ariel*. New York: Harper & Row.

Pollitt, K. 1992. Marooned on Gilligan's Island: Are Women Morally Superior to Men? *The Nation*, December 28, pp. 799–807.

Roth, P. 1969. *Portnoy's Complaint*. New York: Random House.

Sacher-Masoch, L. 1870. *Venus in Furs and Selected Letters of Leopold von Sacher-Masoch and Emilie Nataja*. Trans. U. Moeller and L. Lindgren. New York: Blast Books, 1989.

Samois, ed. 1979. *What Color Is Your Handkerchief: A Lesbian S/M Sexuality Reader*. Berkeley, Calif.: Samois.

Schad-Somers, S. P. 1982. *Sadomasochism: Etiology and Treatment*. New York: Human Sciences Press.

Shainess, N. 1984. *Sweet Suffering: Woman as Victim*. Indianapolis, Ind.: Bobbs-Merrill.

Skinner, B. F. 1957. *Verbal Behavior*. New York: Appleton-Century-Crofts.

Strindberg, A. 1889. *The Stronger. The Plays of Strindberg*. Vol. 1. Trans. M. Meyer. New York: Vintage, 1964, pp. 225–34.

Tavris, C. 1992. *The Mismeasure of Woman*. New York: Simon & Schuster.

Thurber, J. 1942. The Secret Life of Walter Mitty. In *My World—And Welcome to It*. New York: Harcourt, Brace & World, 1965, pp. 72–81.

Updike, J. 1984. *The Witches of Eastwick*. New York: Penguin, 1985.

Walsh, M. R., ed. 1987. *The Psychology of Women: Ongoing Debates.* New Haven, Conn.: Yale Univ. Press.

Weldon, F. 1963. *The Fat Woman's Joke.* London: Hodder and Stoughton, 1981.

———. 1983. *The Life and Loves of a She-Devil.* New York: Pantheon.

Welldon, E. V. 1992. *Mother, Madonna, Whore: The Idealization and Denigration of Motherhood.* New York: Guilford.

Wilson, E. O. 1975. *Sociobiology: The New Synthesis.* Cambridge: Harvard Univ. Press.

Wolman, B. G., ed. 1973. *Dictionary of Behavioral Science.* New York: Van Nostrand Reinhold Co.

Woolf, V. 1925. *Mrs. Dalloway.* New York: Harcourt Brace Jovanovich, 1990.

Chapter Six
Masquerade:
A Feminine or Feminist Strategy?

Véronique Machelidon

In psychoanalytic criticism, the concept of "masquerade," which goes back to Joan Riviere's "Womanliness as a Masquerade" (1929), has attracted feminists' attention as a promising way to theorize femininity and to subvert the patriarchal gender hierarchy based on a male economy of the gaze. Laura Mulvey (1975; for the cinema) and John Berger (1972; for painting) have convincingly demonstrated that the visual arts in Western culture contribute to the construction of man as subject and of woman as object of the gaze. To some feminist critics the masquerade has appeared as a strategy perhaps capable of undermining this phallocratic dichotomy. More recently, however, Emily Apter (1991) has questioned the usefulness of the theory of the masquerade as "inextricable from essentialist commonplaces associated with femininity." She remarks in *Feminizing the Fetish:* "With its language of veils, masks, and sexual travesty, the discourse of masquerade seems always to participate in the very obfuscation of femininity that it seeks to dispel. . . . The theory of the masquerade—associated with the art of camouflaging masculine as feminine—may ultimately qualify as just another mask of phallocentric psychoanalysis. . . . Is the masquerade feminism's fetish?" (90). Although this complex concept serves to illuminate and problematize central aspects of nineteenth-century women's fiction, it may be worthwhile to consider which definition(s) of femininity masquerade promotes—femininity as essence or construction or both—and to ponder whether it subverts or reinforces patriarchal representations of womanliness.

This chapter is the revised and expanded introduction of an unpublished essay that applies theories of masquerade to Charlotte Brontë's *Villette* (1853).

In her 1929 paper Riviere describes the cases of three educated American women who "wish for masculinity [and] put on a mask of womanliness to avert anxiety and the retribution feared by men" (303). Because of her rivalry with her father in her intellectual profession (speaking in public for work of a propagandist nature in the case of the first and main patient, teaching at university in the case of the second), this "masculine" type of woman unconsciously feels guilty at having stolen the father's power (the father's word, the father's penis); she therefore displays herself as typically feminine (i.e., castrated) by coquetting and flirting with father-substitutes. Femininity, Riviere implies, is a kind of reaction-formation compensating for a woman's masculinity. Riviere posits at the beginning of her paper:

> Womanliness therefore could be assumed and worn as a mask, both to hide the possession of masculinity and to avert the reprisals expected if she was found to possess it—much as a thief will turn out his pockets and ask to be searched to prove that he has not the stolen goods. The reader may now ask how I define womanliness or where I draw the line between genuine womanliness and the "masquerade." My suggestion is not, however, that there is any such difference; whether radical or superficial, they are the same thing. (306)

At this point, there is for Riviere no difference between femininity and the masquerade. Both are the same thing: femininity is a mask, a lie, or in Luce Irigaray's words: "The masquerade has to be understood as what women do in order to recuperate some element of desire, to participate in man's desire, but at the price of renouncing their own" (1977, 133). But if, at the beginning of Riviere's paper, genuine womanliness is an illusion, a patriarchal construct, the end of her essay veers into a completely different and more conventional direction. The same patients' cases are now clearly defined as pathological. Riviere distinguishes between the "normal" (healthy, sane) woman and the "homosexual" (or pathological): "Both the 'normal' woman and the homosexual desire the father's penis and rebel against frustration (or castration); but one of the differences between them lies in the difference in the degree of sadism and of the power of dealing both with it and with the anxiety it gives rise to in the two types of women" (313). She tries to identify "*das ewig Weibliche*": "the *essential* nature of fully developed femininity" is "heterosexual womanhood" (313), which Riviere defines as follows:

> The acceptance of "castration," the humility, the admiration of men come partly from the overestimation of the object on the oral-sucking plane; but chiefly from the renunciation (lesser intensity) of sadistic castration-wishes

deriving from the oral-biting level. "I must not take, I must not even ask; it must be given me." The capacity for self-sacrifice, devotion, self-abnegation expresses efforts to restore and make good, whether to mother or father figures, what has been taken away from them. (313)

Whereas, at the beginning of her paper, femininity was the mask, now masculinity is the cocoon that imprisons woman for a while and prevents her from revealing her *essential* femininity to man and to the world. Femininity, in other words, may not be completely innate (it is still defined as a "reaction-formation"), but it is there all along from the beginning as essence, as potential to be activated in every woman through "normal" development. Tackling at the same time the related problem of woman's "original" desire (*"Was will das Weib?"*), Riviere concludes that femininity is primarily phallocentric. Female desire involves penis envy, and the father's penis is the "talisman" of the primal scene reinterpreted in oral terms: "Fully developed heterosexual womanhood is founded as Helene Deutsch and Ernest Jones have stated on the oral-sucking stage. The sole gratification of a primary order in it is that of receiving the (nipple, milk) penis, semen, child from the father. For the rest it depends upon reaction-formations" (313).[1] Similarly, the rivalry with the father (the daughter's desire to speak up, to emulate the father intellectually) is now interpreted as a variation (deviation) of the Oedipus complex: "Thus in its content, such a woman's phantasy-relation to the father (her demand for recognition) is similar to the normal Oedipus one; the difference is that it rests on a basis of sadism" (312).

In Riviere's conclusion, rivalry—that is, identification with the father—fades away in favor of an oedipal love-hate relationship to him. The first patient's ambiguous and complex relationship with her mother is thereby also effaced from Riviere's conclusion: she is killed by the patient in the oedipal scenario envisaged by Riviere (309–10), then met-aphorically killed a second time in Riviere's Freudian reinterpretation of the masquerade. Previously, however, Riviere had diagnosed in her first female patient a very strong homosexual attraction (toward a "rival," her husband's mistress) and the prevalence of "homosexual dreams with intense orgasm" (307), reactivating the patient's past homosexual expe-riences with her younger sister. Originally, Riviere had also emphasized the patient's love-hate relationship with her mother, whom the daughter was at pains to appease, to whom she was trying to restore the stolen penis, and from whom she demanded recognition (310). Thus, the oedi-pal triangle predictably discovered by Riviere at the end of her paper conceals and displaces another triangular relationship in which the phal-lic daughter is the father's rival in her love for and desire to have a child with the mother.[2] The rivalry with the father for access to the Symbolic order (the realm of the word) disguises an earlier rivalry over the common female love object.

Through the curious shift of emphasis that she gives to her argument at the end of her essay, Riviere does not throw light on the "enigma" of femininity as she claims to do (313). On the contrary, she further obscures it through her own masquerade, wherein she disguises herself as Freud's faithful daughter by channelling her unorthodox discovery of the masquerade of femininity (as a cultural, psychological construct rather than essence) into the harbor of Freud's shibboleth of the Oedipus complex. If Riviere at first appeared to oscillate between her recognition of mothers (Melanie Klein, Helene Deutsch) and fathers (Jones, Abraham, and the omnipresent but scarcely mentioned Freud), at the end the final authority on femininity proves to be none other than the father of psychoanalysis. Moreover, Riviere mimics Freud's own procedure in his Dora essay, where he deemphasized Dora's homosexuality in favor of her attraction to the "paternal" Herr K.

As Stephen Heath (1986) suggests, Riviere practiced the strategy of the masquerade not only in her paper but also in her own life, where she compensated for her intellectual achievements by a show of femininity (for instance in her clothing and makeup). Riviere herself attributed her hysterical symptoms (a profound sense of insecurity and an inability to speak in public) to an early and punctilious training in the patriarchal virtue of modesty. As Paula Heimann recalls, during the party thrown by the British Psycho-Analytical Society for her seventy-fifth birthday Riviere made a "charming and humorous little talk" where she "expressed the feeling that she had not really done much for [the] Society, that her merits were small, she had been the receiver, not the giver. And she illustrated these feelings by telling . . . how at a party, when she was a little girl, her mother told her she must entertain her guests. So she said she would paint and they could watch her" (1963, 231). If Heimann optimistically concludes that the "gifted mischievous little girl was alive and glow[ing] in the woman of seventy-five," we may also sense that Riviere's artistic creativity and rebelliousness have been subdued into a masquerade that exposes, mocks, but ultimately does not threaten established gender hierarchies and psychoanalytic authorities.

Interestingly enough, Riviere's masquerade did not bring her the recognition she desired from Jones and Freud, the two father-figures she was trying to placate in her paper and in her life. It did not enable her to preserve her double desire—for Jones's love on the one hand, and for his and Freud's intellectual approbation on the other. Not only did Jones fail to register Riviere's emotional "discontents" (a term significantly used by Riviere in her translation of Freud's *Das Unbehagen in der Kultur* [1930]),[3] not only did his "therapy" result in more conversion symptoms, but he exercised his symbolic authority over her as patriarchal censor as well. Before accepting her contribution to the "Symposium on Child Analysis" for publication in the *International Journal of Psycho-Analysis,* Jones—as he wrote to Freud on October 18, 1927—obliged Riviere to reexamine her "one-sided and therefore misleading" psychoanalytic conclusions and to "modify or omit a great number of her expressions" (Paskauskas 1993, 634). As a result of his editorial censorship, he effectively reduced Riviere from the role of author to that of translator of the master's discourse.[4]

Sending Riviere as a patient to Freud, Jones ignored her as an intellectual subject, and used her instead as an object of exchange in a quintessential example of male "traffic in women." Riviere's own desire was perverted and effaced to qualify her as Jones's gift to the primal father (Freud), whom he was trying to propitiate in order to obtain recognition for himself. The woman's femininity and psychic disorder (her hysteria) were exploited to appease the masculine rivalry and establish a powerful homosocial bond between master and disciple, father and son. Viewing Riviere's intellectuality as a threat and her body as a sort of homoerotic pledge, Jones unconsciously demonstrated the truth that Riviere had uncovered and then disguised in her essay—that is, that heterosexuality, like gender, is neither innate nor normal nor essential, but constructed and normative.

The curious case histories Riviere mentions in her paper and her own "case" reveal a range of issues and problems involved in the notion of "masquerade." First, if femininity per se is a masquerade, as Riviere initially suggests, the logical question is: what, if anything, lies behind the mask? Riviere's involvement with Jones and Freud suggests that masculinity too is a masquerade or, as Lacan puts it in "The Meaning of the Phallus," "the ideal or typical manifestations of behavior in both sexes, up to and including the act of sexual copulation, are entirely propelled into comedy" (1958, 84). As Judith Butler suggests, for Lacan "all gender ontology is reducible to the play of appearances" (1990, 47) because in patriarchy woman *is* not the phallus but *appears as* the phallus, *plays the role of* the phallus for the man. If "woman" and "man" are both appearances, is there anything behind the mask? Certainly, for Lacan, no essential femininity or masculinity seems conceivable. At the beginning of her paper, Riviere indicates that the masquerade of femininity hides "the bisexuality inherent in us all" (1929, 303), while Lacan conceives of the subject's first lack as the loss of a *primordial wholeness* exemplified in Plato's myth of the androgyne. This primordial wholeness would seem to be lost at the moment of sexual differentiation in the mother's womb, but the subject learns of it only after his/her entrance into the Symbolic order (Silverman 1983, 151–54). On the other hand, Lacan inconsistently suggests that an essential femininity *is* lost when the woman takes on her role of "being the phallus" for the male other: "Paradoxical as this formulation may seem, it is in order to be the phallus, that is the signifier of the desire of the Other, that the woman will reject an *essential* part of her femininity, notably all its *attributes,* through masquerade. It is for what she is not that she expects to be desired as well as loved" (1958, 84; italics added). Lacan's hesitation between an essentialist and a constructivist definition of femininity is here betrayed by the blatant contradiction between "essential" and "attributes."

This complex quotation could be understood in Michèle Montrelay's (1977) terms as showing that, in the patriarchal economy, woman appears to be castrated, a lack, so that the other, the male, can have the illusion of having the phallus. In fact, the male does not have the phallus and the woman is not castrated, but she has to play that role for the man—and for herself:

> From now on, anxiety, tied to the presence of this body, can only be in-sistent, continuous. This body, so close, which she has to occupy, is an object in excess which must be "lost," that is to say, repressed, in order to be symbolised. Hence the symptoms which so often simulate this loss: "there is no longer anything, only the hole, emptiness . . . " Such is the *leitmotif* of all feminine cure, which it would be a mistake to see as the expression of an alleged "castration." On the contrary it is a defence produced in order to parry the avatars, the deficiencies, of symbolic castration. . . . It is a ques-tion of organising a representation of castration which is no longer sym-bolic, but imaginary: a lack is simulated and thereby the loss of some stake—an undertaking all the more easily accomplished precisely because feminine anatomy exhibits a lack, that of the penis. At the same time as being her own phallus, therefore, the woman will disguise herself with this lack, throwing into relief the dimension of castration as *trompe-l'oeil.* (1977, 91–92)

Thus, in this passage, Montrelay apparently agrees with Riviere: femininity ("castration" as show or performance) is a masquerade, a strategy of defense against anxiety. It is a psychological cultural, social construct. At the same time, she insists that behind this show "woman" manages to preserve her specifically female eroticism, to remain "her own phallus," that is, her own (narcissistic) object of desire. The difficulty in this enterprise is nevertheless reflected in Montrelay's paradoxical choice of words, in the contradiction between "own" and "phallus": if "woman's" desire remains defined in phallic terms, how can a nonphallo-centric, essential femininity be retained?

Because Montrelay's complex theory has often been reduced to her remarks on masquerade and the above passage is usually quoted with no respect for its context, thus allowing some critics to view her as a feminist rewriter of Lacanian thought, I would like to dwell for a while on "Inquiry into Femininity" in order to reveal the (Lacanian) limitations of this difficult essay. Montrelay's avowed aim is to overcome the opposition between Freud's and Jones's interpretations of femininity by defining female sexuality as a conflict between concentricity and phallocentricity.[5] But the scenario of female development that she envisages traces the "necessary" (although often incomplete) passage from "woman's" concentric jouissance to a sublimated pleasure procured by the penis and by "the law and the ideals of the father" (94). It is only through psychoanalytic therapy or through (hetero)sexual intercourse—that is, through the power of the phallus—that a woman can have access to the (patriarchal) Symbolic and replace the claustrophobic anxiety of an unmediated concentricity by the sublimated orgasm of (the paternal?) metaphor. As for female concentricity, it may, like the Sphinx's riddle, ruin Oedipus's representations, but it remains unable to speak for itself and is therefore always dependent upon the power and the perverting words of the (masculine) analyst or writer:

> The "true" woman, the "femme" woman would be drawn as she who has *"forgotten" her femininity,* and who would entrust the *jouissance* and the representation of it to an other. [She] could in no way talk about herself, her body or "the word it conceals." . . . It is someone else's ["un autre"] task to hold the discourse of femininity, in love and/or in a novel. . . . Understood in this way, interpretation can perhaps help us to locate a certain cultural and social function of psychoanalysis. . . . We can ask whether psychoanalysis was not articulated precisely in order to repress femininity (in the sense of producing its symbolic representation). . . . In response to the analysand's phantasy, the analyst enunciates a certain number of signifiers necessarily relating to his own desire and his listening place. These words are *other:* the analyst's discourse is not reflexive but different. As such it is a *metaphor,* not a mirror, of the patient's discourse. And precisely, metaphor is capable of engendering pleasure [in the patient]. (95–96)

We may thus wonder whose aims the masquerade defined in the previous passage really serves and who generates woman's anxiety, if not patriarchy, which is "terrorised by the threat that femininity raises for his [man's] repression" and by "woman's direct relation to *jouissance*" (93). Whose law prescribes this repression of the female body, this separation from the Maternal and consequent aphanisis? Her excess in body, in "being" (Lacan), is not represented by Montrelay as pleasure but rather as a constraint that bars women's access to the Symbolic, and which they therefore eagerly attempt to repress and to symbolize, with the help of a paternal agency. Thus, if Montrelay insists that the penis is not the phallus, that "woman" remains her own phallus, she also recognizes (like Irigaray) that this female "phallus" has no currency in a masculine Symbolic economy that she legitimizes because it replaces female anxiety by the pleasure of male discourse. Whether castration is symbolic (Lacan) or imaginary (Montrelay), woman's masquerade may disturb but remains contained within the gender hierarchy according to which symbolic power belongs to men and "sublimated" desire is phallic.

If Montrelay first suggests that femininity is both essential and constructed, concentric and phallocentric, thus apparently putting an end to the Jones/Freud debate, she finally argues in favor of Freud's masterful and self-appointed heir, Lacan. The masquerade she describes and enacts does not subvert the patriarchal Symbolic order but is a direct, compulsive, and compulsory result of the hegemony of the phallus. This is revealed by the conflation between penis and phallus that, as in Lacanian theory, continues to lurk, first denied then unacknowledged, in Montrelay's account. If man can repress his desire better, thus guaranteeing his participation in the Law of the Father, it is after all due to his anatomy: "The anatomy of the boy, on the other hand, exposes him very early to the realization that he is not master either of the manifestations of his desire or of the extent of his pleasures. He experiments, not only with chance but also with the law and with his sexual organ: his body itself takes on the value of stake" (90).

Montrelay's deceptively seductive Lacanian theory may offer an accurate (but bleak) representation of the vicissitudes of female sexuality within patriarchy, but it ultimately authorizes an economy that requires an "exterritorialization" of woman's concentricity: "If the exemplar of the hysterical, neurotic woman is *one who never lets up wishing to be her sex,* inversely, isn't the 'adult' woman *one who reconstructs her sexuality in a field which goes beyond [i.e., her] sex?*" (94).

All three critics—Riviere, Lacan, Montrelay—seem to me to oscillate between a definition of femininity as a patriarchal construct and as a biological essence (in Riviere's words, "fully developed womanhood"). Their definition of the masquerade suffers from this unresolved articulation of the roles of culture and nature in the production of femininity. For instance, Lacan's theory of gender as comedy is hard to reconcile with his notion of an undefined *essential* femininity that gets lost in the Symbolic order. Despite Jane Gallop's insistence (1982, 54–55) that Lacan is using the term "essence" on purpose, to "wear it out" until it is "threadbare" and thoroughly "hackneyed," and thereby deprived of its exchange value and its patriarchal meaning, the self-consciousness and irony she detects do not seem to me to be clearly present in the passages she quotes. The contradiction between "essence" and "construct" remains pervasive in Lacan's text.[6]

These three critics also exemplify the difficulty of defining the femininity behind the mask without adopting a phallocentric point of view or, as Irigaray would put it, falling prey to the logic of the Same. The notions of "bisexuality" (Riviere and Montrelay) or of "primordial wholeness" (Lacan) are themselves products (dreams?) of a patriarchal ideology based on a strict and all-pervasive sexual differentiation. Bisexuality is the fantasmatic mirror-image of heterosexuality. To me, the impasse involved in the notion of "masquerade" reflects the difficulty of defining the nature of femininity, which cannot be identified outside the Symbolic order or then becomes a riddle. This paradox is clearly evoked in Irigaray's answer to the question "*Are you a woman?*" (1977, 120). Irigaray can beautifully deconstruct this nonsensical question by reducing it to the logic of the Same, but when she brings up the notion of "speaking (as) woman" ("parler-femme"), she can only point out: "it is spoken, but not in metalanguage" (144). She thus suggests the impossibility of theorizing femininity or a feminine language outside the patriarchal Symbolic order.[7]

Perhaps Judith Butler offers an alternative to this critical deadlock, by insisting that "gender is neither a purely psychic truth, conceived as "internal" and "hidden," nor is it reducible to a surface of appearance; on the contrary, its undecidability is to be traced as the play *between* psyche and appearance" (1993, 234). Because there is no "I" that preexists discourse and its invocation of norms (such as heterosexuality), and because "becoming a subject" is a matter of assuming a predetermined but historically variable place in speech, it is also hopeless to attempt to retrieve a preexisting, presymbolic subject, as Riviere, Montrelay, and at times Lacan seem to do. The nostalgic desire for a lost jouissance (Lacan), for a primary female concentricity (Montrelay), or for a radically Other femininity that would no longer be "the blind spot of an old dream of symmetry" (Irigaray) is itself a discursive production of the law that is said to repress that desire. Thus, if subversion is possible, it is not to be found *outside* the Symbolic but in the history of the subject's complicated inscriptions and its (programmed but not necessarily successful) engendering through a "set of disavowed attachments or identifications" (236). Using Freud's "Mourning and Melancholia" (1917), Butler argues that

> gender performance allegorizes a loss it cannot grieve, allegorizes the incorporative fantasy of melancholia whereby an object is phantasmatically taken in or on as a way of refusing to let it go. . . . What does seem useful in

this analysis . . . is that drag exposes or allegorizes the mundane psychic and performative practices by which heterosexualized genders form themselves through the renunciation of the *possibility* of homosexuality, a foreclosure that produces a field of heterosexual objects at the same time that it produces a domain of those it would be impossible to love. Drag thus allegorizes *heterosexual melancholy*, the melancholy by which a masculine gender is formed from the refusal to grieve the masculine as a possibility of love; a feminine gender is formed (taken on, assumed) through the incorporative fantasy by which the feminine is excluded as a possible object of love, an exclusion never grieved but "preserved" through the heightening of feminine identification itself. (235)

It is precisely drag's hyperbolic performance of gender that allows this reading of gender as cultural sign and the exposure of compulsory heterosexuality as a cultural imperative.

This interesting theory raises at least two sets of questions; the first concerns the relation of masquerade to drag. What Butler describes as "heterosexual melancholy" corresponds to her analysis of masquerade in *Gender Trouble*, where she notes that "the donning of femininity as mask may reveal a refusal of a female homosexuality and, at the same time, the hyperbolic incorporation of that female Other who is refused—an odd form of preserving and protecting that love within the circle of the melancholic and negative narcissism that results from the psychic inculcation of compulsory heterosexuality" (1990, 53). Does masquerade, like drag, result from the inability to grieve the loss of a prohibited (homosexual) love object? Is there no difference between the structure of masquerade, where a compulsory (and not necessarily joyful) performance of hyperbolic femininity compensates for an appropriation of male prerogatives, and drag, which is a theatrical and playful impersonation of the opposite gender? Are all gender performances forms of melancholy? Is masquerade specifically a refusal of female homosexuality or is it rather a grieving of this homosexual loss in a process of mourning? Is it a display of enforced oblivion or rather a tribute to (and retention of) the lost love object, or both? And if Butler concludes by insisting on the necessity of heterosexuals' grieving for their lost homosexuality (1993, 236), doesn't that nostalgic desire contribute to the reinforcement of the heterosexual imperative and thus to the accommodation of the "subject" to the self-reproductive aims of patriarchy?

The definition of drag (and masquerade?) as a hyperbolic, ironic citation of the norm (like Irigaray's concept of hysterical mimicry) returns us to the allied question of subversion. As Butler notes, femininity and masculinity as cultural imperatives are hyperbolic: one can never "be" the embodiment of perfect femininity or masculinity; the norm remains an impossible ideal. What then separates masquerade as irony from the hyperbolic norm? Isn't masquerade a desperate attempt to approximate the norm? When is the Law exposed and when is it merely re-presented? Is, for instance, the hyperfemininity exhibited in fashion magazines and its display by fashion-conscious women a form of masquerade (and to what effect?) or is it merely a reproduction of the norm? Doesn't this hyperfemininity too reveal the naturalization of "heterosexually ideal genders," thus "undermining their power by virtue of effecting that exposure" (231)? Butler herself recognizes this difficulty: "There is no guarantee that exposing the naturalized status of heterosexuality will lead to its subversion" (231).

If what she calls the "presentist" illusion that one can freely redefine femininity, that "language expresses a 'will' or a 'choice' rather than a complex and constitutive history of discourse and power" (228), does not offer any solution to this dilemma, then in what contexts is masquerade legible as subversion? Even if intention, choice, and identity are necessarily an error, masquerade ought not to be entirely separated from some form of agency or "subject," precisely because this constructed subject is the site where different laws converge and possibly clash, where norms may fail to produce their desired effect, thus opening the possibility for contestation, even if this subversive failure of the law can never be programmed with certitude. Who masquerades, how, and to what effect all need to be taken into account. In George Sand's novel *Indiana* (1832), when the eponymous heroine's creole servant Noun exaggerates her femininity and stages herself as object of desire by donning her mistress's clothes, this masquerade does not undermine patriarchal representations of femininity and its equation with whiteness and aristocracy, nor does it shortcircuit the sublimated desire of her and Indiana's lover, Raymon de Ramière. Noun attempts to approximate the ideal of (white, upper-class) femininity, and even though she fails to do so, the norm is not subverted but rather reinforced, as Raymon's compliance and continued idealization of Indiana reveal. On the contrary, the masquerade of the mistress, who disguises herself with the maid's scarf and hair in order to prove Raymon's responsibility for Noun's suicide, effectively deflates male fetishistic desire and reveals Raymon's social, racial, and sexual prejudices.

In feminist film criticism Mary Ann Doane has used the theory of masquerade for a double purpose: on the one hand, to reconsider the representation of femininity in classical (Hollywood) cinema; and on the other, to redefine the position of the female spectator. Defining masquerade as "hyperbolisation of the accoutrements of femininity," Doane concludes that "by destabilising the image, the masquerade confounds this masculine structure of the look. It effects a defamiliarisation of female iconography" (1982, 82). Doane's argument, however, reveals the same ambivalence regarding the subversiveness of masquerade as Butler's definition of drag as irony. Doane explains that "masquerade doubles representation. . . . A propos of a recent performance by Marlene Dietrich, Sylvia Bovenschen claims, 'we are watching a woman demonstrate the representation of a woman's body.' This type of masquerade, an excess of femininity, is aligned with the *femme fatale* and, as Montrelay explains, is necessarily regarded by men as evil incarnate." The difficulty of ascertaining the rebelliousness of masquerade is reflected in Doane's use of the words "doubles" and "aligned." We may agree with her that the image of the femme fatale defamiliarizes female iconography to the extent that it represents femininity as uncanny and threatening, but whose interests does this defamiliarization serve? Does this excess of femininity seriously undermine masculine systems of viewing or, on the contrary, is it recuperated by a masculine economy of the gaze that recontains the "femme fatale" as demonic femininity, as the hysterical (but familiar) witch? The defamiliarization by excess of woman's image may indeed "double"—that is, repeat and reinforce—classic cinema's patriarchal and phallocentric representations of the female body.

Yet Doane raises another set of interesting questions when she reformulates masquerade as spectatorship. "What might it mean [for a woman] to masquerade as spectator?" she asks, "to assume the mask in order to see in a different way?" (82). Doane is here addressing the tendency in recent theories of female spectatorship to view the female spectator as the (bisexual) site of an oscillation between a feminine position (the passive and narcissistic female object of the camera's gaze) and a masculine position (the active hero whose voyeurism appears to double that of the camera):

> Above and beyond a simple adoption of the masculine position in relation to the cinematic sign [i.e., identification with the male hero] the female spectator is given two options: the masochism of over-identification and the narcissism of becoming one's own object of desire, in assuming the image in the most radical way. The effectivity of the masquerade lies precisely in its potential to manufacture a distance from the image, to generate a problematic within which the image is manipulable, producible and readable by the woman. (87)

One might wonder here how the distanciation of the female spectator would differ from the voyeurism typical of the male viewer as defined by feminist theories of the cinema such as Mulvey's.[8] What enables the female spectator to read traditional images of women in a radically different way, uncontaminated by classic cinema's ideologies and reductive definitions of femininity? Is this distanciation from the female body, which Doane finds so useful in Montrelay's essay, not another appropriation of a masculine position that is not contested but rather reinforced through the reformulated opposition between proximity (associated with femininity, concentricity, narcissism, and an "incorrect" type of female spectatorship) and distance (identified with masculinity, specularization, the "correct" spectatorship of a woman masquerading as a man)? There is after all the possibility—disavowed by Doane (1988–89, 46), exemplified by Montrelay, and theorized by Irigaray in *Speculum*—that the discourse of distance and differentiation is itself a male epistemology.

Nevertheless, Doane is highlighting a crucial aspect of masquerade, which has been underestimated in previous theories: the influence of spectatorship and reception. Riviere had already suggested that masquerade's effectiveness depends upon the cooperation of the audience. Her masquerading intellectual patient is successful with specific spectators identified as "unmistakeable father-figures, although often not persons whose judgment on her performance would in reality carry much weight" (1929, 304). These odd father-figures are further described as "the type who themselves fear the ultra-womanly woman. They prefer a woman who herself has male attributes, for to them her claims on them are less" (311). Is female masquerade successful when matched by some "feminization" of the male audience? Does masquerade's effectiveness depend precisely on the fact that it awakens in the male spectator some repressed femininity? And why does Riviere, unlike Doane, exclude the possibility of a solidarity between a female audience and the masquerader? Why does she describe the woman's mask as "transparent to other women" (311) and successful with men only?

Contrary to Riviere's association of masquerade with female rivalry, Charlotte Brontë's *Villette* (1853) shows that the success of Lucy Snowe's masquerade during the school performance of a vaudeville depends upon the solidarity of the two female actors—Lucy herself and Ginevra Fanshawe in the role of a coquette flirting with two male rivals, a "fop" played by Miss Snowe and an "ours" (i.e., a bear), "a good and gallant but unpolished man, a sort of diamond in the rough" (203). While Ginevra exemplifies the image of woman as excess, as concentricity and closeness, Lucy insists on playing her male part while retaining her "woman's garb without the slightest retrenchment, . . . merely assuming in addition a little vest, a collar and a cravat" (209)—that is, the token signs of masculinity. "Seconded by Ginevra," she completely transforms her role, outrivals the good and gallant "ours," and rewrites her prescribed "beauty and the beast" plot, queering it by a grotesque turn into a parody of heterosexuality. Superimposing femininity and masculinity like empty layers of garments, Lucy denaturalizes both genders as constructed, while perhaps alluding to a repressed bi- or homosexuality.

The performance of gender by Brontë is shown to rely not only on Lucy but also on Ginevra, who plays along in this parody of conventional romantic endings and simultaneously ridicules the rivalry of her male admirers in the audience. In some ways Ginevra could be said to stand for the female reader of the novel who, beyond Lucy Snowe's display of excessive humility and insignificance, cannot fail to perceive the stakes of Lucy's performance as narrator and character: the appropriation of the male pen(is) and the birth of a female author writing a script of her own, with an ending of her own.

The relative subversiveness of Lucy's performance in the vaudeville can be gauged by the differing responses of various male spectators of the show. Dr. John, the prototype for the "ours" in the play, recognizes that Miss Snowe has indeed enacted "with no little spirit the part of a very *killing* fine gentleman" (251), yet he continues to view her as an "inoffensive shadow" (403) and a nice case of hysteria, which he treats as would a psychotherapist: by attempting to reconcile her to her fate as a déclassée and a spinster who has to earn her living in a foreign environment. On the other hand, Paul Emmanuel, the authoritarian director of the vaudeville, admires Lucy's performance and begrudgingly learns to recognize her intellectual abilities. It is he who will set her up as an independent schoolmistress and teach her the art of rewriting endings and masquerading between two languages, English and French. If he ultimately responds so positively to Lucy's ambitions, revealing an almost maternal affection behind a constant show of authority, it is perhaps because he too, the rather ugly duckling of obscure Spanish origins, is an outcast.

From this necessarily limited theoretical overview, it would seem that both the critical potential and weakness of masquerade lie in its representation of femininity as undecidability. Flirting between definitions of femininity as essence and as construction, masquerade is perhaps the only possible description of gender within the Symbolic order. With its many contradictions and interrogations, this theory appears to offer a suggestive account of the naturalization of gender in patriarchy. Whatever its ironic possibilities for depicting gender hyperbolically, the subversiveness of masquerade can probably never be calculated, for its actors as well as its spectators (not to mention its readers) are themselves located within the power they are hoping to expose. But neither should the possibility of subversion ever be underestimated because power always generates contradictions and because "subjects" will respond idiosyncratically to its multiple, complex, and at times inconsistent cultural imperatives.

Notes

1. Note the literal and graphic repression of "nipple, milk"—that is, female body parts and products—by male ones: "penis, semen, [male?] child"; a similar lumping together is to be found in Lacan's categorization of these as *"objets petit a."*

2. Riviere's account of the "oral-biting" phase in her patient's psychological development seems to anticipate Freud's description of the phallic stage in "Female Sexuality" (1931). In fact, Freud had introduced this concept in "Infantile Genital Organization" (1923) and he had expounded some of his ideas on the little girl's psychic development in "Some Psychical Consequences of the Anatomical Distinction between the Sexes" (1925). It is likely that Riviere also discussed psychoanalytic issues with Freud during her analysis with him in 1922. Yet Freud's "Taboo of Virginity" (1918) is only briefly mentioned, as it were in passing, whereas Riviere dwells on her indebtedness to Jones.

3. Heath (1986) recalls that Freud had proposed as a translation "man's discomforts in civilization." Riviere's solution conspicuously avoids the use of the generic "man," which erases women's subjectivity from representation by pretending to include them in a general and supposedly neutral category.

4. For an account of this tumultuous triangle, see Appignanesi and Forrester (1992, 352–71). Freud seems at first sight to have been considerably more receptive to Riviere's professional claims than Jones had been. Yet it is difficult to assess Freud's behavior with any certitude. Was his treatment of Riviere more successful because of his greater respect for her personality or was his analysis merely a subtler form of manipulation of a woman whom Freud characterized as "a concentrated acid" (354) but managed to transform into a rather faithful follower? By proposing to Jones that Riviere assume the title of "translating editor," Freud in fact subjected her to his English disciple's supervision, since Jones had insisted on remaining "the one definite head to be responsible for . . . editing and publishing" (Paskauskas 1993, 481).

5. Montrelay explains Jones's view at the beginning of her essay: "For Jones, and for the English school (Klein, Horney, Muller), feminine libido is specific. From the start, the girl privileges the interior of the body and the vagina: hence the archaic experiences of femininity that leave an indelible trace. It is therefore not enough to give an account of feminine sexuality from a 'phallocentric' point of view. It is also necessary to measure the impact that anatomy, and the sexual organ itself, has on the girl's unconscious. Thus Jones and his school were answering the Viennese school when they proposed the precocious, even innate character of femininity. Freud spoke of one libido, whereas Jones distinguished two types of libidinal organisation, male and female" (1977, 83). The term "concentricity," which Montrelay punningly uses to refer to this specifically feminine sexuality, is borrowed from Béla Grunberger (1964, 76). By bringing together and contrasting concentricity and phallocentricity, Montrelay would at first seem to

give a new legitimacy to female eroticism (the cunt heard in "concentricity") and to undermine the primacy of the phallus. However, as I will show, this is not really the case. On the Freud/Lacan-Jones debate, also see Jane Gallop (1982, 15–32).

6. Gallop suggests that Lacan uses other terms such as "phallus" and "castration" to the same purpose: "Maybe he is using them up, running the risk of essence, running dangerously close to patriarchal positions, so as to wear 'phallus' and 'castration' out until they are thoroughly hackneyed. But probably not completely, *pas-tout*. In every alternative practise . . . *un peu de mal*, a bit of difficulty, a bit of maleness returns" (1982, 55). Of course Lacan cannot deprive these words of their old meaning, nor is he able to do without them. More than a bit of maleness surges up when he says in *Encore:* "There is no such thing as The woman since of her essence—having already risked the term, why think twice about it?—of her essence she is not all" (1972–73, 144). Even if the word "essence" is here used jokingly or at least self-consciously, the effect is not to question patriarchy but rather to reinforce it. "Woman" is doubly not-all or not-whole: first as a sexed being, in relation to the original, hypothetical androgyne (in this sense too, man is not-whole); then in relation to man (as a hole, deprived of his sex organ). If Lacan's description of "woman" is relational and descriptive (rather than prescriptive) of the construction of femininity in patriarchy (the only way for a feminist to rescue this statement), why does the word "essence" crop up so insistently under his pen, except as a way of saving his masculinity?

7. This, of course, does not imply that "écriture féminine" does not exist, but rather that Irigaray will not identify it, because this would be possible only according to patriarchal criteria. Defining "speaking (as) woman" ("parler femme") in opposition to phallogocentric discourse would reinscribe it and thus imprison it within the logic of the Same, whereas for Irigaray "écriture féminine" and femininity in general are characterized by fluidity, by the subversion and refusal of all closure. Irigaray prefers to practice this type of writing in her own work: in the initial and final chapter of *This Sex* ("The Looking Glass, from the Other Side," "When Our Lips Speak Together"). The question remains whether her "écriture féminine," which attempts to speak through the female body, to express it in a language based on contiguity, proximity, nonclosure, the tactile, and so forth is a really liberating and (de)constructive feminist strategy. To me, Irigaray's deconstruction of phallogocentric discourse (as practiced, for instance, in the middle chapters of *This Sex*) is more convincing than her "écriture féminine," which runs the risk of being conflated with biological essentialism and confines women to her positively valued, but always dangerous patriarchal stereotypes.

8. Doane elsewhere attempts to clarify this difference: "masquerade seemed to provide a feminine counter to the concept of fetishism which had dominated the discussion of (male) spectatorship. Both concepts theorize subjectivity as constituted both spatially and temporally by a gap or distance; but fetishism does so through a scenario which is dependent upon the presence-in-absence of the phallus. While masquerade . . . is also haunted by a masculine standard, mas-

culinity as measure is not internal to the concept itself (the masquerade designates the distance between woman and the image of femininity, the fetish is the substitute maternal *phallus*). Rather, in masquerade, masculinity is present as the context provoking the patient's reaction-formation" (1988–89, 48–49). If masquerade is indeed "haunted by a masculine standard," how can the normative phallus not be "internal to the concept," as it is in the theories of Riviere, Montrelay, and Lacan? Would there be any need for a female masquerade if femininity were not already defined in relation to the phallus? If the masquerading actress has internalized the law (the rule of the phallus), as Riviere's essay shows, what guarantees that the female spectator as masquerader can escape this same internalization?

References

Appignanesi, L., and J. Forrester. 1992. *Freud's Women*. New York: Basic Books.

Apter, E. 1991. *Feminizing the Fetish: Psychoanalysis and Narrative Obsession in Turn-of-the-Century France*. Ithaca, N.Y.: Cornell Univ. Press.

Berger, J. 1972. *Ways of Seeing*. London: Penguin Books.

Brome, V. 1983. *Ernest Jones: Freud's Alter Ego*. New York: Norton.

Butler, J. 1990. *Gender Trouble: Feminism and the Subversion of Identity*. New York: Routledge.

———. 1993. *Bodies that Matter*. New York: Routledge.

Doane, M. A. 1982. Film and the Masquerade: Theorising the Female Spectator. *Screen* 23:74–87.

———. 1988–89. Masquerade Reconsidered: Further Thoughts on the Female Spectator. *Discourse* 11 (Fall–Winter):42–54.

Freud, S. 1931. Female Sexuality. In *The Standard Edition of the Complete Psychological Works*. Ed. and trans. J. Strachey et al. 24 vols. London: Hogarth Press, 1953–1974 (hereafter *S.E.*), 21:223–43.

———. 1933. Femininity. *S.E.*, 22:112–35.

———. 1905 [1901]. *Fragment of an Analysis of a Case of Hysteria*. *S.E.*, 7:3–122.

———. 1923. The Infantile Genital Organizaiton. *S.E.*, 19:141–45.

———. 1917 [1915]. Mourning and Melancholia. *S.E.*, 14:243–58.

———. 1925. Some Psychical Consequences of the Anatomical Distinction between the Sexes. In *S.E.*, 19:243–58.

——— 1918 [1917]. The Taboo of Virginity. *S.E.*, 11:193–208.

Gallop, J. 1982. *The Daughter's Seduction: Feminism and Psychoanalysis*. Ithaca, N.Y.: Cornell Univ. Press.

Grunberger, B. 1964. Outline for a Study of Narcissism in Female Sexuality. In J. Chasseguet-Smirgel, ed., *Female Sexuality: New Psychoanalytic Views*. Ann Arbor: Univ. of Michigan Press, 1970, pp. 68–83.

Heath, S. 1986. Joan Riviere and the Masquerade. In V. Burgin, J. Donald, and C. Kaplan, eds., *Formations of Fantasy*. New York: Methuen, pp. 45–61.

Heimann, P. 1963. Obituary Notice for Joan Riviere. *Int. J. Psychoanal.* 44:230–33.

Irigaray, L. 1977. *This Sex Which Is Not One.* Trans. C. Porter. Ithaca, N.Y.: Cornell Univ. Press, 1985.

Lacan, J. 1958. The Meaning of the Phallus. In J. Mitchell and J. Rose, eds., *Feminine Sexuality: Jacques Lacan and the école freudienne.* Trans. J. Rose. New York: Norton, 1985, pp. 74–85.

Montrelay, M. 1977. Inquiry into Femininity. Trans. P. Adams. *M/f* 1 (1978): 83–101.

Mulvey, L. 1975. Visual Pleasure and Narrative Cinema. *Screen* 16.3 (Autumn): 6–18.

Paskauskas, R. A., ed. 1993. *The Complete Correspondence of Sigmund Freud and Ernest Jones.* Cambridge: Harvard Univ. Press.

Riviere, J. 1929. Womanliness as a Masquerade. *Int. J. Psychoanal.* 10:303–13.

Silverman, K. 1983. *The Subject of Semiotics.* New York: Oxford Univ. Press.

Part III
Gendered Mirrors

Chapter Seven

Sadomasochism as Intersubjective Breakdown in D. H. Lawrence's "The Woman Who Rode Away"

Barbara Schapiro

No writer has explored the complex interplay of love and domination with such fervent intensity as D. H. Lawrence. A target for feminist critics, particularly since Kate Millett's blistering attack in *Sexual Politics* (1969), Lawrence's work is nevertheless richly valuable by virtue of its very problematic nature. Male domination is a conundrum in the fiction that is dramatized, not solved; the psychological complications of such domination are acutely detailed and more often lead to impasse than to resolution or freedom. Although its attractions are vividly manifest, prompting Millett and others to charge that he celebrates male domination, so are its troubling, even tragic consequences. For all of his single-minded preaching, Lawrence, in the best of his fiction, displays a remarkable aptitude for what Keats calls "negative capability"—a capacity for sustaining uncertainty, contradiction, and paradox—as well as a fluidity of identifications and an ability to play out, though not resolve, deep ambivalence.

Jessica Benjamin's feminist psychoanalytic study *The Bonds of Love* (1988) focuses, like Lawrence, on the dynamic intersection of love and domination. Her work offers a new and rewarding perspective from which to examine Lawrence's fiction. In brief, Benjamin argues that "domination and submission result from a breakdown of the necessary tension between self-assertion and mutual recognition that allows self and other to meet as sovereign equals" (12). What she calls mutual recognition involves the types of experiences currently described in empirical studies of mother-infant interactions: "emotional attunement, mutual influence, affective mutuality, sharing states of mind" (16).

The need for recognition from a primary, nurturing other is inextricably, and paradoxically, bound up with self-assertion and the realization of one's own agency. "Recognition is that response from the other which makes meaningful the feelings, intentions, and actions of the self. . . . But such recognition can only come from an other whom we, in turn, recognize as a person in his or her own right" (12). The fundamental dynamic in psychic development, then, involves a subject relating to another subject—intersubjectivity—rather than the more traditional psychoanalytic view of a subject relating to its object. Drawing on the research of Daniel Stern (1985), which suggests that the infant does not begin life in symbiotic union with the mother but "is primed from the beginning to be interested in and to distinguish itself from the world of others," Benjamin asserts that the key psychological issue is not only how we separate "or become free of the other, but how we actively engage and make ourselves known in relationship to the other" (1988, 18).

Intersubjectivity has become both gendered and problematized in our culture, however, because of the denial of self-assertion and agency to women. If women are the primary caretakers but only men are granted subjectivity, then everyone suffers from this subject/object split. Benjamin compares the problem to Hegel's formulation of the master-slave dynamic, with women in the position of the slave. The master's domination and objectification of the slave deprive the master himself of what he most needs: recognition from an other who is strong and independent enough to give it. A mother's recognition of her child is not simply a matter of her acting as a mirror: her "recognition will be meaningful only to the extent that it reflects her own equally separate subjectivity" (24). Indeed the failure to conceive of the mother as a subject in her own right, with her own desires and bodily reality outside of the child's experience of her, is a problem many feminist critics have found with object relations theory. The problem resides not only in psychoanalytic theory, however, but within our culture at large: it is the problem that Benjamin critiques and that Lawrence wrestles with so passionately in his art.

The intersubjective arena thus offers new ground for psychoanalytic investigation of Lawrence's work. Previous post-Freudian psychoanalytic studies of Lawrence, such as Judith Ruderman's influential *The Devouring Mother* (1984) and, more recently, Margaret Storch's *Sons and Adversaries* (1990), have worked within the framework of British and American object relations theories. These studies emphasize Lawrence's difficulties in separating out of an original symbiotic union with an omnipotent, devouring, preoedipal mother, and they indeed offer valuable insights into the intrapsychic dimensions of Lawrence's texts. If we now, however, begin to look at symbiotic or narcissistic union not as a universal, original condition but as a retroactive fantasy stemming from failures of intersubjective attunement and recognition, still further psychic territory opens up in the fiction.

The struggle for intersubjectivity is, in fact, one of Lawrence's most obsessive themes. The self-realization his characters urgently seek is possible only in relation to a fully recognized other, a separate other capable of granting recognition to the self. The conflict or dilemma in his work generally assumes one of two forms: either the other lacks full subjectivity and collapses under the weight of the self's clamorous needs, or the other's independent subjectivity threatens to suffocate, constrain, or negate the self. Both problems are interrelated since the fantasy of the other's overwhelming and destructive power stems from the failure of mutual recognition and the collapse of intersubjectivity in the first place.

This dilemma is especially apparent in his short stories. "Odour of Chrysanthemums" (1911a), for instance, builds precisely to a climactic awareness of failed recognition and intersubjective breakdown. As Elizabeth Bates views the naked, dead body of her husband, she realizes, with sudden, paralyzing fear and shame, that "she had never seen him, he had never seen her. . . . They had denied each other in life. Now he had withdrawn. An anguish came over her" (301). If the other is not realized in his or her external otherness and separate subjectivity, then the self too remains unrealized, blocked from experiencing its own authenticity or sense of aliveness. "The Shadow in the Rose Garden" (1911b) also ends with the female character in a state of paralysis and shock, though in this case the emphasis is not on the woman's failure to recognize, but on the failure of the beloved other to recognize her. The woman's discovery that her former fiancé has gone mad and does not know her has the effect of nullifying her entire existence:

> [His eyes] were black and stared without seeing. . . . The whole world was deranged. . . . She wondered, craving, if he recognised her—if he could recognise her. . . . Could he recognise her, or was it all gone? She sat motionless with horror and silence. . . . Her eyes searched him, and searched him, to see if he would recognise her, if she could discover him. "You don't know me?" she asked, from the terror of her soul, standing alone. (226–27)

She leaves in a "blind" haste, feeling totally depleted and drained, "without any being" (228). The repeated emphasis on eyes—on seeing and being seen by the beloved other—runs throughout Lawrence's fiction and draws its emotional and psychological force from the eye contact, the subtle but profound attunement play of early mother-child interaction. Such attunement, as Stern and others have argued, sets the very foundation for the development of a sense of a subjective self, the base for how one experiences self in relation to other and to the external world.

Christopher Brown has discussed the preponderance of eye imagery in "The Fox" (1922), and he equates vision in that work with domination—"to see is to dominate, to be seen is to be dominated" (Brown 1980, 61). That equation, however, is the result of a prior process gone awry, of a traumatic break, as in "The Shadow in the Rose Garden," of attunement, of recognition by and of the primary other. Thus the woman in the rose garden, unrecognized by the other to whom she is erotically attached, is terrified and overwhelmed by his alien power: "She had to bear his eyes. They gleamed on her, but with no intelligence. He was drawing nearer to her. . . . Her horror was too great. The powerful lunatic was coming too near to her" (Lawrence 1911b, 227–28). Without attuned recognition, in other words, the erotic or desired other is experienced as a dominating, overpowering presence. The woman's failure to "discover" the real other and be "recognised" by him also leaves her with an unbounded hostility and destructive rage—"now she hated everything and felt destructive" (230). She turns this hostility on her husband and behaves coldly and cruelly toward him, just as he, out of an equivalent wound (her lack of recognition of him), seeks to hurt and control her. The erotic relationship thus dissolves into a destructive power play, the most familiar scenario in Lawrence's fiction.

The masochistic and sadistic strains in Lawrence's writing are rooted in such breakdown of mutual recognition and the failure to "discover" the other or the self. Masochism, as Emmanuel Ghent has argued, reflects a distorted bid for recognition; sadism, a twisted attempt at discovery. According to Ghent, erotic submission is the "defensive mutant" of the healthy and positive desire for "surrender"—for letting down the defensive barriers that inhibit authentic self-experience. Ghent could be describing any number of Lawrence's characters when he states, "There is, however deeply buried or frozen, a longing for something in the environment to make possible the surrender, in the sense of yielding, of false self" (1990, 109). This longing, he believes, is part of "an even more general longing to be known, recognized" and is "joined by a corresponding wish to know and recognize the other" (110). Thus masochism—enslaving oneself to a powerful master—is a "pseudo-surrender" and conceals "the longing for, the wish to be found, recognized, penetrated to the core, so as to become real, or as Winnicott put it in another context, 'to come into being' " (116).

In order to understand the psychodynamics of sadism, Ghent draws on Winnicott's notion of "object use" and the necessity of the object's surviving the subject's psychic "destruction" of it. According to Winnicott, the capacity to use an object involves "the subject's placing of the object outside the area of the subject's omnipotent control," perceiving it as "an external phenomenon," and recognizing it as "an entity in its own right" (1971, 89). The subject must "destroy" the object internally in order to make it external. In terms of the mother-child dynamic, in other words, the child must feel free ruthlessly to unleash his or her full aggressive and erotic potential without excessive concern for the mother's survival. If the mother or object "survives," the subject can then *use* it, or in Ghent's terms, the subject is then able to "un-cover" or "dis-cover" the real other (1990, 125).

Contrarily, if the other fails to survive (which refers not only to traumatic death or absence, but to any number of defensive or retaliatory responses, such as emotional withdrawal and rejection) the self may then feel trapped in its own omnipotent destructiveness. (Recall the rose garden woman's boundless hostility at her failure to discover her former lover.) "If the subjective object never becomes real . . . and externality is not discovered," Ghent says, then the subject is "made to feel that he or she *is* destructive; and finally, fear and hatred of the other develops, and with them, characterological destructiveness comes into being. In short, we have the development of sadism . . . the need to aggressively control the other as a perversion of object usage, much as we have seen in masochism as a perversion of surrender" (124).

Ghent's analysis illuminates the deeper motivational yearnings and fears behind both the masochistic and the sadistic aspects of Lawrence's fiction. It allows us to appreciate the rich psychodynamic territory Lawrence was courageously exploring, even if we are offended by the sadism of his (usually, but not exclusively) male characters and the masochism of his (usually, but not exclusively) female characters. The point is that Lawrence is identified with both. Norman Mailer's contention that Lawrence understood women "with all the tortured fever of a man who had the soul of a beautiful, imperious, and passionate woman" (1971, 152) indeed contains some truth. Lawrence's narcissistic identification with his own mother, though the source of profound rage and ambivalence, is also at the root of an empathic imagination that endows his female characters with the "tortured fever" of his own soul, with his own psychological complexity. Feminist critics who want to dismiss Lawrence have, I believe, missed this crucial identification. His female identification and his masochistic fantasies can, in fact, tell us much about the cultural phenomenon of female masochism.

Such fantasy is essential to "The Woman Who Rode Away" (1924), one of Lawrence's most hotly debated stories. Millett calls this hypnotic tale about an educated white woman who rides off into the mountains and finds herself the sacrificial victim in a barbaric Indian religious rite "Lawrence's most impassioned statement of the doctrine of male supremacy and the penis as deity . . . a pornographic dream" (1969, 403). Although she claims the story devotes equal attention to the masochistic and the sadistic, she perceives "a peculiar relish . . . a wallowing in the power of the Indian male, his beauty and indifference and cruelty, exerted not only on the silly woman, his victim, but on Lawrence too. It is the author himself standing fascinated before this silent and darkly beautiful killer, enthralled, aroused, awaiting the sacrificial rape" (405). True enough, but Millett does not pursue the implications of this insight in her wholesale indictment of the story as a sadistic fantasy of male vengeance and humiliation of women. The authorial identification with the Woman makes for a profound ambivalence that, as with so many Lawrence stories, complicates the surface plot and accounts for an ambiguity of tone and attitude.

The ambiguity is evident in the widely divergent critical readings of the story. Like Millett, R. P. Draper sees much sadistic pleasure in the story's ending; he refers to the "'glittering eagerness, and awe, and craving'" attributed to the Indians as betraying Lawrence's own vindictiveness toward independent women (1988, 161). Peter Balbert, on the other hand, believes there is "ample evidence of an antagonistic attitude toward the primitive 'darkness' of the story" (1989, 116), and that the Woman's "evaluation of the Indians as dangerous creatures is shared by Lawrence, who is willing to choose the 'educated' antagonism of the Woman over the barbarism and coldness of the Chilchui" (121). The story indeed contains both attitudes toward the Indians—a pleasureful identification with their power *and* savagery and a resistant terror of it. David Cavitch is most on the mark when he notes that "none of the story's portended violence *occurs* . . . even the sacrificial thrust is arrested, in a conditional verb—'Then the old man would strike'—. . . . The allegory is evidently about a state of ambivalence so intense that neither the desire for a demonic sexual experience nor the anxiety over its destructiveness can be dramatized by conclusive actions" (1969, 166).

Interpretations that stress only the devaluation and objectification of the Woman—the perspective of the Indians—miss the Woman's own perspective, the perspective from which the major part of the story is indeed told. Although the Indians deny her personal being, her personal feelings and sensations are acutely rendered by the narrative as the experience unfolds. The Indians are actually far more abstracted and depersonalized than the Woman. Despite the fact that she is nameless (as are many of the characters in Lawrence's short stories), she is not a mere abstraction; she is granted an inner life or soul, even if it is the typically suppressed or deadened soul that Lawrence sees as endemic to modern civilization. The Woman, we are told, has been living an empty existence in stuporous subjection to a husband who "had never become real to her, neither mentally nor physically" (1924, 547). Without a "real" other to confer her own reality, she feels herself shriveling into nothingness.

The Woman's expedition to the mountains to find the "mysterious, marvellous Indians" is a last-ditch effort to discover that real otherness and her own reality. As usual in Lawrence's work, however, the self-affirmative desire for surrender, for yielding up the false self in hopes of recognition of one's true or authentic being, becomes distorted by the deficiency and desperation out of which it springs. Self-affirmative surrender to an external other becomes self-destructive submission to an idealized, tyrannical other. Although there is authorial identification with both the sadistic and the masochistic in this story, I would, like Millett in her initial insight, give greater weight to the latter. The story is less a vengeful celebration of the Woman's subjection than a disturbing enactment of the psychological dilemma inherent in masochistic fantasy.

In *The Bonds of Love*, Benjamin analyzes Pauline Réage's sadomasochistic tale *Story of O* (1965) as a reflection of intersubjective breakdown and "the struggle to the death for recognition" (Benjamin 1988, 55). Millett independently points out the similarity between Réage's pornographic story and Lawrence's; Benjamin's analysis of *O* can thus shed light on "The Woman Who Rode Away" as well. In *O*, for instance, Benjamin observes that O's masters "must perform their violation rationally and ritually in order to maintain their boundaries and to make her will—not only her body—the object of their will" (57–58). Similarly, the Indians treat the Woman in an utterly impersonal, ritualistic manner that ensures distance and denies commonality. Just as O is told by her masters that she is being flogged "'to teach you that you are totally dedicated to something outside yourself'" (56), so the Woman is told her sacrifice will "serve the gods of the Chilchui," will reclaim the potency of the sun and empower the Indians once more. As Benjamin says of O, "her sacrifice actually creates the master's power, produces his coherent self, in which she can take refuge. Thus in losing her own self, she is gaining access, however circumscribed, to a more powerful one" (61).

The Indians' sadism also differs significantly from that in Lawrence's other overtly sadomasochistic tale, "The Prussian Officer" (1914). In the earlier story, the Captain's sadism is desperately personal; the Indians', on the other hand, is profoundly disinterested. From the Woman's perspective, that absence of personal interest offers a fantasy of protection and containment. Because the Indians have objectified her and do not need her *personally*, the Woman is reassured of their strength since it is not dependent on her own fragile selfhood. The masochistic fantasy is consequently played out much more fully in this story than in the former. As Benjamin notes, the protective power of the sadist's disinterestedness "constitutes the all-important aspect of authority, without which the fantasy is not satisfying" (1988, 64). The Woman not only gains access to the Indians' greater power by giving up her own, she can also lose herself and "let go" (like Juliet in the story "Sun") without fear of destroying the other through the full expressive force of her erotic being.

The scene in which she is oiled and massaged in preparation for her sacrifice is highly erotic, even orgiastic. The description again emphasizes the Indians' remote, impersonal power, a power on which the pleasure of the masochistic fantasy depends:

> Their dark hands were incredibly powerful, yet soft with a watery softness she could not understand. . . . They were so impersonal, absorbed in something that was beyond her. They never saw her as a personal woman . . . the eyes were fixed with an unchanging, steadfast gleam, . . . the fixity of revenge, and the nascent exultance of those that are going to triumph— these things she could read in their faces, as she lay and was rubbed into a misty glow by their uncanny dark hands. Her limbs, her flesh, her very bones at last seemed to be diffusing into a roseate sort of mist, in which her consciousness hovered like some sun-gleam in a flushed cloud. . . . She knew she was a victim; that all this elaborate work upon her was the work of victimising her. But she did not mind. She wanted it. (Lawrence 1924, 577)

The woman is paradoxically willing to risk annihilation of her self in search of her self, which is the masochistic predicament. The pleasureable aspects of her experience are nevertheless equally mixed with fear and ambivalence in the story as a whole, evident in the narrative emphasis on the Indians' "cruel," "sinister," and "inhuman" nature, and as Cavitch notes, in the hesitancy of the ending, in the failure to actualize the violence.

As in *Story of O,* a father-son recognition dynamic is also prominent in this story. Benjamin describes the young man René's delivery of O to the older Sir Stephen as "a way of surrendering himself sexually to the more powerful man . . . the desire for recognition by the father wholly overtakes the love of the mother; it becomes another motive for domination" (1988, 59). In Lawrence's story, a young Indian forms a bond with the Woman—"He came and sat with her a good deal—sometimes more than she wished—as if he wanted to be near her." He is described as "gentle and apparently submissive with . . . black hair streaming maidenly over his shoulders" (1924, 567). His femaleness and identification with the Woman, in other words, are both affirmed and ultimately repudiated in his alliance with the father. The young Indian, who is being groomed to become the next chief, accompanies the Woman in her meetings with the old chief and serves as translator. As the old man runs his fingers over the Woman's naked body, "the young Indian had a strange look of ecstasy on his face" (564).

Benjamin believes that the father's recognition is as important as the mother's, and that an identificatory bond with the father is vital for children of both sexes. Indeed, if the mother is deprived of full subjectivity and is thus incapable of recognition, the relationship with the father becomes all the more desperate. If the father (or father-figure) is physically or emotionally unavailable (as he was in the emotional constellation of Lawrence's family), then the child, as Nancy Chodorow (1978) has argued, may seek a fantasy—an idealized other. The search for recognition from a real father thus transforms into urgent identification with an idealized, omnipotent father. Because such idealization rises out of frustration and deficiency, however, it masks a deeper shame, envy, and rage. This dynamic underlies the petrifying ambivalence that frequently accompanies homoerotic fantasy in Lawrence's fiction. The Indians' sadism reflects such projected envy and rage; their power is dreaded as much as it is desired.

Finally, eye imagery in this story is also conspicuous. The Indian chief's power, in particular, is specifically located in his black, fixed eyes: "the old chief looked at her as if from the far, far dead, seeing something that was never to be seen" (Lawrence 1924, 563); "She was fascinated by the black, glass-like, intent eyes of the old cacique, that watched her without blinking, like a basilisk's, overpowering her" (573); "Only the eyes of the oldest man were not anxious. Black and fixed, and as if sightless, they watched the sun, seeing beyond the sun. And in their black, empty concentration there was power, power intensely abstract and remote, but deep, deep to the heart of the earth, and the heart of the sun" (581).

The fixation on eyes again signals the Lawrentian obsession with being seen, known, recognized deep to the heart of the self. The Indian chief/father's eyes hold that power, the penetrating, dark power of the Lawrentian sun to "know" the self and bring it into full erotic being. The Woman, as Benjamin says of O, is "the lost soul who can only be restored to grace by putting herself in the hands of the ideal, omnipotent other . . . [her] great longing is to be known, and in this respect she is like any lover, for the secret of love is to be known as oneself" (1988, 60). Only a real other, however, not an idealized projection, can provide such recognition. The narrator is aware of the Woman's "foolish romanticism" in seeking the Indians in the first place. Her masochistic fantasy, however, as a derailed bid for recognition, is nevertheless the story's prevailing fantasy, and one with which Lawrence deeply identifies.

The assertion of male dominion in the story's final lines—"Then the old man would strike, and strike home, accomplish the sacrifice and achieve the power. The mastery that man must hold, and that passes from race to race" (Lawrence 1924, 581)—and the rigid gender polarity on which the story rides reflect a defensive splitting apparent throughout Lawrence's writing, a splitting that is especially blatant in many of his essays and letters. Often in the fiction, however, such polarity is simultaneously undermined by a capacious, flexible imagination that includes a strong female identification and an equally firm, intuitive grasp of the importance of the other's independent subjectivity to the realization of one's own. The recognition the self craves, the stories make clear, can come only from an other who is recognized as a whole, independent subject in her or his own right. Lawrence's work powerfully dramatizes the consequences of collapsed intersubjectivity—a collapse Benjamin sees as historically embedded in our culture. "The negation of the mother's independent subjectivity in social and cultural life," she claims, "makes it harder for her to survive her child's psychic destruction and become real to him" (1988, 214). This is the problem that Lawrence explores with great imaginative force and insight, even if he fails to solve it.

References

Balbert, P. 1989. *D. H. Lawrence and the Phallic Imagination: Essays on Sexual Identity and Feminist Misreading.* New York: St. Martin's.

Benjamin, J. 1988. *The Bonds of Love: Psychoanalysis, Feminism, and the Problem of Domination.* New York: Pantheon.

Brown, C. 1980. The Eyes Have It: Vision in "The Fox." *Wascana Review* 15:61–68.

Cavitch, D. 1969. *D. H. Lawrence and the New World.* New York: Oxford Univ. Press.

Chodorow, N. 1978. *The Reproduction of Mothering: Psychoanalysis and the Sociology of Gender.* Berkeley: Univ. of California Press.

Draper, R. P. 1988. The Defeat of Feminism: D. H. Lawrence's "The Fox" and "The Woman Who Rode Away." In D. Jackson and F. B. Jackson, eds., *Critical Essays on D. H. Lawrence.* Boston: G. K. Hall, pp. 158–69.

Ghent, E. 1990. Masochism, Submission, Surrender. *Contemp. Psychoanal.* 26:108–36.

Lawrence, D. H. 1976. *The Complete Short Stories.* 3 vols. Harmondsworth: Penguin.

———. 1911a. Odour of Chrysanthemums. In Lawrence 1976, 2:283–302.

———. 1911b. The Shadow in the Rose Garden. In Lawrence 1976, 1:221–33.

———. 1914. The Prussian Officer. In Lawrence 1976, 1:95–116.

———. 1924. The Woman Who Rode Away. In Lawrence 1976, 2:546–81.

Mailer, N. 1971. *The Prisoner of Sex.* Boston: Little, Brown.

Millett, K. 1969. *Sexual Politics.* New York: Ballantine.

Ruderman, J. 1984. *D. H. Lawrence and the Devouring Mother.* Durham: Duke Univ. Press.

Stern, D. N. 1985. *The Interpersonal World of the Infant.* New York: Basic Books.

Storch, M. 1990. *Sons and Adversaries: Women in William Blake and D. H. Lawrence.* Knoxville: Univ. of Tennessee Press.

Winnicott, D. W. 1971. *Playing and Reality.* London: Tavistock.

Chapter Eight

"He's More Myself than I Am": Narcissism and Gender in *Wuthering Heights*

Michelle A. Massé

Women, especially if they grow up with good
looks, develop a certain self-contentment
which compensates them for the social
restrictions that are imposed upon them in
their choice of object. Strictly speaking, it is
only themselves that such women love with an
intensity comparable to that of the man's love
for them. Nor does their need lie in the
direction of loving, but of being loved; and the
man who fulfills this condition is the one who
finds favour with them. The importance of this
type of woman for the erotic life of mankind is
to be rated very high. Such women have the
greatest fascination for men. . . . For it seems
very evident that another person's narcissism
has a great attraction for those who have
renounced part of their own narcissism and
are in search of object-love. The charm of a
child lies to a great extent in his narcissism, his
self-contentment and inaccessibility, just as
does the charm of certain animals which seem
not to concern themselves about us, such as
cats and the large beasts of prey.
—Freud, "On Narcissism"

My thanks to Joanna Marshall, Anna Nardo, and Peter Rudnytsky for their comments on versions of this essay.

Feminist analyses of "On Narcissism" (1914), "Some Psychical Conse-quences of the Anatomical Distinction between the Sexes" (1925), "Female Sexuality" (1931), and "Femininity" (1933) have prompted inci-sive critiques of and innovations in psychoanalytic theory. One of the most far-reaching of these changes is the reclamation of the narcissistic realm Freud populates with women, animals, "children and primitive peoples" (1914, 75) as the preoedipal. The most significant feminist work on preoedipal experience in recent decades (by Carol Gilligan, Nancy Chodorow, Marianne Hirsch, and Madelon Sprengnether, to cite just a few conspicuous instances) has established its crucial importance as a developmental stage and its positive significance for adult functioning.

In what Jessica Benjamin calls "the implicit sexual politics" of the "debate over Oedipus and Narcissus" (1988, 156), the preoedipal realm has become the ground on which to lay the foundation for a new developmental model that assumes the worth of the maternal, that values connection as much as (or more than) separation, and that constructs femininity as something other than masculinity manqué. Yet, as Ben-jamin insightfully argues, mature object relations based upon intersubjectivity—the mutual recognition of subjects—require separa-tion as well as connection.

What I propose to do in this essay is to return, with some trepida-tion, to the aspect of narcissism, grounded in the preoedipal, that Freud calls its "morbid process" (1914, 86) and to question its relationship to gender through investigation of one female character, Catherine Earn-shaw of Emily Brontë's *Wuthering Heights* (1847). My aim in choosing a character who embodies much of Freud's problematic description is not to resuscitate the portrait of the adult woman, whose charm, like that of the child, lies in her "self-contentment." Instead, while conceding the descriptive accuracy of Freud's sketch, what I want to explore is the character and story he prescribes for the female narcissist who attempts to fulfill the traditionally masculine aims of *Bildung*. Neither Freud's nor Brontë's narrative can come to a close because of the gendered terms of their own plotting. The woman caught in the self-destructive spiral of using narcissism to achieve object relations by "being loved" cannot develop the intersubjectivity Benjamin establishes as one of the hall-marks of maturity. And the would-be *Bildungsroman* protagonist who, like Catherine Earnshaw, tries to love herself through the roundabout route of "the man's love" is stalled in development: she is replaced by another woman (in this case, her daughter) so that plot can continue. The be-havior of the female narcissist can indeed fit Freud's description. What he identifies as her central "need," however, may be active agency and not passive recognition. The frustration of that need can result only in a truncated saga of development.

In the larger project of which this investigation is a part, tentatively titled *Great Expectations: Narcissism, Masculinity, and the Bildungsroman,* my interest is in how the novel of formation defines itself through its focus on narcissism and in how both the genre and the psychoanalytic category are "gendered" and thus further delineate cultural expectations. Psychoanalysis glosses the *Bildungsroman,* but the *Bildungsroman* in turn explicates the fictions of psychoanalysis. This mutual illumination is nowhere more evident than in the representation of gender within the plots of the *Bildungsroman* and of psychoanalysis. Both question who wants to be a "hero" (or a narcissist), what cultural factors prompt taking that path, and what social constraints may cause its abandonment or rerouting.

My argument is that the *Bildungsroman* is "about" narcissism, whether in mapping the path from adolescent self-regard to adult reciprocity or in displaying the would-be polymath's adult refusal to admit limitation in career, choice of mate, and ability. The genre's innovations in narrative technique are intimately allied to its representation of the protagonist's psychology and to the adolescent's expectations of wish-fulfillment in the external world. In theory, the novel of formation traces a protagonist's transition from pleasure principle to reality principle (as earlier critics maintained in different terms). In practice, the bulk of the novel is far more often the justification of a claim of immunity from social or emotional demands, the insistence that characters are what Freud called, in "Character Types," "exceptions" (1916, 311).

In the temporary refusal to move from the self-love of childhood to an acknowledgment of the separate identities of others, the worldview of narcissists is marked, according to Freud, by "an over-estimation of the power of their wishes and mental acts, the 'omnipotence of thoughts,' a belief in the thaumaturgic force of words, and a technique for dealing with the external world—'magic'—which appears to be a logical application of these grandiose premises" (1914, 75). Freud's "exception," like Karen Horney's "seeker of glory" (1950), creates an idealized image of self. In order to sustain that image, the individual treats events and persons as props in a privately directed drama—just as, in the *Bildungsroman,* narrative point of view, time, secondary characters, and plot often shift to accommodate the perspective of the protagonist. For both the "exception" and the "seeker of glory" (labels that apply to all *Bildungsroman* protagonists at some stage of their development), potentiality is worth more than activity.

Novels and case histories show boys and girls as having the same ambitious dreams in early adolescence. During maturation, however, a sharp distinction emerges between "normal" female and male development. The difference is seen in what is represented as socially possible for girls and boys, but also in how they incorporate those social expectations as part of their identities. As theorists such as Gilligan, Chodorow, and Benjamin argue, girls, finding little social endorsement for outward journeys toward careers and upward mobility, may take an inward course and define identity through relationships.

Girls schooled in the ideology of romance internalize its strictures, waiting for that impossible moment when they are good enough, pretty enough, and docile enough to earn love (i.e., to achieve object relations through passive narcissism). Boys trained in active narcissism close the gap between what they are told they should be and the inevitable limitations of what they are by identification with the ideal. Both pay a serious psychological price—a ruinous "company store" price, particularly for the working class or minorities, who nonetheless have nowhere else to shop.

In "On Narcissism," Freud acknowledges that both girls and boys go through narcissistic stages of development and, like "His Majesty the Baby" (91), have grandiose expectations during infancy and later. Strangely enough, however, they come to love differently, "although these differences are of course not universal" (88). Men's love tends to be anaclitic, "complete love of the object type," based upon love of "himself and the woman who nurses him," while women, like "perverts and homosexuals," "are plainly seeking *themselves* as a love object" (88).

For the purposes of this discussion, I would like to put aside the vexed distinction between anaclitic and narcissistic love (Kernberg 1991, 138) and instead, following Freud's argument in "Instincts and Their Vicissitudes" (1915), simply posit an active and a passive mode of narcissism suggested by the phrase "loving . . . [and] being loved" (1914, 89). My premise is that there is a realm of narcissistic entitlement endorsed by social and cultural expectations that Freud does not register systematically. Narcissistic entitlement can be constituted by race, ethnicity, class, and so forth, but the aspect that interests me here is heterosexual sex/gender expectations. Thus, just as Freud in a number of essays understands "overvaluation" as a mistake that the dominant make about the subordinate, so too he sees narcissistic object relations as a primarily feminine (passive) phenomenon while remaining blind to much of masculine (active) entitlement.

My passive/active distinction does not assume an absolute polarity, but instead is a means to determine how and why certain expectations or modes of behavior predominate in a given instance. For example, the active articulation of narcissism that attempts to impose one's will or desires upon another can be accompanied by a passive strain that presumes fond admiration in return; similarly, someone belonging to what Horney calls the "self-effacing" type can use abnegation to extort responses from others. Nonetheless, the distinction between active and passive components is useful in that it identifies both modes as manifestations of narcissism. Although Freud notes that the distinction is not sex-specific, his discussion presumes a strong gendering of patterns and, as is true elsewhere in his work, a devaluation of the passive feminine pole. If, in suggesting a certain gender malleability, Freud provides an alternative to essentialism, so too he hints at a cultural critique as he sets forth the first formulation of the ego ideal and begins to move from a topographical to a structural model of the psyche. In the 1914 argument, the individual's ego ideal and conscience are said to arise from "the critical influence of his parents (conveyed to him by the medium of the voice), to whom were added, as time went on, those who trained and taught him and the innumerable and indefinable host of all the other people in his environment—his fellow-men—and public opinion" (96). Freud is not inclined to question what those voices are saying, and, indeed, elsewhere in the essay he ascribes instinctual repression to an intrapsychic conflict with "the *subject's* cultural and ethical ideas" (93, emphasis added). Yet he also strikingly associates feminine narcissism with social constraint at a late stage of development: women "develop a certain self-contentment *which compensates them for the social restrictions that are imposed upon them in their choice of object*" (88–89, emphasis added). The frustration of object-choice, then, and the resulting turning of libido inward upon the self are not only intrapsychic or even interpersonal events, but ones that can be considered in light of larger cultural patterns.

The character of Catherine Earnshaw demonstrates all of the behaviors Freud attributes to women who love narcissistically. What she displays, however, is not only a splitting of the ego in the process of defense but, more startlingly, a gendered splitting of narcissistic modes in her relationships with Heathcliff and Edgar Linton. In addition, the briefly sketched history of her development suggests that analysis of cultural and familial channeling of girls' aggression may confound male-specific developmental models and explicate "normal" female patterns.

Although a number of critics have noted Catherine's egoism,[1] the peculiarities of her behavior are more often obscured by the cultural credence given to the heterosexual romance plot: Catherine and Heathcliff, in this reading, are a superb instance of star-crossed lovers, their merger not bizarre but an intense articulation of what love "should" be. I would argue instead that Catherine is doomed, not by the stars but by the *in*ability to love, where love is understood as intersubjective reciprocity. Freud claims that "in the last resort we must begin to love in order not to fall ill, and we are bound to fall ill if, in consequence of frustration, we are unable to love" (1914, 85). What I would like to trace briefly here is the frustration of aggressive, active drives that leaves this girl unable to love and that leads to different modes of narcissism (active and passive) as well as to forms that fulfill both preoedipal and oedipal demands.

Brontë beautifully delineates the difference between merger and mirroring (a less extreme form of narcissistic bonding) in Catherine's impassioned speech to Nelly. Catherine distinguishes her sense of an eternal bond with Heathcliff ("he") from her love for Edgar (to whom she refers by his surname):

> "If all else perished, and *he* remained, I should still continue to be; and, if all else remained, and he were annihilated, the Universe would turn to a mighty stranger. I should not seem a part of it. My love for Linton is like the foliage in the woods. Time will change it, I'm well aware, as winter changes the trees. My love for Heathcliff resembles the eternal rocks beneath—a source of little visible delight, but necessary. Nelly, I *am* Heathcliff—he's always, always in my mind—not as a pleasure, any more than I am always a pleasure to myself—but as my own being." (1847, 74)

The bond with Heathcliff Catherine so vehemently asserts is the active embodiment of her ego ideal in another (or overvaluation)—what Freud, in fact, might well call an anaclitic or masculine type of love, since the libido "leans on" the ego-instincts and Catherine is ensuring her very psychic survival through this love. At the same time, however, the absence of boundaries between self and other that characterizes preoedipal attachment is conspicuous.

Catherine's changeable love for Edgar, on the other hand, is perfectly feminine and narcissistic according to Freud's model: she passively accepts being loved and emphasizes her self-containment in relation to him. Yet, although the narcissistic form of love suggests a "lower" form of object relations in Freud's schema, for women in particular accepting the passive form also means accepting oedipal dynamics, separation of self and other, and establishment of the conscience and superego that acknowledge social expectations and oversee behavior.

What we have, then, is something of a conundrum in which Freud's sequence from "lower" to "higher" (preoedipal to oedipal, narcissistic to anaclitic) is confounded by "normal" feminine development. It may help if, instead, we consider both relationships as narcissistic, but fulfilling narcissistic needs and social expectations at different stages of development and in different modes. Freud outlines four ways in which the narcissist may "love": "(a) what he himself is (i.e., himself), (b) what he himself was, (c) what he himself would like to be, (d) someone who was once part of himself" (1914, 90). Catherine's love for Heathcliff is the attempt to restore object relations and identity itself: he is the embodiment of what she herself was, and someone who was once part of herself.

Edgar, on the other hand, personifies what she would like to be according to all of those parental and social voices that form the superego. Catherine's representation of her relationship with Heathcliff moves past identification and toward incorporation. The power of their bond is a perennial analytic rebus. Philip Wion (1985, 146) and Jeffrey Berman (1990, 93), for example, both suggest in their sensitive explications of separation and attachment in the novel that Catherine's symbiosis with Heathcliff points to his function as a maternal surrogate. Barbara Schapiro, also recognizing the bond as preoedipal, views him as a "projection of her enraged, 'bad', instinctual self that she cannot fully accept or acknowledge" (1994, 48), while Margaret Homans, assigning him a later developmental role, argues that he is "for Cathy . . . a proponent of the Law of the Father" (1986, 79).

Each of these readings demonstrates significant insight and explanatory power, but none quite accounts for how Heathcliff and Catherine become what John Matthews calls "the haunting spectre of the other" (1985, 64). Wion's and Berman's hypothesis, for example, traces an important strain of loss in the novel but—even given the human propensity for inappropriate object choices—cannot explain Catherine's strikingly bizarre need for a maternal surrogate without consideration of the aggressive drives Heathcliff also embodies for Catherine. And while I agree with Homans that Catherine is trying, in Lacanian terms, to maintain both Imaginary and Symbolic orders, Homans' representation of feminine preoedipal development obscures the active, aggressive drives of that period that Catherine projects upon Heathcliff; Schapiro's reading, which credits those drives, nonetheless plays down their worth and the cultural values responsible for their repudiation and distortion.

Different as these explications are, they all minimize the positive role of agency and aggression in the preoedipal period, Catherine's "unfeminine" inclusion of them as integral parts of her core self, and her insistence that those who cherish her must accept them as well. Her choice of a twin, rather than a parental or hierarchical partner, to establish what Leo Bersani calls a "stabilizing mirror" (1976, 208) is significant in this regard, since it shifts the balance of power and enables her to assert an active narcissism that would otherwise be impossible. Heathcliff is what D. W. Winnicott would call a "good-enough" mother insofar as he mirrors Catherine's activities with wholehearted approval; it is crucial to note, however, that he mirrors and endorses "masculine" activity for which he later becomes a surrogate when Catherine assumes the socially endorsed role of a passively narcissistic "lady."

Considering gender helps us to trace the tortured process that results in the apparent "self-contentment and inaccessibility" of Freud's passive female narcissist, whose "very high" worth can only be assessed through her impact upon the "erotic life of mankind" (1914, 89). As Sandra Gilbert and Susan Gubar discern, Catherine's yearning for masculine power is, paradoxically, part of what enables her feminine "oceanic" merger with Heathcliff (1979, 265).[2]

In arguing the need to reconsider gender in our understanding of narcissistic modes and developmental stages, I am not trying to establish the figure of Catherine Earnshaw as a feminist heroine thwarted by plot and history. My interest here is rather in investigating how, despite the sketchy developmental trajectory delineated in the novel, active and passive narcissism become the gendered means through which she provisionally shores up a frail core identity in adolescence and how, as an adult, the inability to adapt to external events or move toward intersubjective object relations and "healthy" narcissism leads to the disintegration of identity and of life itself.

What is sadly missing in the tallying of interpretative possibilities, including my own, is what Horney would call the "actual self": "an all-inclusive term for everything that a persona is at a given time, body and soul, healthy and neurotic" (1950, 158). That self remains as shifting as Catherine's inscriptions of "Catherine Earnshaw . . , Catherine Heathcliff . . . and Catherine Linton" (Brontë 1847, 25), which Lockwood spells over in old books as he tries to determine her identity. She herself does not know. At the novel's beginning, Lockwood dreams about this enigmatic figure. Even in death, however, the representation of Catherine can only pursue the narcissistic strategies that she used in life. The revenant's repeated "'let me in'" is a plaintive, aggressive, problematic, and unheeded attempt to establish object relations, and Lockwood's disingenuous insistence on separation—"'Let *me* go, if you want me to let you in!'"—is no more comprehensible to her dead than alive (Brontë 1847, 30).

What we see of the very young Catherine is far removed from that weeping child-ghost: she prefers the active mode for each component instinct (scopophilia/exhibitionism, sadism/masochism, epistemophilia/not knowing). For example, the six-year-old requests no Beauty-and-the-Beast rose as a gift from her father before his trip to Liverpool but a whip, useful for a girl who can already "ride any horse in the stable" (38). She looks, judges, and acts with pleasure in her own activity.

> Her spirits were always at high-water mark, her tongue always going—singing, laughing, and plaguing everybody who would not do the same. A wild, wicked slip she was—but she had the bonniest eye, and sweetest smile, and lightest foot in the parish. . . .
>
> In play, she liked, exceedingly, to act the little mistress, using her hands freely, and commanding her companions. (42–43)

When Catherine and her brother receive Heathcliff instead of the promised gifts, fourteen-year-old Hindley weeps at the loss of his fiddle, but Catherine "showed her humour by grinning and spitting" at the foundling (39).

Between the ages of eight and twelve (her ages when her mother and father, respectively, die), Catherine's mode of dealing with those around her is active and aggressive. Indeed, her interaction with her father displays a striking oedipal competition. She willfully does "just what her father hated most, showing how her pretended insolence, which he thought real, had more power over Heathcliff than his kindness; how the boy would do *her* bidding in anything, and *his* only when it suited his own inclination" (43). Her father's inability to see anything *but* her "insolence"—the inappropriate display of agency and will in a girl—triggers verbal sparring as well. In "praising" her for a gentle mood, he dismisses the actual child, who responds with an rejoinder as sharp as any that the equally precocious Jane Eyre gives to her supposed guardian, Mrs. Reed, when faced with adult aggression.

> "Why canst thou not always be a good lass, Cathy?"
> And she turned her face up to his, and laughed, and answered—
> "Why cannot you always be a good man, father?" (44)

Mr. Earnshaw rarely indicates to Catherine that she can indeed be a "good lass," or that a good lass might be articulate and independent. His decidedly unproductive means of encouraging empathy for others is to deal her "a sound blow . . . to teach her cleaner manners" (39) because of her anger at Heathcliff when he's first introduced to the household; when she comes to him for "fondling" after "behaving as badly as possible all day" (43), she is thoroughly rejected, as Nelly reports.

> "Nay, Cathy," the old man would say, "I cannot love thee; thou'rt worse than thy brother. Go, say thy prayers, child, and ask God's pardon. I doubt thy mother and I must rue that we ever reared thee!"
> This made her cry, at first; and then, being repulsed continually hardened her, and she laughed if I told her to say she was sorry for her faults, and beg to be forgiven. (43)

With almost all forays at reciprocal object relations rebuffed, it is not surprising that the girl retreats to narcissistic modes of behavior and finds a haven for the active, aggressive self that is her only firm identity in merger with Heathcliff.

Although Catherine and Heathcliff are "very thick" (39) before her father's death, it is only afterwards that they join forces fully, becoming symbiotically united in their desperate attempts both to assert an identity and to rebel. "More reckless daily," both "promised fair to grow up as rude as savages" (46). Unlike Freud's "children and primitive peoples" (1914, 75), each resists "degradation" (46) to passive, subordinate status by dint of the other's reinforcement. In recounting the expedition to the Grange that introduces Catherine to the Lintons, Heathcliff uses "we" throughout his narration[3] and is bemused by the evident separation between Isabella and Edgar: "'When would you catch me wishing to have what Catherine wanted?'" (48). Even after physical separation, Catherine avers that she and Heathcliff remain psychically joined: "'he's more my-self than I am. Whatever our souls are made of, his and mine are the same'" (72).

Paradoxically, it is only by narcissistic merger that each achieves some measure of autonomy and identity. At the same time, however, there are indications of inequality in their *unio mystica* that make Heath-cliff what Heinz Kohut would call a safe self-object for Catherine, one who is "not experienced as separate and independent from the self" (1971, 3). On the one hand, Heathcliff represents a unified self and a cool self-sufficiency. The very singularity of his name suggests an ele-mental essence: not for him debates about which name is the "right" one. The child who can stand "blows without winking or shedding a tear" (40) is seemingly impervious to the actions of others. On the other hand, however, Heathcliff remains subordinate to Catherine by dint of eth-nicity and class: the "gypsy" foundling, whose epistemophilia has been so halted that he "had extinguished any curiosity he once possessed in pursuit of knowledge" (62–63), cannot command Catherine in the way she commands him.[4]

For the same reasons, while Heathcliff can function as the ego ideal through which Catherine preserves the active component instincts, the boy with "slouching gait, and ignoble look" (63) cannot supply the social reinforcement necessary to support a narcissistic personality structure. Furthermore, she cannot receive that social esteem in an active mode: the only gender-appropriate way for her to be praised and admired is by assuming the passive characteristics of a "good lass."

Catherine's narcissistic needs remain the same, then, but she must adapt her strategies and find a second object. In a commentary on Freud's "On Narcissism," Nikolaas Treurniet elucidates such an impasse.

> The *denial of separateness* from objects creates the illusion that the object is part of the self and cannot be lost or destroyed. The other person has to fulfill the function of (part of) the patient's structure. The *denial of connect-*

edness, the defense of noncommunication, on the other hand, means having to sustain the belief in a state of omnipotent self-sufficiency, side by side with an intense and overwhelming dependency, expressed as a craving for admiration. It is a striking paradox that in these defenses both the tie to the object and the separateness from the object can be denied. (1991, 83)

Catherine enacts both denials—and their paradoxes—in her object choices. She denies psychic separateness from Heathcliff, yet demonstrates, as J. T. Matthews notes, an "unquestioned devotion to *maintaining* the very barriers that keep them apart*" (1985, 59), as well as an uneasy recognition of Heathcliff's potential autonomy. By forming a new alliance with the proper Edgar Linton in which she fulfills passive, "feminine" narcissistic aims, she denies connectedness, asserts self-sufficiency, and gains social admiration; but the heterosexual marriage pact inevitably also implies connection and regulation.

If Heathcliff is the archaic ego ideal, Edgar represents the advent of the superego and the conscience with their replication of cultural expectations and monitoring of behavior. The small world that could only deplore a hoyden who was "'half savage, and hardy, and free; and laughing at injuries'" (Brontë 1847, 107) applauds the fifteen-year-old young lady with her Tartan silk dress and carefully arranged ringlets who refuses the contamination of touch when she returns from the Grange.

Catherine wants that applause, for "she was full of ambition" (62), and it is only by practicing what Freud seems to assume is woman's "natural" passive skill of "being loved" that she can achieve it. Thus, for example, when she strikes Edgar early on, she realizes with dismay that *he,* not she, will assert separation. She draws him back with "'I'll cry myself sick'" (66), a promise Nelly dourly endorses and a lesson in passivity that Catherine learns well.

Edgar brings all a passive narcissist could want, as Nelly points out in her disquisition upon the shallow basis of Catherine's "love": "'he is handsome, and young, and cheerful, and rich, and loves you. . . . [Y]ou will escape from a disorderly, comfortless home into a wealthy, respectable one; and you love Edgar, and Edgar loves you'" (71). Yet, just as Catherine denies any possible separation from Heathcliff (while her choice of another nonetheless provides a margin of safety), so too she denies all deep-rooted connection to Edgar, while becoming increasingly dependent.

Catherine simultaneously maintains her active and passive narcissistic attachments without any acknowledgment that they may be in conflict or that their objects may have desires of their own. When Nelly sensibly points out that Heathcliff will be again abandoned with her marriage, Catherine is aghast at Nelly's obtuseness: "'He quite deserted!

we separated!' she exclaimed, with an accent of indignation. . . . 'Every Linton on the face of the earth might melt into nothing, before I could consent to forsake Heathcliff' " (73). In continuing to seek support for her "unruly nature" and active self from Heathcliff while at the same time having "no temptation to show her rough side" in the company of the Lintons, according to Nelly, Catherine adopts "a double character without exactly intending to deceive anyone" (62).

Heathcliff's departure is an abrupt assertion of autonomous identity that precipitates Catherine's psychic and physical collapse. She reaps pronounced secondary gains, however. Illness assures that Catherine's active drives, agency, and determination will be rewritten as the symptom of weakness and not preclude her being loved. She can continue to be a "haughty, headstrong creature" (61) and still have the Lintons indulge her, like "the honeysuckles embracing the thorn" (81).

Catherine's inability to be anything but willful, even in passivity, is medically authorized, as she never tires of pointing out. Nelly reports:

> she esteemed herself a woman, and our mistress, and thought that her recent illness gave her a claim to be treated with consideration. Then the doctor had said that she would not bear crossing much, she ought to have her own way; and it was nothing less than murder, in her eyes, for any one to presume to stand up and contradict her. (79)

Catherine, then, learns the hypochondria that Freud associates with narcissistic personality disorders, not primarily as the means of redirecting libido to the ego (although it surely serves that purpose also), but so that her helplessness and pain will prompt the speedy return of others to mirror status. Through achieving the properly feminine passivity of "a woman," she also gains the authority to be "our mistress" and enforce compliance to her will through class as well as sex.

In accepting the narcissistic gratification that comes from others' admiration, Catherine must also accept being the passive object of others' knowledge and scrutiny. Whereas in her active merger with Heathcliff she remains resolutely unaware of his responses as separate from her own or as factors to consider in her speech or behavior, with Edgar she is on guard against his critical assessment, concerned lest he " 'have a glimpse of her genuine disposition,' " as Nelly threatens (66). She calibrates her behavior so that, in general, it adheres to the pattern of passivity that Edgar, as representative of the superego and society, will approve. Nonetheless, she often chafes under the gaze of this externalized conscience, which Freud associates with the sense of "being *watched*" (1914, 95), and which soon approaches the paranoia that he also links to narcissistic disorders.

Catherine's sensitivity to Edgar's judgments, however, is not empathy. She shows no signs of being able to recognize the responses of others in either relationship, and her emphasis on potentiality rather than actuality, simultaneous adherence to contradictory stances, inability to recognize causality, and erratic relationship to durational time all bespeak the narcissist. She cannot fathom that her actions set in motion responses and events that will persist through time regardless of her intention. She tells Nelly, "'I have only to do with the present'" (Brontë 1847, 71), but both the past and the future are inescapable.

She is shocked, for example, when Edgar does not share her joy at Heathcliff's return (83) and the restoration in reality of the object whom she has cherished in fantasy for the last three years. That Heathcliff has developed an identity and plans other than her own also startles her, although she quickly moves to reestablish their symbiosis, assuming a split in his character similar to her own. Her marriage to Edgar and her bond with Heathcliff present no contradiction for Catherine; the only mystery is why both men are so grudging of her pleasure.

And, in a pregnancy as central and as absent as that in Hemingway's "Hills Like White Elephants," Catherine's and Edgar's unborn child does not function as the feminine narcissistic extension Freud postulates. The pregnancy doesn't "show" much in the text, but Catherine's narcissistic oblivion does. Neither pregnancy's physical changes, nor its emphatic reminders of causality and the passage of time, nor the existence of a future other seems to register for Catherine. Both Heathcliff's return and her pregnancy—clear instances of what Kohut calls "external shifts"—instead mandate the "replacement of one long-term self-representation by another [that] endangers a self whose earlier, nuclear establishment was faulty" (1972, 128).

Catherine's pregnancy must come to term; her attempt to maintain active and passive narcissistic attachments simultaneously must likewise come to conflict. Reality and its concomitant, irreversible time, intrude. Heathcliff will marry Isabella, not as part of the homosocial swap Catherine proffers in her "'offer of a wife'" (Brontë 1847, 97), but as an indication of his separate will and identity. Edgar, invoking the authorized connection of spouse, will insist that she choose between them, and his gaze will change from admiration to censure.

As Catherine's world crashes around her, the only new self-representation she can muster is of herself as a victim of that world, which inexplicably refuses to mold itself to her needs. Through the rest of the novel, she rallies her narcissistic forces to extort compliance through rage; when that strategy proves unavailing and others persist in acting autonomously, projection and paranoia escalate rapidly. From her perspective, all are against her and she stands alone. Her increasingly phantasmagoric thought processes, loss of reality testing, and accelerated splitting of affect, signal a turning inward of aggression that finally results in the ultimate gesture of grotesque narcissistic triumph—selfinduced death.

Catherine cannot adapt her self-representation, nor can she abandon her narcissistic strategies. Instead, she furiously increases the intensity and quantity of the defenses that have maintained her identity in the past. "Consumed by inner rage" (Berman 1990, 91), she "converts her self-love into a force of chaos" (Spark and Stanford 1960, 253) that is "directed both inward and outward, at self and other" (Schapiro 1994, 47). She attempts to extort compliance from others through active and passive means and thereby wrench her universe back into its Catherinecentric alignment.

Catherine's conviction that something is awry with the world and not with her is, as Kohut points out, a common one:

> The enemy who calls forth the archaic rage of the narcissistically vulnerable, however, is seen by him not as an autonomous source of impulsions, but as a *flaw in a narcissistically perceived reality*. The enemy is a recalcitrant part of an expanded self over which the narcissistically vulnerable person had expected to exercise full control. The mere fact, in other words, that the other person is independent or different is experienced as offensive by those with intense narcissistic needs. (1972, 148)

Catherine is not only offended but appalled when Heathcliff, Edgar, and Nelly assert separate existences that are not extensions of her own. If not her appendages, they must be, as she says accusingly to Nelly, "'my hidden enemy'" (Brontë 1847, 110). Through projective identification, she insists that *their* rage and vindictiveness, not hers, is the issue. She is unable, as Kohut predicts, to "acknowledge the inherent limitations of the power of the self, but attributes its failures and weaknesses to the malevolence and corruption of the uncooperative archaic object" (1972, 159). Such projective identification represents what Otto Kernberg characterizes as "a last-ditch effort to differentiate self from object, to establish a boundary between the self and the object by means of omnipotent control of the latter" (1992, 196–97).

The fragile identity Catherine has maintained through simultaneous passive and active narcissistic identifications is threatened. Earlier, she castigates both Lintons as "'spoiled children [who] fancy the world was made for their accommodation,'" and claims that it is she who "humours" others; now she perceives herself as betrayed. "'I'm delightfully rewarded for my kindness to each! After constant indulgence of one's weak nature, and the other's bad one, I earn, for thanks, two samples of blind ingratitude, stupid to absurdity!'" (Brontë 1847, 99). Catherine refuses to acknowledge that, as Nelly tells her, "'You can well afford to indulge their passing whims, as long as their business is to anticipate all your desires'" (86). Instead, she casts others as narcissistic exploiters (with partial justification), and herself as the victim of others' narcissistic expectations.

Catherine's world collapses because of Heathcliff's and Edgar's refusal of the narcissistic pact and the frightening suggestion that, at this point, they are more in accord with one another than with her. Heathcliff not only asserts separation through his appropriation of Isabella for his own aims, but by *judging* Catherine—an analysis that casts even the memory of their symbiotic bond into doubt. "'I want you to be aware that I know you have treated me infernally—infernally! Do you hear? And if you flatter yourself that I don't perceive it, you are a fool; and if you think I can be consoled by sweet words you are an idiot'" (97). Heathcliff's insistence upon his own knowledge and upon her "hearing" his speech sharply contrasts with earlier episodes in which he accepts Catherine's determination that he "'know nothing and say nothing'" (64).

Similarly, by asserting the right of monogamous connection, Edgar demands an agency from Catherine that had previously characterized her relationship with Heathcliff: he will no longer love unquestioningly while she allows herself to be loved. "'You *must* answer it; and that violence does not alarm me. I have found that you can be as stoical as any one, when you please. Will you give up Heathcliff hereafter, or will you give up me? I absolutely *require* to know which you choose'" (102).

Catherine is at an impasse. As the self-objects she needs to maintain simultaneous active and passive narcissism spring to fuller representational life, she regresses to an ever narrower psychic existence. Kernberg notes that "intolerance of psychic reality also brings about a self-directed attack on the patient's cognitive functions" (1992, 211), and Kohut confirms that "the secondary processes tend to be pulled increasingly into the domain of the archaic aggressions" (1972, 158). Language and logical thought yield to hallucination, and the external world fades away to be replaced by a more vivid primary universe in which Catherine can merge with nature and self-objects.

Projective identification joins with an "exacerbation of splitting mechanisms" (Kernberg, 1992, 214) that lets her distinguish "'*my* Heathcliff'" (134) from the simulacrum who lays claim to that name in the real world, just as she dissociates the "real" Catherine, restored to the moor in fantasy, from the sorry shadow trapped by the exigencies of the mundane here-and-now. Her rage has nowhere else to direct itself with any efficacy except that shadow. As Kohut observes, when narcissistic rage "is blocked from being directed toward the selfobject . . . [it] may shift its focus and aim at the self or at the body-self" (1972, 159n15).

Catherine's outward-directed rage and her collapse are equally unavailing; both active and passive objects refuse to stay in place. Her only "choice" is between annihilation and survival, as she tells Nelly: "'I'll choose between these two: either to starve at once . . . or to recover and leave the country'" (Brontë 1847, 104). She can imagine no psychic survival in a nonnarcissistic mode, however, and there is no new source of narcissistic gratification, as there was after her first collapse. "'How strange! I thought, though everybody hated and despised each other, they could not avoid loving me'" (104).

Catherine has no knowledge of a love that is intersubjective and reciprocal. Hence she chooses death as fit vengeance and a final display of superiority through pain. For the first time, then, all her libido and aggression are directed to her own ego in a self-destructive strategy that nonetheless assures a narcissistic coherence through martyrdom. "'Well, if I cannot keep Heathcliff for my friend, if Edgar will be mean and jealous, I'll try to break their hearts by breaking my own'" (101). And she does. Although once described by her doctor as a "'stout, hearty lass'" (111), she quickly becomes an anorexic, dissociated wraith who can no longer function in the world.

Catherine's dying is the grim proof of her "success" and of both Heathcliff's and Edgar's "failure": she maintains her standards of identity and "wins" the competition of pain. The frantic investment of energy that is her dying ensures that she will, for a brief while, maintain her centrality as she defines it. Finally and dreadfully, punishing herself is worthwhile because it lets her punish others and demand their allegiance. As Kernberg observes about patients with malignant narcissism, "to commit suicide, in these patients' fantasy, is to exercise sadistic control over others or to 'walk out' of a world they feel they cannot control" (1992, 78).

Catherine insists that others' suffering pales next to her own: she is the one who has "real" emotion (and "real" identity). "'You and Edgar have broken my heart, Heathcliff! And you both come to bewail the deed to me, as if *you* were the people to be pitied! I shall not pity you, not I. . . . I care nothing for your sufferings. Why shouldn't you suffer? I do!'" (Brontë 1847, 132–33). While her self-pity is real, so too is her pain. Catherine does suffer, and "'my agony'" (107) is not only an attention-getter but an excruciating truth.

Unable to sustain mature self-esteem or object relations, Catherine can only regress in the course of the novel to increasingly archaic, grandiose, and destructive articulations of her needs. The weakness of her core identity undoubtedly comes from circumstances specific to the childhood represented, such as the lack of genuine recognition by her parents and their early deaths. Yet the structural split caused by an actively disposed girl having to assume a passive role to gain familial and social approval also shapes Catherine's adult identity. That adult identity conforms to Freud's description of feminine narcissism, but an analysis of how it got to be that way demands that we consider gender.

Catherine welcomes death as the restoration of primary narcissism, her final, unanswerable assertion of grandiosity, and her last chance for a world in which she can be active: " 'That is not *my* Heathcliff. I shall love mine yet; and take him with me—he's in my soul. . . . I'm tired, tired of being enclosed here. I'm wearying to escape into that glorious world, . . . really with it, and in it. I shall be incomparably beyond and above you all' " (134). She dies "having never recovered sufficient consciousness to miss Heathcliff, or know Edgar" (137). She never was able to do either in life as well. That, perhaps, is the real tragedy of *Wuthering Heights*.

Notes

1. In his 1857 review of Elizabeth Gaskell's *Life of Charlotte Brontë*, W. C. Roscoe commented upon the "vivid and terrible delineation" of "self-love" in *Wuthering Heights* (1857, 71), an observation reaffirmed by Mrs. Humphry Ward in 1900 when she declared Catherine a stellar instance of the Romantic "exaltation of the Self" (1900, 98). Later critics also have singled out Heathcliff and Catherine as "transcendent narcissists" (Spacks 1975, 176), remarked that Catherine "is a curious case of self-love carried to the extreme" (Spark and Stanford 1960, 252), noteworthy for her "self-centered nature" (Leavis 1969, 28), and existing within a "self-created environment" (McKibben 1960, 42).

2. Other critics have also commented upon Heathcliff's role in representing Catherine's "own energies . . . uncurbed by the restraint which her sex imposes" (Montégut 1857, 75) and "her 'male' traits of anger, desire, and the power to harm" (Jacobs 1986, 81), as well as the way in which, through the delineation of Catherine, the novel hands over "power of motivation to the female" (Armstrong 1987, 197).

3. Heathcliff's "we" has a purpose similar to that pointed out by Eve Sedgwick in Catherine's " 'I *am* Heathcliff' " speech: " 'I will myself to be one with Heathcliff. To assert that I *am* Heathcliff feels like effecting this magically. Thus as I become identical with Heathcliff, my language becomes identical with reality' " (1980, 101). The ontic freight of language in *Wuthering Heights,* which I ascribe to narcissistic omnipotence of thought, is also noted by Miller (1982, 61), Homans (1986, 68), and Matthews (1985, 57).

4. As Terry Eagleton notes of Heathcliff, "he can, it seems, be endowed with impressive ontological status only at the price of being nullified as a person"

(1976, 124). Heathcliff's lack of individuation in relation to Catherine, however, is determined by the narcissistic needs of both characters as well as by class differences.

References

Allott, M., ed. 1992. *Emily Brontë's "Wuthering Heights": A Casebook.* New York: Macmillan.

Armstrong, N., 1987. *Desire and Domestic Fiction: A Political History of the Novel.* New York: Oxford Univ. Press.

Benjamin, J., 1988. *The Bonds of Love: Psychoanalysis, Feminism, and the Problem of Domination.* New York: Pantheon.

Berman, J., 1990. Attachment and Loss in *Wuthering Heights.* In *Narcissism and the Novel.* New York: New York Univ. Press, pp. 78–112.

Bersani, L. 1976. *A Future for Astyanax: Character and Desire in Literature.* Boston: Little, Brown.

Brontë, E. 1847. *Wuthering Heights.* Ed. W. M. Sale. 1972. New York: Norton.

Chodorow, N. 1978. *The Reproduction of Mothering: Psychoanalysis and the Sociology of Gender.* Berkeley: Univ. of California Press.

Eagleton, T. 1976. *Myths of Power: A Marxist Study of the Brontës.* New York: Macmillan.

Freud, S. 1914. On Narcissism. In *The Standard Edition of the Complete Psychological Works,* ed. and trans. J. Strachey et al. 24 vols. (hereafter *S.E.*). London: Hogarth Press, 1953–74, 14:67–107.

———. 1915. Instincts and Their Vicissitudes. In *S.E.,* 14:117–40.

———. 1916. Some Character-Types Met with in Psycho-Analytic Work. In *S.E.,* 14:311–33.

Gilbert, S. M., and S. Gubar. 1979. *The Madwoman in the Attic: The Woman Writer and the Nineteenth-Century Literary Imagination.* New Haven: Yale Univ. Press.

Gilligan, C. 1982. *In a Different Voice: Psychological Theory and Women's Development.* Cambridge: Harvard Univ. Press.

Gregor, I., ed. 1970. *The Brontës: A Collection of Critical Essays.* Englewood Cliffs, N. J.: Prentice Hall.

Hirsch, M. 1989. *The Mother/Daughter Plot: Narrative, Psychoanalysis, Feminism.* Bloomington: Indiana Univ. Press.

Homans, M. 1986. The Name of the Mother in *Wuthering Heights.* In *Bearing the Word: Language and Female Experience in Nineteenth-Century Women's Writing.* Chicago: Univ. of Chicago Press, pp. 68–83.

Horney, K. 1950. *Neurosis and Human Growth: The Struggle toward Self-Realization.* New York: Norton.

Jacobs, N. M. 1986. Gender and Layered Narrative in *Wuthering Heights* and *The Tenant of Wildfell Hall.* In Stoneman 1993, pp. 74–85.

Kernberg, O. F. 1991. A Contemporary Reading of "On Narcissism." In Sandler et al. 1991, pp. 131–48.

———. 1992. *Aggression in Personality Disorders and Perversions.* New Haven: Yale Univ. Press.

Kohut, H. 1971. *The Analysis of the Self: A Systematic Approach to the Psychoanalytic Treatment of Narcissistic Personality Disorders.* New York: International Universities Press.

———. 1972. Thoughts on Narcissism and Narcissistic Rage. In *Self Psychology and the Humanities: Reflections on a New Psychoanalytic Approach,* ed. C. B. Strozier. New York: Norton, 1985, pp. 124–60.

Leavis, Q. D. 1969. A Fresh Approach to *Wuthering Heights.* In Stoneman 1993, pp. 24–38.

Matthews, J. T. 1985. Framing in *Wuthering Heights.* In Stoneman 1993, pp. 54–73.

McKibben, R. C. 1960. The Image of the Book in *Wuthering Heights.* In Gregor 1970, pp. 34–43.

Miller, J. H. 1982. *Wuthering Heights:* Repetition and the "Uncanny." In *Fiction and Repetition: Seven English Novels.* Cambridge: Harvard Univ. Press, 1982, pp. 42–72.

Montégut, Émile. 1857. Charlotte Brontë: Les Oeuvres. In Allott 1992, pp. 74–75.

Roscoe, W. C. 1857. Rev. of Mrs. Gaskell's *Life of Charlotte Brontë.* In Allott 1992, pp. 70–73.

Sandler, J., E. S. Person, and P. Fonagy, eds. 1991. *Freud's "On Narcissism: An Introduction."* New Haven: Yale Univ. Press.

Schapiro, B. 1994. The Rebirth of Catherine Earnshaw: Splitting and Reintegration of Self in *Wuthering Heights.* In *Literature and the Relational Self.* New York: New York Univ. Press, pp. 46–61.

Sedgwick, E. K. 1980. Immediacy, Doubleness, and the Unspeakable: *Wuthering Heights* and *Villette.* In *The Coherence of Gothic Conventions.* New York: Methuen, 1986, pp. 97–139.

Spacks, P. M. 1975. *The Female Imagination.* New York: Avon.

Spark, M., and D. Stanford. 1960. *Emily Brontë: Her Life and Work.* London: Peter Owen.

Sprengnether, M. 1990. *The Spectral Mother: Freud, Feminism, and Psychoanalysis.* Ithaca, N.Y.: Cornell Univ. Press.

Stoneman, P., ed. 1993. *New Casebooks: "Wuthering Heights."* New York: St. Martin's.

Treurniet, N. 1991. Introduction to "On Narcissism." In Sandler et al. pp. 75–94.

Ward, M. A. 1900. Introduction to the Haworth edition of *Wuthering Heights.* In Allott 1992, pp. 95–103.

Wion, P. K. 1985. The Absent Mother in Emily Brontë's *Wuthering Heights.* *American Imago* 42:143–64.

Chapter Nine

Looking Back at the Mirror: Cinematic Revisions

Maureen Turim

"Baby's first mirror," a toy with an unbreakable mirror surrounded by a blue and white plastic sky, arrived on the market just as educated Lacanians reached a stage that they for the most part had delayed and deferred, if not altogether renounced—parenthood. The instruction booklet prepared for the toy seems slyly to know Lacan's (1949) theory of the mirror stage and to want to leave nothing of its outcome to chance. It offers its safe version of a reflective surface not as mere distraction, but as a tool for helping the child through this stage, as if failure to purchase and display this object would leave the poor infant forever unable to develop an imago or accede to the Symbolic. The booklet likewise instructs the parents who wish to guide the child into self-awareness, including suggestions of games they can play while placing their reflections alongside the child's in this "first mirror." Many other versions of this baby mirror appear on the market, along with advice from sources in popular culture such as parenting magazines about the play of reflections to be practiced in front of the bathroom vanity.

As soon as children reach the *Sesame Street* stage, they can find this first mirror evoked nostalgically in a song entitled "Monster in the Mirror." Here the child hears the babytalk narration ("wabba wabba wabba wabba woo woo woo" is the chorus) of the baby encountering a monster in the mirror, which, over the course of several verses, his gaze accommodates and tames. The lyrics suggest the progression from the transliteration of babytalk to recognizable English phonemes. "Wabba wabba wabba wabba woo woo woo" cedes to "I will wabba you and you will wabba me." Violence, proxemics, and touch are hinted at when the monster's "wabba" seems to become meaningfully transitive and even aggressive, sounding like a threatening "rubba." Finally, it seems contextually to become merely babytalk for "love" as if what is being said is "I will lova you if you will lova me." In the visual images that surround the lyrics in *Sesame Street*'s music video for kids, what appears is not the reflection of the child viewer but a montage of television pop culture images, drawn not just from kids' shows or even PBS, but a collage of all aspects of television viewing not proscribed for the under-five age group. This is you, your mirror, your culture, never first or last, but in one looping, eternally present surround. This is how you will learn to see, to speak, to move, and to love—watch and learn, *Sesame Street* seems to say in a self-conscious gesture. However, I think it's altogether likely that the convergence of elements in this song is just one of the ways that the fairy tale tells us more than it knows. It illustrates the assumption of the imago in all its potential monstrousness, combined with the access to language, sexuality, and love.

For if a self-conscious knowledge of the mirror stage appears to be ubiquitous in our culture, this may be a misapprehension. Popular culture seems to miss the significance of mirror-stage theory when it proffers explanations of our troubled psyches. In a recent television documentary on Alzheimer's disease, we are told of a woman who insists on sharing half of her medicine with her mirror reflection. Her case is presented as an emblem of the bizarre irrationality of the disease, rather than as a decipherable and highly poetic gesture whose unconscious logic is quite clear. Equally, Jeffrey Dahmer's acts are deemed incomprehensible, as if there were nothing in the theory of the mirror stage in its references to aggressivity, desire, and the double to help us understand the eroticism of necrophilia or the desire to eat the other's fragmented body parts, and as if the desire to incorporate a fragmentary, lifeless other into the self were entirely beyond imagination. Of course, we need not go to Lacan alone for help in understanding such cases as Dahmer, the Alzheimer's victim, or even *Sesame Street*'s "The Monster in the Mirror"; we might instead return to Freud's discussion of the uncanny and to Otto Rank's theory of the double, for as Mikkel Borch-Jacobsen reminds us, the principal ingredients in the mirror stage are "the mirror, the image, the double, narcissism, imaginary fragmentation (and by implication castration) and death" (1991, 45), all of which are to be found in Freud and Rank.

THE STORY OF THE EYE AND THE GENDERED SUBJECT IN INTERSUBJECTIVE SPACE

Significantly, the mirror-stage essay has met lately with much criticism and rejection, after having exerted considerable influence over theories of visual representation in film and other media. Some of that rejection stems from the lack of empirical evidence in Lacan's formulation of the theory. Borch-Jacobsen refuses to seek further empirical proof, insisting that "it will not be particularly useful to spend too much time on this 'spectacular' observation, available to any parent who is even slightly attentive" (1991, 46). Let me suggest that we should accept the degree to which the mirror stage *is* a fable, an enabling fiction, and a metaphor. It may never happen once and for all in the way that it appears to do in one version of Lacan's narrative explanation. It is an ongoing and iterative process that "begins" in moments of uncertainty of body image and selfhood and "ends" in a dialectic between the self conceived of as a whole and as fragmentary. Cultural images of all sorts conjoin with mirror images as mediators of this dialectical process.

Others' objections are aimed less at Lacan's observation and theory itself than at the uses made of it by Althusser and elaborated by such critics as Stephen Heath (1981) and Jacqueline Rose (1980, 1986), as well as at its subsequent overlay on Foucault's theorization of Bentham's panopticon. Although I cannot enter into these debates in detail here, I would submit that the history of the deployments of the mirror stage and its critiques is one of partial readings, some of which (like those just mentioned) are quite productive, even if in other respects they mislead in what they leave out.[1]

Laura Mulvey (1975) and Jacqueline Rose (1986), among others, usefully recast these psychoanalytic issues in terms of gender. For Rose, the mirror stage seems to divide into an Imaginary and a Symbolic phase; female subjects must overcome a too-close relation to the mirror (narcissism) as well as the danger of being encased within another's representation without ever establishing a sense of themselves or learning to speak as women. I would like now to revisit this gendered view of the mirror stage by opening its premises to a more dialectical interrogation, one that will not try to close off the Imaginary by dreaming that the subject could ever ascend completely to the Symbolic. This more troubled mirror stage is certainly there in Lacan, alongside the notion that the child learns to construct an image of his or her self and thereby begins to enter into the Symbolic order of language.

This duality is linked to Lacan's theory of the gaze and its relation to anxiety and the function of the *objet petit a*. Recent reassertion of the Hegelian aspects of Lacan, found in the writings of Borch-Jacobsen (1991) and Slavoj Zizek (1991), has brought renewed attention to dialectical operations in Lacan's work. Nowhere is the complexity of the mirror stage hinted at better than in the teasing allusion Lacan (1981, 17) makes to Louis Aragon's poem "Contre-chant" (Counter-melody), which I will cite in full and retranslate here:

> Vainement ton image arrive à ma rencontre
> Et ne m'entre où je suis qui seulement la montre

Toi te tourant vers moi tu ne saurais trouver
Au mur de mon regard que ton ombre rêvée

Je suis ce malheureux comparable au miroirs
Qui peuvent réfléchir mais ne peuvent pas voir
Comme eux mon oeil est vide et comme eux habité
De l'absence de toi qui fait sa cécité.

[In vain your image comes to meet me
And does not enter me where I am who only shows it
You turning yourself toward me you could find
At the wall of my gaze only your dreamt-of shadow

I am this unhappy one comparable to mirrors
Who can reflect but cannot see
Like them my eye is empty and like them inhabited
By your absence which makes it blind.]

Aragon narrates a love conflict in which "an image" of the speaker's lover remains outside the self and "comes to meet me and does not enter me where I am." As in much of his poetry, the voice is autobiographical (this poem appears in *Le Fou d'Elsa,* where one of the referents of Elsa is Elsa Triolet, a poet and Aragon's wife). Yet the voice is also fictional, set in a highly imaginative mythologized history, here referring to Spain in the 1490s as a site of political and ethnic confrontation and reconfiguration.

The poem's speaker can only turn the image back, as a mirror does. It does not enter him. The lover, in turn, is said by him to experience his gaze as a wall, for it is preoccupied with her dreamt-of shadow, *another* image that is not her image but his image of her. The address of this poem to "you," the lover, is all the more ironic as she never appears, can never be seen except as the "you" shown in and turning toward the mirror. The lover is an image whose place is taken by an imaginary shadow. Of course, the reader also hears that "you" as a direct address. In Alan Sheridan's translation of the poem (Lacan 1981, 17), however, we lose the trajectory culminating in the last line; the antecedent of "sa" in "sa cécité" has to be "mon oiel" (my eye), but is mistakenly rendered as "them," whose antecedent is "mirrors."[2] As a result, the complex chain of actions becomes hard to follow to the end; in the original French, the actions are diagrammatically clear, if delightfully double. In fact, the progression of the actions in the poem resembles the diagrams Lacan makes of the "two mirrors" in *The Technical Writings of Freud.*

Lacan calls the poem an "admirable work in which I am proud to find an echo of the tastes of our generation, so much so that I am forced to turn to friends of my own age if I am to make myself understood" (1981, 18). This aside reveals an anxiety about aging and that his students may not appreciate his sensibilities, a surrealism tinged with Romanticism, which he shares with Aragon. He makes their task more difficult by not divulging the title of the book in which the poem appears or the fact that it was published only one year earlier (the seminar took place in 1953). He does, however, reveal in one of his phallic jokes that the poem is accompanied by a tag line, "Thus said an-Nadjdî once, as he was invited to a circumcision." (Another such joke comes during his exposition of the gaze later in the same seminar, when he speaks of anamorphosis as a prophylactic, thus emphasizing the relationship of the gaze to sexual desire as embodied by erection.) By his joke, Lacan wants us to understand this imputation of voice to an-Nadjdî and the reference to circumcision as underlining a correspondence with his own concepts of the lack and the trajectory of desire. The entire poem is to be read in the frame of a ritual that centers on a transformation of the penis as an initiation into the community, a community that will in turn be persecuted because of this mark. The joke entails rethinking circumcision as at once a form of castration (it marks the Jewish male as other, outsider) and its opposite (it allows entry into Jewish manhood).

Lacan neglects to indicate that the line he cites attributing the poem to an-Nadjdî is the first part of a long and complex paragraph in *Le Fou d'Elsa* that establishes an even more self-conscious relationship to these notions of lack and the trajectory of desire, as well as the fusion of joy and sorrow, life and death, in the sexual drive. It is intriguing that he does not directly bring up the poem's reference to the mirror or its speaker's identification with the mirror and the way the mirror is presented as a wall (which could be correlated with Lacan's frequent references to the mirror as "screen"). This reticence is coupled with his bypassing of the fact that mirrors, love, memory, singing, desire, loss, and historical change are themes throughout *Le Fou d'Elsa*. (The preceding poem in the volume is entitled "Le Miroir," while a later one is "Fable du miroir-temps.") This is Lacan's famous elliptical style, which proceeds by nuanced gestures and oblique references, yet he indicates how interconnected the mirror-stage theory is with all that follows in *The Four Fundamental Concepts*—the *Tuché*, the automaton, the eye and the gaze, the picture, anamorphosis, and transference.

In "The Orthopsychic Subject" (1989), Joan Copjec makes much of the diagram of two interpenetrating triangles in which the gaze and the subject of representation meet on a line that forms both the image and the screen (diagram 1). She argues that film theory has depended too much on the optical aspect of Lacan's myth and recognized too little of how representation is an opacity that is the cause of the subject's desire;

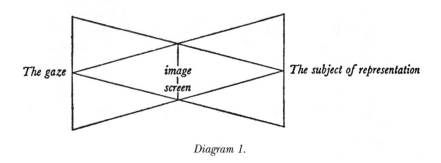

Diagram 1.

she believes that Lacan meant the mirror to be conceived of *primarily* as a screen. Her emphasis on the screening aspect of the mirror metaphor highlights the complexity of Lacan's dialectic, but she ultimately inverts the usual reading of the diagram and goes to the opposite extreme, emphasizing those moments in which Lacan has representation and spatiality themselves transfix the subject.

Copjec claims that Lacan sees no transitivity in the mirror, but she misses how he wants to have it both ways. Her implicit polemic is with the Althusserian strategies by which film theory is linked to the mirror stage, and as a result she detaches the mirror stage from a larger social critique as well as from the optical components that connect it to the scopic drive. However, if Lacan spends so much time expounding optical concepts and sees scoptophilia as a prototype for desire, it is for a good reason. The complexity of the mirror myth encompasses many scenes, including ones in which the subject identifies with and reacts aggressively against the imago. This aggressivity is underlined in Lacan's use of the term *stade,* which is routinely translated as "stage" but also means "stadium." This double meaning subtends his argument that the "I" conceives itself as a fortress or stadium in which an agon takes place.

If the mirror stage is to continue to enhance film theory, it will not be because it is used either simply to reiterate or dismiss the more or less Althusserian positions originally mobilized in reference to it, but because of its fundamental duality. We must comprehend more subtly how the mirror stage speaks to fascination, identification, empathy, aggression, and desire. Its poetics need to be appreciated before its meanings can be understood.

One way of grasping the complexity of the mirror metaphor is to look at yet another diagram—that of the double mirrors, which appears in *The Technical Writings of Freud* and again in *The Four Fundamental Concepts of Psychoanalysis.* In this diagram (diagram 2), a still life is inverted in the mirror, forming what Lacan calls the "inverted bouquet," which serves

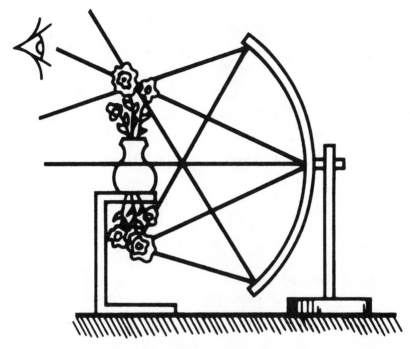

Diagram 2. The experiment of the inverted bouquet

to illustrate the camera obscura. This preliminary version of this diagram displays the effects of a concave mirror; subsequently the concave mirror is bounced off a flat mirror (diagram 3).

Lacan's use of these diagrams resembles conceptual art. Although he invokes the science of optics, he displays these diagrams as representations of the processes of representation. It is no accident, then, that the object represented in the mirror of the diagram is an inverted bouquet, rather than the human body. To have the still life stand in for a corporeal image implies that artistic representation and the mirror stage, as well as the object and the ego, are to be seen in reciprocal relationship. The purpose of the inverted bouquet is to describe a situation in which the spatial configuration of an object undergoes an impossible reordering that nonetheless corresponds to a process of optical refraction.

When we move from the single curved mirror to the double mirror diagram, what is at stake is the reconstitution of the "correct" or "normal" image of an object in reference to a hypothetical subject (*sujet virtuel*) that is the Other, which is what the "I" is not. Here the inverted bouquet of the convex mirror is rearranged to appear in the planar mirror in its whole form (properly ordered and unified). One of the tricks played by

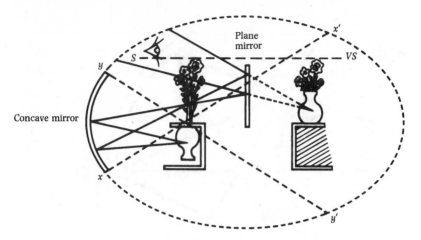

Diagram 3. Schema of the two mirrors

Lacan with this mirror diagram is to suggest its relationship to a double reflection in a store window where self and an object of desire are simultaneously reflected. One can take this metaphor in several directions: the child at the bakery window, the woman looking at the mannequins of high fashion, the man at the auto showroom. My gender and age typing of these consumer preferences is meant to help us understand the power of Lacan's metaphor to explain the arrangement of self and image. We might say that "identification" becomes an inadequate term with regard to the mirror stage because it leaves out the resonance of the desire for the self as object and for other objects that Lacan seeks to elucidate.

Yet another diagram, that of the 0-0′ connection to the mirror, adds to this increasingly difficult series the notion of a shimmering, an oscillation back and forth between positions in the mirror-illusion that have no transcendent location in an externalized consciousness (diagram 4). Here Lacan introduces us to his distinction between the ideal ego and the ego-ideal and locates the 0-0′ position as that of the ideal ego.

These diagrams remind me of a specific mirrored wall in a living room of my childhood. I sat in this room at the age of five wondering which world was real—the one with me in it or the wholly other one I saw from where I sat. I have watched my daughter at age four replay this game as she pivoted a door-mirror on its hinge with her face next to it, in profile, while the mirror reflected the rest of the room, including another large vanity mirror also displaying more of the room. "I'm not looking at myself in the mirror," she announced, "I'm looking at the rest of the room, and it is changing." The optics of her experiment are, of course, in Lacanian terms a *way* of looking at the self, for the mirror stage

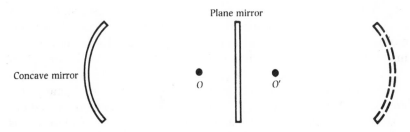

Plane mirror

Concave mirror

•
O

•
O'

Diagram 4. Simplified schema of the two mirrors

is really a complex treatise on spatiality and self; the shifting of perspectives forcibly extracts the self from the image, as the self strives to remain constant, fixing its own gaze. In these games we enact the paradox of the looking glass, of wanting to enter that other mirror, that representation, that double.

In my essay "The Place of Visual Illusions" (1980), I suggested that the viewer of avant-garde film might be compared to a child playing with a three-way mirror, in which the image of the self was not so easily delineated and appropriated as was implied by Lacan's model of a child before an ordinary, two-dimensional mirror. This was a serious joke on my part, one that attempted to rescue a playful, visually imaginative, and innovative avant-garde cinema from a framework that sought to dismiss it. A certain purportedly Lacanian critique could not see such play as having any value because it simply trapped the subject in the Imaginary. Since then, I have become increasingly convinced that what was once taken as *the* Lacanian critique is only an extrapolation to which Lacan's writings do not easily lend themselves. The Lacan who invoked Holbein's *The Ambassadors* as he asked "What is a Picture?" and quoted Aragon's poem with confessional identification has been rewritten by those who demand that art repudiate an imaginary appeal, a demand that he himself held to be impossible (though art can acknowledge this appeal more or less self-consciously).

When Constance Penley (1985) charged that the British school of avant-garde filmmakers failed due to an "insufficient critique of the imaginary," she did not ask whether this judgment precluded the complex explorations of visual representation that Lacan develops in *The Four Fundamental Concepts*. The argument of her article overlaps with one made by Jacqueline Rose (1980), who read my metaphor not as exploratory and paradoxical, but as one in which the young girl is enclosed in the mirror, trapped in primary narcissism, unable to grasp or address representation.

Yet if the mirror stage is significant, it is surely as a limit to the knowledge that anyone desires to have. I did not choose the child in my example solely *because* she is a girl, though Lacan does allude to the image of a young girl pointing out her genitals as she looks at herself in the mirror; and the only way for girls to see their own genitals is by using a mirror. We recognize here the "forgotten vagina" of Luce Irigaray's *Speculum of the Other Woman* (1974). But feminism is beginning to understand that remembering the vagina is not as simple as either embracing its reflected image or pointing to the places of its absence. These are the paradoxes of epistemology that Lacan traces in the ovals of the double mirror; metapsychology can diagram, but its diagrammatic functions don't suddenly evoke a reconstitution of the self outside their borders and mirror games.

What is at stake here is not simply our judgment of avant-garde visions, but the possibility that Lacan's theories are far more sophisticated with respect to the problem of vision and identification than earlier accounts have acknowledged. If avant-garde films have been provocative and moving, it is because they self-consciously thematized the act of vision, using it to explore the subject in space. Their deployment of sight as a metaphor was far less innocent than some have supposed. Lacan's own preoccupation with the mechanisms of optics and mirrors is replicated in these films, which impel us to rethink vision, identification, and spatiality. If my earlier arguments referred to the pleasure in the visual attained through abstraction at a time when that was a heresy in film studies, if they were seen as a defense of merely fetishistic imaging, the turns of theory in the intervening years have renewed their urgency. How space, gender, and self interact in the enunciation of the visual field is a crucial question whose implications are still being unfolded.

MIRROR SCENES AT THE MOVIES

It is perhaps in search of a simpler approach to the same issues that Christian Metz returns to the mirror in his last book, *Impersonal Enunciation, or the Site of Film* (1991). In Metz's examination of modes of enunciation in film, the mirror becomes an internal frame, a means of marking elements and describing not only the scene, but also the interior thoughts of a character. In this new approach Metz leaves behind the problem of identification except insofar as its most basic aspects underlie the viewing of these images:

> We know that since Cocteau, and long before that, the mirror is a privileged filmic object. I will not return here to the psychoanalytic roots of this

affinity, which do not consist—contrary to what it is sometimes claimed I have said—of a pure and simple identity between the screen and the mirror, or even a large-scale empirical analogy between them. The idea would be absurd because the screen doesn't reflect the spectator's own body. Their only affinity is deeper, and in the development of the psychic mechanisms.

Metz goes on to cite Ed Branigan's work on subjective mirror shots, then speaks of a second sort of mirror shot that reflects something other than the person looking at the mirror. These two types of shot are then further broken down into a list of five shots that (1) bring in another space, contingent but separate; (2) bring in imaginary space; (3) lead to a new narrative tack, adding suspense, surprise, fear, danger; (4) work like a superimposition that overlays one image with another; and (5) create a multifaceted mirror, reduplication, and mise-en-abîme.

Implicit in this discussion is an interweaving of theories of enunciation with previous psychoanalytic work, though Metz does not complete this synthesis. I would like to extend his ideas here by resituating these "enunciative" mirrors within filmic representation through exploratory readings derived from psychoanalytic theories of the mirror. My first move in this direction is to indicate how all five points Metz makes define processes of addition and multiplication, the "bringing in" of elements. The uncanny function of the mirror as offering "the double" is here redoubled in distinct ways. In reduplicating and reinitiating narrative, in giving us a space that exceeds planar limits and always accesses another space, the mirror becomes a device that has the potential to transgress the boundaries of whatever is more finite, bounded, and limited. There is magic inherent in this object-device that always promises something else that we have not yet perceived. It is this fundamental affinity with motion pictures, narrative, and a multiplicity of perspectives that gives the mirror so much evocative power in the cinema.

Cinema's inscription of the mirror borrows from various pictorial and narrative traditions, including myth, literature, theater, opera, and iconography. Let us recall the myth of Narcissus pivotal to the mirror stage, as it figures in Freud's theory of narcissism. Borch-Jacobsen (1991) analyzes the myth's relation to the theory and links it to the fiction of Blanchot, where the interplay between Echo and Narcissus becomes the focus. Blanchot's narrative, in turn, is intertextually related to paintings of this myth, notably Renoir's *Echo and Narcissus*. The myth is replete with doubling and cross-referencing, the same annexing that we find so prominently in mirrors found in film narratives.

From a feminist perspective, it is noteworthy that the enuciative mirrors in film are often associated with women, in a manner reminiscent of the pictorial association of Venus with a mirror. Marcel Carné slyly refers to this tradition in *Children of Paradise* (1944), where Garance (Arletty) is presented as the featured attraction of a sideshow on the Boulevard des Capucines. Those who have paid the entrance fee see her sitting in a revolving tub, naked but discretely covered by its high sides, looking at herself in a hand-held mirror; the camera lingers on this ironic evocation of specularity tied to a myth of female narcissism (figure 1). Later in the film, the mirror reappears, this time in Garance's dressing room as she discusses her desires with one of her three suitors, the actor, Fréderic Lemaître (Pierre Brasseur), here in his early incarnation as the *commedia dell'arte* Harlequin. This reinscription (figure 2) self-consciously juxtaposes the woman's gaze at her reflection in the mirror with masculine desire (and not only the desire of men for her). The irony of Garance's sideshow display as an object of desire becomes apparent, as she is never simply available to a male gaze or to male possession; the mirror works to indicate, through a flirtation with the image of vanity, a nascent sense of female-generated desire.

Another intriguing example of such ironic mirroring is a *Life Magazine* photo used to illustrate an article on Jeanne Moreau. It shows her at the window of her villa, with her back to the camera, but with her face luminously reflected in a round, hand-held mirror (figure 3). Moreau is figured through a series of ready associations as the ageless Venus, an alluring and powerful goddess. What is less obvious is the manner in which her face, bounded by the oval reflection, gives us that which we would not otherwise be able to see, inscribing into the photograph all the imaginary power of the mirror. In a scene from François Truffaut's *Jules and Jim* (1962), Moreau as Catherine is seen in her vanity mirror taking off her makeup as Jim (Henri Serre) is reflected watching her from the bed across the room. Here the imaginary power of the mirror to show more than we would otherwise see captures the tension of the scene, as the lover's eyes meet in the relay between the mirror and the spectator's view.

As in this scene from *Jules and Jim,* a woman's vanity or dressing table is a frequent fixture in the mise-en-scène of melodrama, particularly the subgenre of "women's film," and film noir. The vanity establishes a quintessentially feminine space, where femininity is "made up" or removed, a mask donned or stripped, in either case revealing a new image of woman, perhaps in a mise-en-abîme. Films mine this territory to explore female narcissism, with its corollaries of self-posession and self-doubt. They likewise use the vanity mirror to adumbrate darker aspects of the female psyche, such as duplicity and jealousy. Far from having a single symbolic meaning, the connotations of the mirror are manifold,

Figure 1. Ironic specularity and female narcissism

Figure 2. A reflected play of male and female gazes

Figure 3. Moreau as the ageless Venus

called into play by complex contextual associations in both diegesis and image construction.

Early examples of the "vanity mirror" can be found in D. W. Griffith's *The Painted Lady* (1912) and *The New York Hat* (1912), in both of which the mirrors are hung over a chest of drawers, since the women in these films—still teenagers, really—are of modest backgrounds and strict upbringings, precluding the vanity proper. The imperative of modern allure for women is linked in *The Painted Lady* to madness and a mirror. A woman is initially presented as being of such purity as to eschew facial powder, a refusal articulated by her moment of doubt and her renunciation of artifice in front of the mirror. Then she finds herself taken in by a swindler who romances her despite her refusal to follow fashion; she shoots him during his attempt to rob her father, though not at the time knowing his identity. Her subsequent delusions are depicted in part by a return to the shot of her reflected in the mirror as she repetitively powders her face.

The New York Hat concerns a dying mother who bequeathes to her daughter a fancy hat, though she transmits this female legacy indirectly through money and a note left with her minister. When he purchases the hat for the daughter, this precipitates a scandal among his shocked parishioners. The marriage of the girl and the minister at the end of the film sanctifies the desire for beautiful adornment. A shop window is the privileged site in which the minister views the hat, and a mirror shot later shows the daughter reveling in her finery; this suggests the connection between the mirror and shop window in Lacan that I discussed earlier. These shots convey a relay of desire associated with both adornment and the mother, who uses the talisman of the hat to speak from beyond the grave to her daughter. Recapitulating the symbiotic dyad of the mirror stage, the daughter inherits her mother's projected self-image and desire.

An understated and elegant variation on the female-mirror scene is found in Jean Renoir's *Rules of the Game* (1939), where the Marquise de la Chesnaye (Nora Grégor) and her chambermaid, Lisette (Paulette Dubist), are both reflected in a vanity mirror as they discuss infidelity and pleasure; the mirror becomes a site of female bonding and class contrast. This mirror scene is coupled with constant doubling and comparison of the two characters, as well as of the pair formed by the Marquise and her husband's lover, Genevieve de Marrast (Mila Parely). By the same token, the dressing room scene in Joseph Mankiewicz's *All About Eve* (1950) depicts Margo Channing (Bette Davis) reflected in a vanity mirror, her face covered with cold cream as her entourage chastises her for her jealous suspicions of Eve (Anne Baxter), the ingenue who ingratiates herself only to attempt to usurp Margo's place. Here the mirror insinuates a cruel reflection on Margo's less glamorous off-stage personality, but the scene aims at a greater irony. Its mirror suggests an inversion of images in which rivalry and jealousy will take forms that the entourage does not yet see. In both of these examples, mirrors associate diegetic doubles and their inversion in unpredictable ways.

In Robert Bresson's *Four Nights of a Dreamer* (1968), a full-length mirror heralds the shy heroine's nascent sexual self-awareness and even insinuates masturbation. This is unexpected, insofar as one hardly associates Bresson's rigor, understatement, and "pure" cinema with onanism, but his films do hint at sexual motifs they don't fully portray, as is the case here. This shot also adds a lingering self-doubt to other connotations of the cinematic mirror; the heroine's reflected gaze and gestures are so tentative that one senses that what the mirror here relays is a far-from-secure narcissism.

Mirror scenes are by no means limited to U.S. and European film, and it is instructive to turn to Japanese culture and film for a comparison. In Japan, mirrors have an ancient cultural history, which I rehearse at greater length in *The Films of Nagisa Oshima: Images of a Japanese Iconoclast* (1998). Here it suffices to note that the mirror moves from being an image of wealth and authority following the initial importation of Chinese bronze mirrors of the Han dynasty during the Yayoi period (200 B.C.–A.D. 300) to being a symbol of the "god body," a luminous perfection in Shinto shrines (Amakasu 1973). Mirrors were soon incorporated into Japanese Imperial symbolism, where they became a token, along with the sword and the jewel, of the authority of the Emperor (Singer 1973). A further psychoanalytic association with the mirror is supplied by the Japanese folktale "The Mirror of Matsuyama," where it is linked to commoners. This folktale turns on the gift of a mirror to an individual whose village is unfamiliar with them; in one version, the mirror becomes a repository of the daughter's memory of the mother, much as it does in *The New York Hat.*

Beyond these historical contexts, Japanese filmmakers such as Kenji Misoguchl and Yasuhiro Ozu borrow directly from the Ukiyo-e (woodblock print) tradition in which prostitutes and actresses who are sexually coded as "loose" women are associated with mirrors. For example, in Ozu's *A Woman of Tokyo* (1933) the sister, Chikako (Yoshiko Okada), is shown transforming herself in her room. She sheds a domestic appearance, including an apron, to reveal her street-wear kimono. This scene includes cuts to a series of three shots from various distances and angles of her applying makeup as she kneels in front of a large mirror over her makeup box. In the last, she is shown in close-up reflected in the mirror, but toward the end of the shot she exits, leaving the "empty" mirror. In one of Ozu's abrupt-cut transitions, this shot is followed by one of a table on which rest the white gloves of a police official, who we learn in the ensuing scene has come to inform her employer of her moonlighting as a prostitute. In the understated associations constructed through Ozu's formal filmic montage, the mirror is a sign of the prostitute, but an ambiguous one; its emptiness leaves us with the suggestion of Chikako's absent and uncertain self-image, rather than the fixed image of her as a fallen woman. It also suggests that Chikako's behavior and roles perhaps elude her subsequent categorization and condemnation.

Similarly, Ozu's *Floating Weeds* (1959) uses actresses' makeup mirrors to stage a scene in which they converse about their sexual affairs. Mizoguchi acknowledges the woodblock heritage of much Japanese cinematic imagery in *Utamaro and His Five Women* (1946), where he deploys mirrors in the mise-en-scène in a manner analogous to that of the master artist, Utamaro. Yet here the psychoanalytic coding is less dynamic than in most European and U.S. films; it displays a category of women, rather than the psyche of any particular woman. A more explicit psychoanalytic dimension can be found in Teinsuke Kinugasa's *Page of Madness* (1926), where the woman, a former dancer who has been locked up in an insane asylum, is associated with a mirror. The montage and narrative exposition of this film use objective correlatives to evoke the notions of both a "break" and "fragmentation," as the woman's janitor-husband breaks a bowl. Some aspects of the history of the wife's mental illness are presented, but rather than merely providing an explanation, these flashes increase the atmosphere of shared mental disorder.

Given the psychoanalytically intertwined focus on women and mirrors in film, it is not surprising that self-conscious feminist alternatives should emerge. Indeed, there is a scene in Diane Kurys's *Entre Nous* (1982) in which the two women who will eventually leave their husbands in order to live together first acknowledge their mutual attraction after one voices dissatisfaction with her body as the two stand before a mirror. When the first woman's insecurity is met by a compliment from the other, the bond between them is established.

The films of Jean-Luc Godard offer a fascinating commentary on women and mirrors, as they become increasingly self-conscious in their use of this trope. As Colin McCabe and Laura Mulvey (1980) suggest, Godard's protofeminist moments are always ambivalent, simultaneously perpetuating and deconstructing the display of women as objects. Sometimes his films even ridicule or demean a particular woman to mount a critique of women's social roles. As early as *Breathless* (*A Bout de Souffle;* 1959), Patricia (Jean Seberg) mimics Michel's (Jean-Paul Belmondo) gestures in the hotel room mirror, setting off a series of visual doublings throughout the film, which assimilates the amorous protagonists to images garnered from art and popular culture. In *Masculine Feminine* (1965), the young couple meet in a bathroom where their flirtation is relayed across two mirrors, a hand-held one used by Madeleine (Chantal Goya) to adjust her makeup and another on the wall, which frame and reframe the two in dialogue. Such uses of mirrors, while deliberate and reflexive, are in keeping with their function as a privileged site for romance in many films. In *Two or Three Things I Know about Her* (1966), the scene in the "maison de passe," the prostitution hotel, brings the commentary on mirrors to the forefront. The young client, a subway worker, places a mirror on a chair to reflect the sexual encounter for which he has paid the heroine, Juliette (Marina Vlady). The dialogue presents a fragmented commentary on this desire to see oneself in sexual activity, which begins with an earlier shot of Juliette looking at herself thoughtfully in another mirror, the one over the sink at which she washes. And in *A Married Woman* (1964), Charlotte (Mache Méril) measures the proportions of her breasts in front of her bathroom mirror, using a magazine article to guide her through the calculations. While Charlotte is perhaps being mocked for her gullibility, this scene (which confirms Godard's bra fetishism) also functions as a metacommentary on the way that women assess themselves through society's mirrors. This depiction of obsessive self-doubt, as the self turns on its own image, epitomizes the "arrested" mirror stage to which women are relegated in our cultural Imaginary.

Male subjectivity, too, can be articulated through mirrors, but it is striking how different the context and signification of male mirror shots often are. Rarely has the mirror been used as poetically as in Marcel Carné's *Daybreak* (*Le Jour se lève;* 1939), where scriptwriter Jacques Prévert deploys mirrors as tropes of memory, interior thoughts, and images of the self. François's (Jean Gabin) thoughts are first associated with a mirror on an evening three weeks after his initial meeting with Françoise (Arletty), when he poses in front of a mirror in her room, as he holds her teddy bear up next to his face, covering his ear to match the tattered bear. Sexually rebuffed by Françoise, he takes the bear with him as a souvenir and sign of hope for a commitment from her in the future. This scene is a flashback from François's perspective as he is holed up in his room under siege by the police as a suspect in his rival's murder. The return to the present takes place through a dissolve to a shot showing François at a window whose pane has been shattered by bullets. He repeats the gesture he made in Françoise's room in the flashback, as he looks in his mirror while clutching the teddy bear that he still possesses. As François's barricade against the world is systematically destroyed, we see first the shattering of the window, then the breaking of the mirror that fragments his self-image.

The male, then, tends to be associated with a mirror that eventually shatters, an image of projected violence that leads to self-destruction. In Bresson's *Balthazar* (*Au Hazard, Balthazar;* 1966), the long mirror typical of the French café is shattered by the antihero Gérard (François Lafarge). The film image catches Gerard's reflection as he launches an empty wine bottle at the mirror, then his frenzy of destructiveness in its shards. Lacanian theory allows us to appreciate the rich signification of such scenes, their link of violence to specularity and self-destruction.

The psychoanalytic nexus of mother and son is refigured in relation to the mirror in a scene in Robert Siodmak's *Criss Cross* (1949). Steve (Burt Lancaster) is dressing to meet his former wife, Anna, when his mother enters his bedroom to discourage his rekindled love for this femme fatale. While she sits on his bed and watches, Steve bends to straighten his tie in a vanity mirror too low to encompass his frame. He assumes this position twice, once before and once after putting on his suit jacket, a repetition that correlates dialogue with the mirror shot. In the first instance, the mother says, "You're a very nice looking boy. Out of all. the girls in Los Angeles, why'd you have to pick on her?" What ensues is Steve's attempt to escape from the maternal scrutiny that threatens to infantilize him; this danger looms from the moment she enters his room unannounced, catching him polishing his shoes on the bed. To her astonishment, he responds, "Make believe you didn't catch me!" The threat of infantilization recurs as he objects to her surveillance: "You sit around watching me like I'm a ten-year-old boy." Her retort attempts to justify her monitoring: "How old do you think you are?" For the representation of masculinity the vanity mirror poses the threat. not of aging or loss of beauty, as it does in so many figurations of women, but rather of not being able to escape the mother and enter manhood. The encounter in *Criss Cross* depicts a son well into his twenties still fleeing the mother who tries to shield him against harm. Such scenes can be read as a cultural wish for regression to a moment before the mirror stage, in which maternal love and knowledge might protect the infantile male against the evils of a city whose predatory females embody a modernity encroaching on his soon-to-be-duped self. Steve is too "nice looking" for his own good; men who look too often into the mirror are violating a law of the gendered unconscious in post-World War II film noir.

Men are more likely to appear in cinematic mirrors in modes similar to those used to represent women when they are associated with prostitution, hustling, or homosexuality. Chuck Wein and Andy Warhol's *My Hustler* (1965) has a second reel entirely shot in a bathroom, in which Ed McDermott stands before the mirror shaving, combing his hair, and rather obsessively washing his hands, while Paul America occupies the space behind him, preparing to shower and waiting for his turn at the mirror. The film revels in duration, prolonging the moments of delay. As a result of the elaborate exchanges that occur in the interim, the scene endows bodily care with its full meaning of seduction.

It is intriguing to see the translation of this male fixation with mirrors in a later mainstream Hollywood film such as John Badham's *Saturday Night Fever* (1977), where the young Brooklynite (John Travolta) first combs his hair and checks his appearance before a dresser mirror, then perfects his dance duet in a mirrored studio, only to unleash it and his solos on a polished, gleaming dance floor. This sort of imagery, however, differs from that of the female vanity; it is more active, more performative, and more assured in its relation to others, who can be counted on to admire the reflected subject, even though he is markedly obsessed with himself.

The three-way mirror is a prominent feature of the mise-en-scène of expressionist film. In G.W. Pabst's *Joyless Street* (1925), a full-length three-way mirror discloses Grete (Greta Garbo) sitting close to the central mirror, adjusting her makeup, while a servant enters, reflected in all the faces of the mirror behind her. The narrative is less significant than the symbolism of Grete dominated by the needs and desires of men. In Germaine Dulac's *The Smiling Madame Beudet* (1923), the vanity mirror again has three faces that divide the heroine's image into a dynamically fragmented and reiterated composition. In Jean Epstein's *Three-Way Mirror* (*La Glace à trois faces;* 1927), the mirror that gives its title to the film binds together three separate narratives, which dovetail when we realize that all three women of different classes have been disappointed by the same lover. This tripartition depicts the manner in which each woman mirrors the man's desires. Not only is the film composed of three distinct segments, but each utilizes a fragmented and multiple mode of representation, a cubist refraction of the action. Unable really to know or possess this man who elicits their desire only to disappear, the women are also unable to understand their own fascination with his "tyrannical" force over them. Perhaps the most famous three-way mirror in cinema is the one in Orson Welles's *Lady from Shanghai* (1947), where the three protagonists shoot at each other only to kill themselves in the fun-house room of mirrors.

These three-way mirrors allow us to discern the power of the imaginary mirrors that, as Metz suggests, pervade the cinema. He cites Jean Cocteau's *Orpheus* (1949) and *The Testament of Orpheus* (1959) for their self-conscious inscriptions of the mirror's imaginary power. Cocteau renders radically physical a pun on "reflection": "Reflect for me and I will reflect on you." His mirrors grant access to an imaginary world, as in Lewis Carroll's *Through the Looking Glass,* and do so by being transformed from a solid to a liquid state, engulfing the subject in their fluidity. In Philip Glass's operatic version of *Orpheus* (1994), the mirrors are staged as empty frames emitting a violently bright light. This conceit undergoes various transformations, all of which explore the mirror as an imaginary surface, an object of psychic power. This is the magic mirror of fairy tales, which appears in different guises in *Snow White, Beauty and the Beast,* and *The Wizard of Oz.* Vincent Minnelli's *An American in Paris* (1951) accesses this fairy-tale mirror in its café scene where the male rivals all "see" a different version of their beloved in the mirror. This multiplicity subverts any single image of the woman, but the contradiction between images wavers between being a difference of perspective, a benign plentitude, and an absence. The absence of an image in a mirror recurs in vampire myths as the void where the vampire's reflection in any possible mirror might be.

In cinema all mirrors belong to Lacan's Imaginary, even if they are not literally "imaginary mirrors." In this analysis of the inscription of the mirror in film I have tried to show its richness as a site of cultural and psychoanalytic meanings. If women have been closely associated with the mirror throughout most of film history, the issues that psychoanalytic feminists have raised are no less urgent for gender than for film studies. I have remarked on the pervasive cultural differences in the representations of women and men, but I venture to predict that these boundaries will become increasingly blurred. As men take their places before the mirror not just to unleash violence but to imagine a less certain self and less confident seductiveness, we shall find their contours changing.

Notes

1. Jean-Louis Comolli, Pierre Oudart, Stephen Heath, and Christian Metz are among those who belong to what is sometimes referred to—often pejoratively— as the Althusserian-Lacanian school of film theory. This label effaces their differences, particularly in the degree to which Althusserian political ideals are espoused and Lacanian arguments tempered with other readings of Freud. Yet these theorists all refer more or less explicitly to the mirror stage as helping to elucidate the "imaginary of the cinema" or its status as an "imaginary signifier."

2. This problem of translation is perhaps conditioned by the difficulties posed by "sa cécité," which literally means "its blindness." Since a literal translation is awkward in English, I have rendered it as "makes it blind," which changes the possessive to a subjective pronoun and the noun to a verb. Aragon's poem exploits the rhyme *habité/cécité* as part of the trajectory to which I refer. For yet another translation of the poem, see Samuels (1995).

References

Aragon, L. 1963. *Le Fou d'Elsa*. Paris: Gallimard.

Amakasu, K. 1973. Aspects of Yayoi and Tumulus Art. In N. Egami, ed., *The Beginnings of Japanese Art*. Trans. J. Bester. New York: Wetherhill, pp. 166–78.

Borch-Jacobsen, M. 1991. *Lacan: The Absolute Master*. Trans. D. Brick. Stanford: Stanford Univ. Press.

Copjec, J. 1989. The Orthopsychic Subject: Film Theory and the Reception of Lacan. *October* 49:53–71.

de Lauretis, T., and S. Heath, eds. 1980. *The Cinematic Apparatus*. New York: St. Martin's.

Heath, S. 1981. *Questions of Cinema*. Bloomington: Indiana Univ. Press.

Irigaray, L. 1974. *Speculum of the Other Woman*. Trans. G. C. Gill. Ithaca, N.Y.: Cornell Univ. Press, 1985.

Lacan, J. 1948. Aggresivity in Psychoanalysis. In Lacan 1977, pp. 8–29.

———. 1949. The Mirror Stage as Formative of the Function of the I as Revealed in Psychoanalytic Experience. In Lacan 1977, pp. 1–7.

———. 1953–54. *Le Seminaire livre I: Les Ecrits techniques de Freud.* Paris: Editions du Seuil.

———. 1960. Remarque sur le rapport de Daniel Lagache: "Psychanalyse et structure de la personnalité." In Jacques Lacan, *Ecrits.* Paris: Editions du Seuil, 1966, pp. 647–84.

———. 1973. *Le Seminaire livre XI: Les Quatre concepts fondamentaux de la psychanalyse.* Paris: Editions du Seuil.

———. 1977. *Ecrits: A Selection.* Trans. A. Sheridan. New York: Norton.

———. 1981. *The Four Fundamental Concepts of Psychoanalysis.* Trans. A. Sheridan. New York: Norton.

Life Goes to the Movies. 1977. New York: Pocket Books.

McCabe, C., and L. Mulvey. 1980. Images of Women, Images of Sexuality. In C. McCabe, ed., *Godard: Images, Sounds, Politics.* Bloomington: Indiana Univ. Press, 1980, pp. 79–104.

Metz, C. 1991. *L'Enonciation impersonnelle ou le site du film.* Paris: Meridians Klincksleck.

Mulvey, L. 1975. Visual Pleasure and Narrative Cinema. *Screen* 16-3:6–18.

Penley, C. 1985. The Avant-Garde and its Imaginary. In B. Nichols, ed., *Movies and Methods.* Vol. 2. Berkeley: Univ. of California Press, 1985, pp. 576–602.

Rose, J. 1980. The Cinematic Apparatus: Problems in Current Theory. In de Lauretis and Heath 1980, pp. 172–86.

———. 1986. *Sexuality in the Field of Vision.* London: Verso.

Samuels, R. 1995. Art and the Position of the Analyst. In R. Feldstein, B. Fink, and M. Jaanus, eds., *Reading Seminar XI: Lacan's Four Fundamental Concepts of Psychoanalysis.* Albany: State Univ. of New York Press, pp. 183–86.

Singer, K. 1973. *Mirror, Sword, and Jewel: A Study of Japanese Characteristics.* New York: Braziller.

Turim, M. 1980. The Place of Visual Illusions. In de Lauretis and Heath 1980, pp. 143–50.

———. 1998. *The Films of Nagisa Oshima: Images of a Japanese Iconoclast.* Berkeley: Univ. of California Press.

Zizek, S. 1991. *Looking Awry: An Introduction to Jacques Lacan through Popular Culture.* Cambridge: MIT Press.

Part IV
Voyages Out

Chapter Ten

The Woman with a Knife
and the Chicken without a Head:
Fantasms of Rage and Emptiness

Claire Kahane

> Though a seeming paradox at first, the fact is
> that in penis envy nothing matters less than
> the penis itself. This partial object appears . . .
> as a stopgap invented to camouflage a desire.
> —Maria Torok,
> "The Meaning of Penis Envy in Women"

I want to begin with a news story that captured the national imagination several years ago and is still making waves; it has some relevance to my subject:

Dateline: Manassas, Va.

A Virginia woman who cut off her husband's penis told police that her husband raped her and then told her that her objections did not matter to him, a police detective testified yesterday.

"He said he didn't care about my feelings and went back to sleep," said Detective Peter J. Weintz, reading from a transcript of a taped interview with Lorena Bobbitt, who was charged with malicious wounding in the June 23 incident. "Then I pulled back the sheets, and then I did it." . . .

She said her husband forced her to have sex, then pushed her away and went to sleep. . . . Lorena Bobbitt later went to the kitchen to get some water . . . and "turned my back and the first thing I saw was the knife." She told police she returned to the bedroom with the knife and wakened her husband to tell him that he shouldn't have raped her. When he went back to sleep, she cut off his penis.

"He wanted his own satisfaction, and that's not fair," said Weintz, quoting Lorena Bobbitt.

> After severing the penis . . . Lorena Bobbitt ran out of the apartment to
> go to her employer's home. On the way, she threw the penis out of her car
> window and tossed the knife in a trash can. (*San Francisco Chronicle*, Aug. 5,
> 1993: A6)

Clearly, Lorena Bobbitt's actual castration of her husband, aptly named
John Wayne Bobbitt, came from a sense of injustice. If he treated her like
a devalued sexual object, she, in retaliation, would devalue his sexual
being, which she located in his penis, tossing it out of the car window like
a piece of waste—tit for tat, the *lex talionis*.[1]

The public fascination with this story as an uncanny realization of
male fear and female rage was the subject of an elaborate interrogation
by Kim Masters in the November 1993 issue of *Vanity Fair*. After observing
that women seemed to love the story, "their eyes brighten and their pulses
race at its mere mention," Masters went on to describe Bobbitt's act as a

> mythic leap into our collective consciousness, an act so primal that an-
> thropologist Helen Fisher of the New York American Museum of Natural
> History is surprised that it hasn't happened more often, especially given the
> high incidence of violence between the sexes. So reflexive is most women's
> sympathy for Lorena, so deep seated the rage against John, that [the] wife
> [of surgeon John Sehn] has been . . . accosted by women who aren't too
> pleased that her husband sewed the thing back on. "I've heard women say,
> 'I wish she'd put it down the garbage disposal,'" she says. Even Camille
> Paglia, the reigning queen of media-defined sexual politics, gleefully con-
> firms the mythic status of female rage, saying "Lorena Bobbitt committed a
> rather thrilling act of revolution. . . . It's kind of like the Boston Tea
> Party. . . . It's a wakeup call. . . . It has to send a chill through every man in
> the world." (170)

Interestingly, except for occasional references to the name "John
Wayne Bobbitt," no report at the time remarked on other curious ironies
manifest in the proper names circulating in this true story—perhaps
most uncannily, that it takes place in *Manassas*, Virginia. Manasses was
the husband of Judith, who decapitated Holofernes in an act of figurative
castration. The other principal name also evokes the Judith myth, for
"Lorena" is a virtual anagram of "leonor" or lioness, a female figure of
rageful retribution also recognizable as an avatar of the biblical Judith.
Judith's decapitation of Holofernes in Friederich Hebbel's nineteenth-
century play, *Judith* (1840), likewise turns on a plot of rage and retaliation. After having been raped by the potent and charismatic Holofernes,
the previously virginal Judith vents her outrage at having been sexually
violated and then discarded:

And he sleeps so peaceful. . . . That peaceful sleep, after such an hour, is it not the worst sacrilege of all? Am I a worm that he may crush me with his feet and then go to sleep so peacefully as though nothing had happened? I am no worm! (1974, 87)

Judith conveys virtually the same message as Lorena ("Leonor") Bobbitt, but the accompanying affect is different. Although Lorena actually castrates John Wayne Bobbitt, there is no grand emotion evoked in her explanation of the act—no divine lioness she, in spite of her name—but rather a kind of naive artlessness in her almost childlike complaint of having been unfairly treated. Indeed, while Judith's decapitation of Holofernes and Lorena's castration of John Wayne Bobbitt are psychically equivalent acts of retribution, Lorena's seems to occur in a trance of ego-suspension: she later "forgets" exactly what happened, or so it was reported. Judith, on the other hand, communicates the grandiosity of her ego through an expansively articulated rage, a rage specifically provoked by the violation of that ego's integrity.

As Freud pointed out in his brief discussion of the play in "The Taboo of Virginity" (1918), Hebbel added a sexual dimension to the Judith story, transforming the pious Judith of the Apocrypha into a sexually aware but virginal widow whose husband—Manasses—had uncannily shied away from the conjugal bed.[2] Freud in turn used Hebbel's version of Judith to confirm his own analysis of the widespread folk taboo that surrounds virginity, which he derived from men's fear of women's rage. Arguing that a woman inevitably feels hostility toward the man who deflowers her and harbors retaliatory castration wishes, Freud concluded that the taboo developed as a defense against this feared female response. Thus, he writes, "the taboo of virginity which seems so strange to us, the horror with which, among primitive peoples, the husband avoids the act of defloration, are fully justified by this hostile reaction" (208).

In developing his argument, Freud points out that there are real reasons for women's hostility: the first sexual act is typically unsatisfying; it is experienced as a narcissistic injury; the husband is always a substitute, never the right man; and women are bitter about their social subjection to men. These reasons certainly apply in Lorena Bobbitt's case as well as Judith's.[3] But however "real" and legitimate the reasons may be, Freud ultimately attributes the deepest source of women's rage not to reality but to fantasy, to infantile phallic impulses "reactivated during the act of defloration" (204). For Freud it is woman's envy of what she lacks—the male sexual organ—that is aroused during sexual penetration and that provokes her hostility and castration wishes as an appropriate form of retaliation—a wound for a wound, as it were. By this logic, Holofernes' decapitation is equivalent to Judith's rape, both analogues of castration, the psychoanalytic figuration of primal loss.

I want here not to argue with Freud's interpretation but simply to mine its usefulness. First, it reminds us that although this patriarchal logic asserts an underlying psychic equivalence between defloration, decapitation, and castration, some signifiers are more equal than others. Defloration may be a kind of castration, but castration is not a kind of defloration: the phallus is clearly the privileged signifier. Similarly, in his account of castration anxiety in the Medusa myth, which is the obverse of the Judith story,[4] Freud treats decapitation as an upward displacement of castration and psychically equivalent to it (1922, 273). Once again, decapitation is depicted as a symbolic castration, but the reverse does not hold; castration remains the controlling term in the equation of loss. Freud's theoretical mappings depend on this phallic economy that, by figuring the subject's primary loss as castration, establishes the subject, whether male or female, as masculine. This cultural fix on the masculine subject fuels what I will suggest is a pervasive though often un-acknowledged female rage—a rage that is performed by Judith both on stage and in the wings, and given an encore in the Bobbitt melodrama.

If Judith's loss of her maidenhead induces a rage that demands a talionic justice through her beheading of Holofernes, and if both Judith and Lorena are thus caught up in the metaphorics of castration, it is significant that in Hebbel's play it is not only Judith but also Holofernes who feels overwhelming rage. Certainly, the changes Hebbel rings on the apocryphal story not only sexualize Judith and mystify her virginity, but recurrently shift our gaze to Holofernes as a subject of desire. The play opens with Holofernes; it is his narcissistic rage, his desire to find an adequate self-projection, that initiates the narrative movement. In a voice seething with erotic fury, he expresses his longing for a heroic warrior who would offer a challenge to him and not be an easy conquest:

> At times I feel among all these fools that I am alone, as though they could only become aware of themselves if I cut off their arms and legs. . . . If I only had one enemy, just one, who'd dare to confront me! I'd kiss him; indeed, after I'd made him bite the dust in hot battle, I'd throw myself upon him and die with him. (40–41)

Here Holofernes voices his desire for a violent homoerotic merger that would destroy both self and other. The pleasure offered by Hebbel's play lies in great part in the reader's or spectator's identification with this self-annihilating rage.

Indeed, Holofernes' monologues tie his rage with increasing specificity to masochistic desire, a desire that informs a good number of *fin-de-*

siècle representations of male subjectivity at the margins, as Kaja Silver man (1992) has recently argued. This masochistic rage is passionately articulated toward the close of the play:

> Come, all of you whom I have hurt! I'll claim you whom I've crippled, you, whose wives I tore from your embrace. . . . Come, think up tortures for me! . . . Let him come who can hurl me to the ground! I long for him! Let him grind me in a mortar and if it pleases him, fill in the hole I tore into the world with the hash he makes of me! I bore further and further with my sword. If the bloodcurdling screams for help fail to rouse the savior, then none exists. (82)

Holofernes' desperate attempts to provoke a supreme punishment from an absent God, an extreme example of what Freud called moral masochism, are gratified offstage in his climactic decapitation by God's lioness, Judith, the phallic woman who answers his call.

But his impassioned summoning of an absent godhead also suggests that it is absence itself—absence of a savior, of a phallic double—that triggers his rage and its barbarous effects. Indeed, this evocation resembles another deformed representation of rage, that by Mary Shelley of Frankenstein's monster, who also articulates a powerful anguish at being isolated in his singularity, being without an equal, without a mirror for his narcissism. Thus, while the heroic emotions of Hebbel's play are invested in and evoked by both Judith and Holofernes as sexual antagonists, each seems to represent Hebbel's own yearning for a narcissistic other, a desire like that which Freud imputes to Leonardo da Vinci. Freud, we recall, speculates that Leonardo, identifying with his mother's desire for him, takes his own person as a model in whose phallic likeness he chooses his love-objects (1910, 100). Holofernes is also such a man's man, desiring an object like himself to ravish him; what Hebbel gives him is Judith.

In short, Judith and Holofernes dramatize not so much a battle between two heroic exemplars of sexual difference as the ambivalent emotions of a male subject who wants impossibly to be both subject and object, male and female. Insofar as rage is a dominant affect of the play, it repeatedly erupts as the subject's response to wanting and not being/ having all. Inevitably, the subject of this rage seeks a resolution of his perverse desire in a fantasmatic surrender to the summoned other, a way of paradoxically being all by being nothing. Since in Hebbel's text the all is clearly phallic, the characters' rage and their fantasied submission to the other find representation only through a metaphorics of castration. Indeed, both Freud's theory and Hebbel's play are implicated in the same symbolic order that represents desire and rage through the phallic term; without it there is only silence and emptiness.

In the last decade a number of feminist psychoanalysts have pointed to the pernicious effects of this phallocracy of representation on the female subject and traced its relation to rage. Thus, for example, theorists as diverse as Luce Irigaray and Jessica Benjamin both note that the lack of a female economy of desire is a significant factor in promoting female rage. As Irigaray argues in her extensive analysis of Western meta-physical assumptions, *Speculum of the Other Woman* (1974), Freud's theory of penis envy is deeply embedded in a scopic economy that privileges the visible; woman's sexual organ, which is neither seen nor one, is thus counted as none. It is the negative of the visible—and thus the only morphologically designatable—organ, the penis (46–53). Irigaray describes the phallus as a borrowed signifier, deriving from a male imag-inary but offered as the ground of symbolization. According to this logic, because women have no symbol of their own for what is lost, they suffer from a diffuse melancholy and hysteria. In this sense, as Jessica Benjamin also argues (1986, 78–101), "penis envy" refers to a woman's desire for a signifier of her own, for an "image" of her desire not offered by patri-archal discourse and the male tropes that constitute it. As these theorists suggest, what is lost for women is at once more and less than the phallus: the possibility of a return to, and of, the lost object through representa-tion. As I shall suggest below, the effects of this double loss are both an intensification of a rage that cannot be articulated and an emptiness where the object should be.[5]

There are, of course, diverse psychoanalytic readings of the sources of rage and its relation to gender. Whereas for Freud the daughter's rage is a consequence of penis envy and maternal lack, for Melanie Klein rage is initially ungendered, a response to the loss of maternal plenitude that arouses the aggressive desire to rob the maternal body of its fullness, to incorporate it into a totality that is analogous to Freud's concept of primary narcissism. In Kleinian terms, because primal rage has as its goal both the destruction of and reunion with the maternal object, rage threatens to destroy not only that object but also the subject in a fusion that respects no boundaries. Thus, for Klein rage must be contained and loss gradually acknowledged as the subject moves into the depressive position. But in both Freud's and Klein's conceptualizations, it is the mother, the ambivalently constructed other who bears at the same time the traces of self, who is the primal object of this unconscious rage and desire—an object, moreover whose value potentially rivals that of the phallus, and whose loss within a patriarchal symbolic order is made anal-ogous to castration. The analogy returns us to the overdetermined trope of castration at the heart of psychoanalysis and to knife-wielding, castrat-ing women—the mythical Judith as well as the more prosaic Lorena Bobbitt.

    This archetypal confrontation with phallic narcissism undergoes a significant alteration in gender-dynamics in Virginia Woolf's first novel, *The Voyage Out* (1915). In Woolf's depiction of the woman with the knife, the object of female vengeance is not a male but a female figure— literally a hen, but metaphorically a "spring chicken" identified with the novel's heroine, Rachel, whose name has come to signify maternal grief.[6] How might we interpret the scene of woman's rage when the object—or its totemic representative—is not the predatory male but a vulnerable female, and the context a relationship between mother and daughter?

    To give a brief outline of the novel, a Victorian couple, Helen and Ridley Ambrose, embark for a vacation in South America on a ship captained by their widower brother-in-law. Although Helen, introduced as a mother grieving at being separated from her children, seems at first to be the protagonist, once they board the ship the story shifts its focus to her young niece, Rachel, and becomes a female *Bildungsroman*. At her father's request, Rachel becomes Helen's ward, to be educated in what it means to be a woman in late Victorian culture. Once they arrive at the British resort that is their destination, the father as a figure of authority virtually drops out of the plot, and Rachel and Helen become sisterly intimates in a narrative that interrogates love, marriage, and the nature of sexual desire and identity. Rachel becomes romantically involved with a young writer, Terence Hewet; Helen strikes up an ambiguous friendship with his friend St. John Hirst. But these intimacies are disrupted when Rachel, having become engaged to Hewet, abruptly falls ill and unexpectedly dies. The novel ends with an attempt to incorporate this seemingly arbitrary calamity into some schema that gives it an overarching meaning.

    The scene of decapitation by a knife-wielding woman that surfaces in the middle of the novel seems at first to be purely gratuitous. Why does Woolf insert it? It is prefaced by an encounter with a minor character, Evelyn Murgatroyd, a young woman who, during an uncomfortably intimate conversation with Rachel, looks out the window of her hotel room and remarks, "They kill hens down there. . . . They cut their heads off with a knife—disgusting!" (251). Her reference to hens—a recurrent, maternally inflected trope in Woolf's texts—is fulsomely elaborated when Rachel, disturbed by Evelyn's proximity, escapes the room and, having confusedly wandered down "the wrong side of hotel life . . . cut off from the right side," stumbles upon an uncanny sight: "Two large women . . . were sitting on a bench with bloodsmeared tin trays in front of them and yellow bodies across their knees" (252). Before the meaning of this haunting image is clarified by the ensuing sentences, it provokes questions and demands interpretations, from the reader if not Rachel herself. Who are these two women? What are they doing? Are they midwives or murderers? Figures of life or death? What follows tells us that this is not an either/or scene:

> They were plucking the birds and talked as they plucked. Suddenly a chicken came floundering, half flying, half running into the space, pursued by a third woman whose age could hardly be under eighty. Although wizened and unsteady on her legs she kept up the chase, egged on by the laughter of the others; her face was expressive of furious rage, and as she ran she swore in Spanish. Frightened by handclapping here, a napkin there, the bird ran this way and that in sharp angles, and finally fluttered straight at the old woman, who opened her scanty grey skirts to enclose it, dropped upon it in a bundle, and then, holding it out, cut its head off with an expression of vindictive energy and triumph combined. (252)

If "vindictive energy and triumph" seems to be diction more appropriate to Judith's victory over Holofernes than to the capture of a runaway chicken in a hotel, the detailed description of the old woman's action—opening her skirts, enclosing the chicken, holding it out, and cutting off its head—nevertheless insinuates the novel's thematic concern with female identity and desire.[7] The familiar trope of castration, however, is foregrounded by the description of the voyeuristic Rachel as "fascinated"—a word derived etymologically from the Latin *fascinum*, a phallic amulet that is meant to paralyze the viewer. Woolf writes:

> The blood and the ugly wriggling fascinated Rachel, so that although she knew that someone had come up behind and was standing beside her, she did not turn round until the old woman had settled down on the bench beside the others. Then she looked up sharply, because of the ugliness of what she had seen. It was Miss Allan who stood beside her. (252)

Although "the blood and ugly wriggling" suggests castration, the phrase also evokes a repugnant birth-scene, both paralyzing fantasms of an abjected and mutilated body.

Indeed, from this scene onward, Woolf's text moves quickly to associate the trapped chicken with Rachel as she feels repeatedly thwarted in her attempts not only to emerge as a separate subject, to be born as herself, but also to know and to be able to represent her desire. Thus, when Rachel turns her look away from the killing floor, two other women appear who embody and presage onerous destinies she would avoid—the spinster, Miss Allan, and the invalid Mrs. Paley. The latter inadvertently blocks Rachel's passage with her wheelchair, forcing her, as the text notes, into an "intolerable cul de sac." Reiterating the phrase, "block in the passage" (257), the text represents Rachel as caught in the conventions of an oppressive system of social relations, "wriggling" in a crisis of identity figured as a thwarted birth. "For the time her own body was the source of all the life in the world, which tried to burst forth here—there—and was repressed now by Mr. Bax, now by Evelyn, now by the imposition of ponderous stupidity—the weight of the entire world" (258). Insofar as the maternal body is the source of being and birth, these images of blockage in *The Voyage Out* turn the universe itself into an unbearable maternal cul-de-sac that does not allow Rachel a passage of her own.

Not surprisingly, then, trapped like a chicken in the maternal·skirts, oppressed by the weight of the world, which in this context seems yet another trope of the suffocating maternal body, Rachel experiences an intense rage that she directs against the oblivious Miss Allan as its representative: "An uncomfortable sensation kept Rachel silent; she wished to whirl high and strike a spark out of the cool pink flesh" (255). But such rage directed at the female flesh that she too shares is impossible for Rachel to express; threatening too great a loss, it is immediately suppressed, or rather converted, as the text tells us, into a "melancholy lethargy" (258). This particular conversion from rage to melancholy lethargy moves in a trajectory antithetical to that of Hebbel's Judith or Lorena. While they both act out their rage at the offending object, Woolf's young heroine, by contrast, swallows her rage and thus repudiates its affect, as does the novel itself. Melancholy lethargy, a symptom of repressed rage, replaces action in a kind of self-castration that leaves loss and emptiness at the novel's very center.

In a later text Woolf showed she understood that the alternative to this self-castration is a psychological form of matricide—killing the angel in the house. Numerous recent critics have returned to this female dilemma to point out the relation between matricidal impulses and masochism (Butler 1990). Moreover, as Irigaray notes, while the matricidal impulse is culturally encouraged in both men and women, it is more devastating for the woman who, in order to emerge as a separate subject, must disavow her primary identification with the maternal body in an imaginary and symbolic identification with the father. This unconscious maternal disavowal itself generates a crisis of identification in women that compounds rage. For in giving up the mother, "the girl has no consciousness of what constitutes loss, and a loss that radically escapes any representation is impossible to mourn" (Irigaray 1974, 66). Quoting Freud's observation in "Mourning and Melancholia" that, for the melancholiac, "the object has not perhaps actually died, but has become lost as an object of love . . . the patient cannot consciously perceive what he has lost . . . melancholia is in some way related to an object loss which is withdrawn from consciousness" (245), Irigaray, like Butler, relates melancholia to normative female development. Because "the girl's relationship to the lost object is . . . complicated by conflict and ambivalence that remain unconscious" (68), the girl's loss escapes representation. Without a privileged signifier of desire that can recuperate that loss, mourning is impossible and melancholia inevitable.

The thematics of loss thus furnishes the precondition of the female *Bildungsroman;* its affective corollary is a rage that, being repressed, leaves only fantasms of emptiness in its place. *The Voyage Out* opens with references to a mother mourning her children and returns at the end to a scene of mourning, as the principal characters all respond to Rachel's death with a generalized melancholy. But there are periodic eruptions of rage in the text, as in the seemingly gratuitous scene of the woman with a knife. Thus the novel is marked by sudden outpourings of bewilderingly violent imagery, of furious verbs and fierce metaphors that rip through the smooth surface of the prose, like a fin in a waste of water, to use Woolf's own trope. From the opening pages, as the Ambroses make their way through London to the ship awaiting them, "angry glances struck upon their backs"; cabs "plunge"; streets "shrink"; boats "shoot past." "The beauty that clothed things" suddenly unveils "the skeleton beneath" (12). Mrs. Ambrose's mind is "like a wound exposed to dry in the air," a simile of anxiety quickly reified as a real external danger: "At this point the cab stopped, for it was in danger of being crushed like an egg-shell" (13).

Once the story moves from the streets of London to the ship, the deictic center shifts from grieving mother to motherless daughter, but the same violent metaphors continue to resound.

> Down in the saloon of her father's ship, Miss Rachel Vinrace, aged twenty four, stood waiting for her uncle and aunt nervously. . . . As she occupied herself in laying forks severely straight by the side of knives, she heard a man's voice saying gloomily:
> "On a dark night one would fall down these stairs head foremost," to which a woman's voice added, "And be killed." (14)

When Rachel goes out on deck, her gasping words, " 'It blows—it blows!' . . . rammed down her throat" (18). When Helen and Rachel look into a room, "they saw Mr. Ambrose throw himself violently against the back of his chair." Even the description of a tapestry seems to radiate anger, not just visually but in its explosive consonants, especially its *p*'s and *b*'s: "twisted shells with red lips like unicorn's horns ornamented the mantlepiece, which was draped by a pall of purple lush from which depended a certain number of balls" (18). Out of such verbal shrapnel scattered through the opening pages, a narrative emerges in which nothing really "happens" on the level of action but a sporadically disgorged rhetoric of rage suggests havoc being wreaked elsewhere. In the phallic trope of the woman with a knife chasing the young chicken, the fantasy at the core of that havoc is unveiled.

For the most part, however, Woolf suppresses the violence, which, as the narrative moves toward the conclusion, becomes increasingly anesthetized and distanced. Words are emptied of affect; speech becomes "little meaningless words floating high in air":

> "We are happy together." He did not seem to be speaking, or she to be hearing.
> "Very happy," she answered.
> "We love each other," Terence said. . . .
> "We love each other," she repeated. (276)

This dialogue, a hollow parody of romantic courtship, is in every respect antithetical to the lethal embraces of Judith and Holofernes or Lorena and John. Devoid of passion, meaning, desire, or identity, a general melancholy has suffocated both characters and narrative voice. By the end, all the characters come to function as hapless vocalists in a chorus of loss. In emblematic fashion, the matriarchal Mrs. Thornbury, "oddly dazed, and seeking she did not know exactly what, . . . went slowly upstairs and walked quietly along the passages, touching the wall with her fingers as if to guide herself. . . . Something had passed from the world. It seemed to her strangely empty" (357).

If Freud is right that rage is an affect especially common among women and leads to the pervasive cultural fantasm of the woman with a knife, we can see that no less common and perhaps more devastating is women's repression of rage, which leads to a desolate blank space at the center of female identity, to the emptiness of unrepresentable loss. What Woolf records, among other things, is the loss of rage itself.

Notes

1. One might note, as Peter Rudnytsky has, the Solomonic wisdom of the jury verdicts that came in after this chapter was written. Both were found not guilty: he was exonerated of raping her, and she of severing his penis.

2. Interestingly, after her rape Hebbel's Judith derides the value of virginity:

> A virgin is a foolish creature who even trembles with fear before her own dreams because a dream can mortally wound her, and still she lives in hopes of not always remaining a virgin. There is no greater moment for a virgin than the one when she stops being a virgin, and every sensation of her blood which she tried to fight . . . enhances the value of the sacrifice she has to make at that moment. (1974, 86)

For Judith, losing her virginity is the same as Holofernes submitting to the cut, both symbolic castrations.

3. Freud's assumption that Judith's desire lurks in all women who have felt themselves unjustly treated by patriarchal society and the men it empowers also underlies the reading of Artemisia Gentileschi's famous painting of Judith decapitating Holofernes (c. 1615–20) that attributes its fierce and vindictive power to her own rage at having been repeatedly raped by her art teacher when she was fifteen. See Garrard 1982, 147–52.

4. See Mary Jacobus (1986 124–27) on Heine's reading of a painting of Judith as a young Medusa, with short black snakes for hair, the castrating mother to Holofernes, who sleeps like a satisfied child. Jacobus notes the relevance of Heine's own wish, "Let me die like Holofernes," to his reading of the painting. However, the question of male masochism that I take up here is bypassed in Jacobus's provocative discussion.

5. Although in "The Taboo on Virginity" Freud attributes women's hostility to penis envy, he develops a different model in "Mourning and Melancholia" (1917). Whereas in the former account rage is a response to a lack *in* the maternal, in the latter it is induced by the loss *of* maternal plenitude. Melanie Klein (1940) extends this second view into a theory of object relations that centers on a fantasy of emptiness and on the depressive position that develops from maternal loss. Kristeva too deals with melancholia and emptiness in *Black Sun* (1989); Irigaray complicates discussions of female rage and melancholia by suggesting that the female subject is insufficiently narcissistic to experience violent emotions (1977, 58–62).

6. Perhaps the best-known literary allusion to Rachel searching and weeping for her children is Melville's at the conclusion of *Moby Dick*.

7. I am indebted to Professor Rosemary Feal of the University of Rochester for pointing out that Woolf's decapitating crone who swears in Spanish recalls Goya's *Caprichos*, caricatures commenting on the corrupt violence of social relations. (See especially no. 19, "All Will Fall"; no. 20, "They Go Plucked"; and no. 21, "How They Pluck Her," in which the human bird is a girl.) Feal also calls my attention to the story "The Decapitated Chicken," by the Uruguayan writer Horacio Quiroga, in which two idiot brothers witness the cook's decapitation of a chicken and then decapitate their sister. In Italian, a slang word for penis is bird (*ucello*). That birds can serve as phallic symbols was noted by Freud in *The Interpretation of Dreams*. Significantly, the chicken is a bird that cannot fly.

References

Benjamin, J. 1986. A Desire of One's Own: Psychoanalytic Feminism and Inter-subjective Space. In T. De Lauretis, ed., *Feminist Studies/Critical Studies*. Bloomington: Indiana Univ. Press, pp. 78–101.

Butler, J. 1990. *Gender Trouble: Feminism and the Subversion of Identity*. New York: Routledge.

Freud, S. 1910. *Leonardo da Vinci and a Memory of His Childhood*. In *The Standard Edition of the Complete Psychological Works*, ed. and trans. J. Strachey et al. 24 vols. (hereafter *S.E.*). London: Hogarth Press, 1953–74. 11:59–138.

———. 1917. Mourning and Melancholia. *S.E.*, 14:243–58.

———. 1918. The Taboo of Virginity. *S.E.*, 11:191–208.

———. 1922. Medusa's Head. *S.E.*, 18:273–74.

Garrard, M. D. 1982. Artemisia and Susanna. In M. D. Garrard and N. Broude, eds., *Feminism and Art History: Questioning the Litany*. New York: Harper and Row, pp. 147–71.

Jacobus, M. 1986. *Reading Woman*. Ithaca, N.Y.: Cornell Univ. Press.

Hebbel, F. 1974. *Three Plays by Hebbel*. Trans. M. W. Sonnenfeld. Lewisburg, Pa.: Bucknell Univ. Press.

Irigaray, L. 1974. *Speculum of the Other Woman*. Trans. G. C. Gill. Ithaca, N.Y.: Cornell Univ. Press, 1985.

———. 1977. *This Sex Which Is Not One*. Trans. C. Porter. Ithaca, N.Y.: Cornell Univ. Press, 1985.

Klein, M. 1940. Mourning and Its Relation to Manic-Depressive States. In *The Selected Melanie Klein*, ed. J. Mitchell. Harmondsworth: Penguin, 1986, pp. 146–74.

Kristeva, J. 1989. *Black Sun: Depression and Melancholia*. Trans. L. S. Roudiez. New York: Columbia Univ. Press.

Silverman, K. 1992. *Male Subjectivity at the Margins*. New York: Routledge.

Torok, M. 1964. The Meaning of Penis Envy in Women. In N. Abraham and M. Torok, *The Shell and the Kernel*, ed. and trans. N. T. Rand. 2 vols. Chicago: Univ. of Chicago Press, 1994, 1:41–73.

Woolf, V. 1915. *The Voyage Out*. New York: Harcourt, Brace, and World, 1948.

Chapter Eleven

Playing Scrabble with My Mother

David Willbern

Within the arena of almost every utterance an
intense interaction and struggle between one's
own and another's word is being waged, a
process in which they oppose or dialogically
interanimate each other.
—Mikhail Bakhtin, "Discourse in the Novel"

The entry into syntax constitutes a first victory
over the mother.
—Julia Kristeva, "Place Names"

Beginning when I was four or five years old, playing SCRABBLE® with my
mother became an arena wherein I formed a central relation to language, both private and public. Those early contests pitted a petite,
proper, quietly humorous, fifty-year-old woman against a precocious, in-
quisitive little boy. Our games were played in a thickly carpeted, air-
conditioned living room, on a fold-out cardtable also used for the weekly
women's bridge club.

The time could be summer in the late 1940s, hot and dusty on the
Kansas-Oklahoma border. Or it could be winter, dry and cold and bright.
Outside there is a slight breeze, or a strong midwestern thunderstorm.
Inside, it is quiet and temperate, good for concentration. Two pairs of
hands prepare to place small wooden tiles on a thick paper board. One
pair is beginning to be contorted by arthritis, knuckles swollen against
heavy rings. The other is small and soft, quick and dexterous.

For these players, the world contracts to a field of 225 small squares
marked at the center by a black, five-pointed star. Specially coded colored
squares of pink and blue crisscross the board diagonally, designating
spaces of amplified scoring potential: double letter points, triple word
points. Drawn blindly from their protective sack, fourteen smooth
wooden tiles recline on their slanted rests, ready for action.

Player 1	**M**	**I**	**D**	**C**	**L**	**H**	**A**
Player 2	**R**	**H**	**O**	**E**	**T**	**D**	**W**

Some letters are ubiquitous workers, always ready for construction: Es, Is, Ss. Others are privileged citizens, available under special conditions for limited employment: Q, X, Z. Two are magical: blank, omnipotent, the gap that sutures, one might say (not I). Of course, blank tiles carry no scoring value, only facilitating presence, sovereign substitution.

I begin, placing my tiles so that one occupies the center square:

```
C
H
I
L
D
```

"How clever," says my mother. And she places her tiles:

```
        C
O   T   H   E   R
        I
        L
        D
```

A mysterious smile plays on her face. Quick to see a simple advantage, I add only one tile:

```
        C
M   O   T   H   E   R
        I
        L
        D
```

On my mother's next turn, she shifts the vocabulary to another register of self-reference. We seem to be playing a type of metascrabble.

Like most games, Scrabble simultaneously teaches possibilities and limits. Today, without consulting The Rules (I haven't played in decades), I recall that there are strict limits on types of words: no proper nouns, no foreign terms, no slang. It was a good game for post–World War II Kansas: a decent, virtuous, Republican, Cold War pastime. Within an authorized, hegemonic semantic field, proper standard English could be championed against incursions by outside lexical agitators. (Has the game lost popularity because it's no longer politically correct? Does Bill Bennett play it with his sons?)[1] A dictionary, bible of the word police, should always be on hand to settle disputes. Within this disciplined frame, words are formed in a contested context of decorum and desire. For the game also offers the chance literally to play with words, to test limits, to challenge convention, to joke, to self-consciously avoid improper terms, to flirt with the forbidden. So many words, the child discovers, have four letters.

(I *was* only five.) But although my mother grants me the momentary pleasure of this childish transgression, she won't permit this profanation of the language (her father was a Bible-Belt Baptist) nor violation of the rules. I must make another move. Flush with the excitement of my profanity, I revert to simple addition:

```
    W       C
M   O   T   H   E   R
    R       I
    D       L
    S       D
```

Scrabble offers a demonstration of the latent potential of words to become something else: language trembling on the edge of transmutation, ready to jump tracks and head toward other significations. Such textual volatility can be a mark of anxiety and excitement: letters build toward meaning while they remain vulnerable to appropriation by another's intention. Words can turn on you (or turn you on); one man's version is another's perversion. Displaying her advanced adult technique, my mother now crosses *two* words to produce a third:

Now an entire range of the board opens below, and I extend myself into it:

Two quick antinomies continue this overdetermined text:

A central feature of Scrabble is that opponents are also partners: the "*rivals* of the watch," to borrow a phrase from the opening scene of *Hamlet*. As these rivals play, a text is simultaneously co-produced and co-read: it is *derived*. Generally it's produced and read in terms of the possibility of further production: where can a player's letters be most profitably conjoined to the existing text? Yet it can also be read as a text-in-itself, in terms of reception and not production. Once the Scrabble board has a few words positioned on it, it's available for analysis as a kind of poem: a text at cross-purposes. One strategy of play produces a lexically arbitrary text, determined by random drawings of letters and the arithmetic of point-count: a computer would maximize this style. Another strategy, however, suggests itself. What about the unconscious components of Scrabble textual productions, analogous to the unconscious determinants of Ouija board productions? What varieties of messages emerge within the play space of interanimated language?

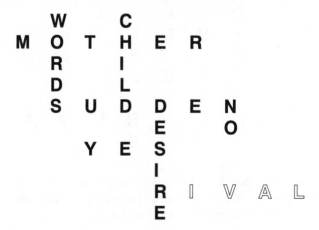

My mother's latest addition (has she been reading *Hamlet?*) elicits a mildly aggressive response, as I transmute words into weapons:

Sensing perhaps that this mock-oedipal drama is getting out of hand (yet, though I would show daggers to her, I would use none), my mother lays down her next word, to which I respond with childish resistance:

And now my mother, from her deep reservoir of maternal wisdom about life and little boys, offers a compromise by introducing another arena of gratified desire. Has she been reading Freud?

As the scrabbled, cross-purposed text emerges, it marks out a field of possibility even as it de/fines it: the outside boundary of the board maps an absolute limit to burgeoning significance. In this implausibly overdetermined game, the **C H I L D / (M) O T H E R** nexus is the aboriginal matrix, the intertext at the center. The emerging compromised text wends its way into the lower right sector of the board. Each advancing letter takes a step toward development while it reduces the available field. Each formed word both encourages and limits potential neighboring words. As players build words—constructing a shared text within a competitive and cooperative relation—the issue becomes one of context: What does the current text enable or limit? Beyond the immediate, contiguous contextuality of possible linguistic permutations are the larger contextual limitations of convention and decorum (proper usage), and the still larger bounds of nationalism (English or American usage), and the largest bounds of sense (patriarchal usage?) and nonsense (*une autre écriture?*).

In this game, I, who have not been reading Freud, but perhaps gripped by unconscious motives, respond to the notion of wishing by associating to my favorite wish-fulfillment story, one that took place in my home state. Lacking the proper tile, however, I boldly add an **O** to a near neighbor:

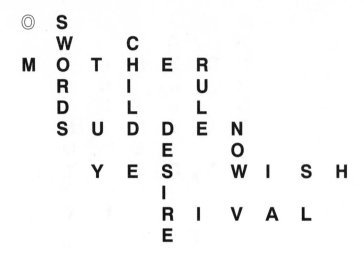

Her mouth slightly agape, my mother looks at me strangely, then asks what word I'm spelling. "Oh," I say, "it could be the plural of the letter *O*, like my morning Cheerios. But it's really *Oz*." (I'm trying not to smile.) "*You* know," I continue. "Dorothy, Toto, the Wicked Witch, the yellow brick road" (to the unconscious). Still staring strangely at me, she slowly nods and says, "Well, it's really OZ, but I suppose we can relax the rules a bit, since it's such a magical place and you're such a clever little boy. But since *you're* revising the rules, I'm going to follow suit." (My mother loved her bridge.) With a gleam in her eye, she makes her next move:

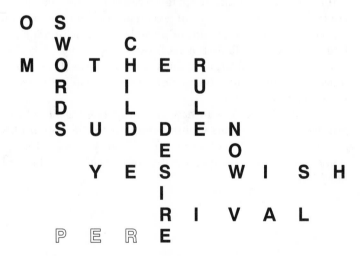

"What's *that?*" I ask. Smiling, then suddenly pensive, she replies: "Oh, it could be *peer,* as in 'look,' or it could be *pair,* as in socks." By now we've thrown caution to the winds; all is permitted. I've been looking for a good place to put one of my big letters, and now find occasion:

"And what might *that* be?" asks my mother. Giggling, I suggest it could be the *vox* who tries to get into the henhouse when the farmer is away. (We had read stories about this, she and I.) We both are pleased with this bit of preschool wit, and my mother ventures upon a lecture. "Actually, she begins, "our language—you know, English—isn't the only language. There are many, many others, spoken and written by people all over the world. And what you've just created . . . " Just then the back door banged opened and my father's booming baritone called out, "I'm home! Is dinner ready?" Quickly my mother said, "We have to quit. Since you started, I'll finish my turn, and you can add up the scores."

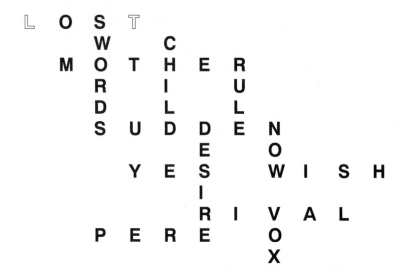

When my mother left the table and went into the kitchen, I starting adding the scores. After all the double letters and such, I managed a three-point victory: 82 to 79. I *won*, I thought. This satisfaction wasn't great, but it was good enough. In the kitchen I could hear my parents talking, low and steady.

A few decades later, my own styles of textual reception and production (let's call them reading and writing) privilege the visual and aural. Don DeLillo once said in an interview that he wrote on an old manual typewriter so he could feel the physical impression of his text as he created it. My style is different: I focus on the sight and sound of words, and their relative positions. My interpretative reading mode is a type of generative acid (both solvent and drug): it dissolves texts into semantic stew, which I can stir at will and then fantasize about in a monitored free association. Within this lax yet lucid reconstruction of texts, conventional syntax surrenders to latent sense. Freud referred to this process as "syllabic chemistry."[2] A recent exhibition of this style is in an essay entitled "Pushing the Envelope: Supersonic Criticism" (1994).[3] By way of examples, here are a preface, a couple of specific readings, and a speculative conclusion:

> [*Preface*] [I envision] Shakespeare's language . . . as an arena of linguistic play in which pun and profundity coexist: a field of deep wit, wherein the nature of particular rhetorical events is as much a function of our attitude toward them as of their intrinsic semantic qualities, or Shakespeare's inferable intent. This essay aims to test some boundaries in our rhetorical attitudes: to draw provisional lines around licit and illicit uses of Shake-

speare's language and to propose some models of close reading. One might call them pilot projects.

[*Example 1*] Isabella has come to Angelo to plead for her brother, who is condemned to die for the crime of fornication (*Measure for Measure*, 2.2). Her first words are not about Claudio but about her own views of sexuality and justice:

> There is a vice that most I do abhor,
> And most desire should meet the blow of justice;
> For which I would not plead, but that I must;
> For which I must not plead, but that I am
> At war 'twixt will and will not. (2.2.29–33)

Since Isabella's first words in the play concern the limits to her liberty when she joins the convent (she wants in fact more restraint than the already strict rules require), one reading of her initial words to Angelo reinforces a psychological view of the character as one who wishes to repress sexual energies. Her image of "the blow of justice" could be connected to her later notorious statement to Antonio that, rather than submit her body to shameful lust, "th' impression of keen whips [she'd] wear as rubies, / And strip [her]self to death as to a bed / That longing have been sick for" (2.4.101–3). Such a psychological reading could speculate about sado-masochistic ambivalences in Isabella, and call into question the posture of severe purity she maintains. A third-ear audition of her opening line ("There is a *vice* that most I do ab*hor*") could hear the genital meaning of "vice" (used more directly in her charge to Claudio, "Wilt thou be made a man out of my vice? / Is it not a kind of incest, to take life / From thine own sister's shame?" [3.1.138]), and an aural echo of the term she cannot say but which characterizes the flip side of the nunnery she intends to join (the play even has a character named "Abhorson"). But to really push the envelope, let me reform the lines in a way that their form provisionally permits, but that many readers may judge out of bounds: "There is a vice which most I do abhor, and most desire." (Period.) Now, can I do that? Is it proper or permissible? The syntactic moment evanesces, resolved into the succeeding clause. But for a moment the line captures the precise paradox of desire that energizes *Measure for Measure* and most of its characters, "at war 'twixt will and will not." But can Isabella mean to have said this? Or is it unconscious? Or is it an aspect of the extradramatic *play of language*? Or is it merely beyond the pale of permissible readings?

[*Example 2*] Now for the acid test. As the first interview is about to conclude, Isabella suddenly offers to bribe Angelo. "How?" he returns. "Bribe me?" "Ay," she says,

with such gifts that heaven shall share with you.
Not with fond sicles of the tested gold,
Or stones, whose rate are either rich or poor
As fancy values them: but with true prayers . . . (2.2.146–52)

Editors tell us that "sicles" derives from the Hebrew "shekel," that "tested gold" is gold proved true on a touchstone, and that "stones" are precious jewels. Fine. And my third ear, by this time acutely attuned to the extraordinarily suggestive language of the entire scene, and further sharpened by Angelo's own quick response to Isabella's offer (in terms of his character's psychology, her answer may respond to his wish that she bribe him with sexual favors)—my third ear, now listening in supersonic registers, breaking sound and syntax barriers—hears Isabella referring to something that she cannot plausibly be referring to: these contiguous syllables, only slightly re-arranged, evoke the term "testicles," immediately glossed by the common synonym of "stones." Now what am I to do with this response? It's on the edge, marginal even for me. Does it make sense to construct an unconscious intention in the character, whereby she produces a brilliant Freudian moment that discloses her own desires while appealing to Angelo's, in a kind of unconscious conversation such as real people may have but rarely become aware of outside of an analyst's consulting room? (Earlier she exclaims to Angelo, "I would to heaven I had your potency.") I could argue that the moment catches a radical ambivalence in Isabella, placed on the threshold between one state (the silence and repression of the nunnery) and another (sudden entry into the slippery sexual economy of Venice). Or I could argue that the moment demonstrates how the sexually charged language of that erotic economy invades Isabella's speech even as she tries to deny it, as if it were unavoidable, a contamination by carnality (this is a condition common to characters in *Measure for Measure:* see for instance the Duke at 1.3.1–6). Or I might contend that Isabella's language, like the character herself, is a masculine invention, constructed with the purpose precisely of invading the privacy of her "true prayers" by a denied and displaced profanity. The textual moment replicates in miniature the large-scale project of the play, which is to move Isabella out of the nunnery and into the Duke's bed. The moment may be a prime instance of the play of language, beyond character, outside local intentionality. Or is it rather a prime instance of a reading distorted by what Timon of Athens, referring to another character's bawdy comments about procreation, calls "lascivious apprehension" (1.1.207)?

[*Speculative Conclusion*] The two interview scenes between Angelo and Isabella are dramatized instances of the problem of *reading*. Both Angelo and Isabella are trying to read the other's character, to detect through language and gesture the other's intention, to discover underlying meaning. When senses and intentions that neither suspects gradually emerge, as when Angelo finds himself aroused by Isabella, who is the agent of this newly constructed meaning?

> What's this? what's this? Is this her fault, or mine?
> The tempter, or the tempted, who sins most, ha?
> Not she; nor doth she tempt; but it is I . . . (2.2.162–4)

From the perspective of character, Angelo's location of meaning-construction is apt and plausible. He is guilty of "reading into" Isabella's speech and gesture, of imposing his own wished-for sense on the text that she presents to him (rather like Malvolio and the forged letter). During the second interview, the readings of the situation by Angelo and Isabella become more obviously a struggle between competing meanings, as Angelo approaches the raw proposition of his scheme and Isabella seemingly is unable to comprehend. "Nay, but hear me," he says to her: "Your sense pursues not mine: either you are ignorant, / Or seem so, crafty; and that's not good" (2.4.73). At this point, both characters may be negotiating "lascivious apprehensions": Angelo is trying to bring them to the surface, while Isabella tries to keep them suppressed. What I suggest is that both characters are subsumed within a play of language wherein such meanings are already in play. Perhaps the characters arrive belatedly at understandings an attentive audience already entertains.

Language, Carnality, and the Feminine

By no accident are my examples predominantly sexual. It's an aspect of my reading style that my third ear is especially attuned to sexual meanings. It is also my theoretical conviction that the deep metaphoric core of language is carnal. At root, many terms relate to the body and to physical action, like Angelo's word, "conception"; "genius" and "genital" have the same root. The phrase "lascivious apprehension" literally means to grasp or lay hold of wanton pleasures. Indeed, tracking the etymology of "lascivious" through Latin *lascivia* and Anglo-Saxon *lust*—both terms cognate with *ludere* (to play, to sport)—I realize that my personal and professional reading project is to conjoin the ludic and the lascivious. My own interpretative style involves a working compromise between literary learning and unconscious response, or (as a colleague has put it) a rhetorical coproduction of my intellect and my primary process.

Yet I would argue that connections between language and sexuality in Shakespeare's texts are not only aspects of my interpretative style or of the carnal core of language. Recent feminist and psychoanalytic studies of

Shakespeare suggest that masculine efforts to manage meaning and to control female sexuality (such as *Measure for Measure*) are powered by an anxiety about threats to the boundaries of conventional significance represented by the exorbitant surplus of "femininity." In an essay on *Hamlet* and *Measure for Measure,* Jacqueline Rose remarks that "slippage of meaning and sexuality as excess seem . . . to be the subtext of the critical focus on Isabella and Gertrude" (1985, 108). The figure of woman presents a destabilizing effect within the conventional system of representation known as "masculine hegemony" or "patriarchy." Femininity or female sexuality, as the site of excess, the ludic and lascivious realm of the infinitely marginal, may embody a powerful background against which traditional (masculine) critical projects enact their exegetical searches for stable meaning. Commenting on T. S. Eliot's famous remark that *Hamlet* is "the Mona Lisa of literature," Rose extrapolates her ideas into a hypothesis about the hermeneutic need for articulatable meaning and recognizable aesthetic form as a defense against anxiety about destabilized, excessive feminine significance. This is a large and provocative claim, one that likely intimates Rose's personal notions of the power and place of her own interpretations. Traditional criticism of Shakespeare, however, as the poet of mixed metaphor and the all-too-willing victim of puns, suggests a similar point. For example, take Samuel Johnson, whose famous criticism of Shakespeare's wordplay is often quoted: "A quibble was to him the fatal Cleopatra for which he lost the world, and was content to lose it."

These excerpts from a recent, purportedly adult, professional publication may supply specific force to my contention, in this artificially autobiographical and necessarily narcissistic essay, that my academic relation to language rests on and derives from my childhood, and a particular kind of childhood *play.* As I reconfigure the event, playing Scrabble with my mother represents and reanimates a potential space of linguistic co-production between mother and child (see Winnicott 1953 and 1967). It's a later developmental model, or high-level, sublimated scene of earlier primordial relationships, such as *reading with* mother and being *read to* by mother. On the foundational ground of a semiotic orchestration of language (the Kristevan *chora*), the newly literate child learns the powers and limits of a semantic or syntactic organization of language (see Kristeva 1974). From an arbitrary *parataxis* of discrete letters resting *in potentia* side by side (in a wooden frame, or in an alphabet), he or she arranges a lexical *syntaxis* of singular meaning within the delimited field of play.[4]

When my mother and I played, I don't recall my father in the scene. He was at the office, or on the golf course, or on the way home for dinner. Yet he was still present: in the dictionary, or on the underside of the boxtop with the rules, or in that proper and propertied sign, the sub-scripted trademark "®" that registers and owns the very term itself: Scrab-ble®. Perhaps a primordial agon is adumbrated in the colors of the board: the field of sublimated struggle between maternal and paternal linguistic principles is marked by the conventional casts of gender: pink and blue.

The word "scrabble" itself has real lexical value: it's not a commer-cial invention. As a verb it derives from (1) *scrape*, to pull together with one's hands. It then branches into the senses of (2) *struggle*, and (3) *scribble:* writing as scratching. Thus the term gestures toward the primitive and preverbal—a scrabbled-together mix of elements in the struggle for life—as well as toward the sophisticated and literate, a scribbled articula-tion of written expression. It denotes the *manipulation of language* at both crude and subtle levels. To me, literature means more if I can get my hands on it, scrabbling it into a new version: ScrabbLit.

Les mots sous les mots: Lacan over Kristeva, with Bakhtin dialogically or ambivalently on the side. The scrabbled field of discourse reaches out literally in two dimensions toward semantic sense, while it reaches figur-atively down into other dimensions: (a) preexisting texts and conven-tions that define a language or discourse (Bakhtin), and (b) the prever-bal matrix that structures or anchors linguistic development (Kristeva). It is a playful enactment of *phenotext* on *genotext*. It sketches a transcendent intertextuality of literary, linguistic, and preverbal registers of language.

> The *genotext* can be seen as language's underlying foundation. We shall use the term *phenotext* to denote language that serves to communicate. . . . The phenotext is constantly split up and divided, and is irreducible to the semiotic process that works through the genotext. The phenotext is a structure . . . ; it obeys rules of communication and presupposes a subject of enunciation and an addressee. The genotext, on the other hand, is a process; it moves through zones that have relative and transitory borders and constitutes a *path* that is not restricted to the two poles of univocal information between two fully fledged subjects. (Kristeva 1974, 121)

The scrabble board game constructs a space-between that connects as it separates, like a bridge or a *copula*. (Now I know why Hamlet made his initial appearance above: that particular oedipal closet game spells **M U R T H E R**.)[5] Within this arena a child can discover lexical possi-bility and restriction, propriety and impropriety, enclosed within the shifting authorities of the mother's voice and the father's law. The thrill of victory within the *jouissance* of play. Writing about the place of identi-fication in analysis, Kristeva implicitly describes the act of deciphering scrabbled language. "The analyst situates himself on a ridge," she writes, "where, on the one hand, the 'maternal' position—gratifying needs, 'holding' (Winnicott)—and on the other the 'paternal' position—the differentiation, distance and prohibition that produces both meaning and absurdity [Lacan]—are intermingled and severed, infinitely and without end" (1983, 246; my interpolation).

> (*To be sung*)
> **M** is for the many things she gave me.
> **O** is for the Other that she was.

I could go on. **I** is for the self she helped to form. Or, **T** is for the word she helped me form. Both constructs were partly out-of-bounds formations, *sous table,* only marginally suitable, occasionally in another tongue (a romance language). The game is a primary stage of my m.o., my *modus operandi.* But before my harmonized sentimentality of a restaged mother-and-child reunion dissolves into clumsy three-stooged clowning—after Mo(e), Curly, and Larry wait in the wings—I'd better end the game and return the tiles to the box. *Modus operandi interruptus.*

Notes

1. Invented in Britain in the 1940s, the game was marketed in America by Parker Brothers. In 1994 Milton Bradley competed with Parker Brothers for U.S. distribution rights. At the same time, different vocabulary restrictions were placed on usage. While Britain liberalized the rules to admit slang, profanity, and even racist terms, the new American edition excluded such terms, and edited out about one hundred previously acceptable words that might be considered racist, sexist, or politically incorrect (*Reuters* news report, September 1994).

2. Although I've lost the specific reference, I'm sure the phrase is somewhere in the Freudian text. It could be in *The Interpretation of Dreams,* one of my favorite and formative books (those rebuses! those cross-language puns!), or it could be in a letter. One of my own critical productions is an essay on "The Interpenetration of Dreams" (1979) in which I assert that interpretation is oedipal: a type of textual intercourse.

3. The editor had some difficulty finding a title for the collection in which it appears. When he finally made his choice and informed the contributors, I responded that he had left out the "*t*" in *Reread.*

4. A recent book (Pinker 1994) describes Chomskyan linguistics and current psycholiniguistics whose theories push language acquisition further back, deeper than the maternal *chora,* into the neural networks of the brain. Contemporary psychoanalysis, like gender theories a theory at the interface of biology and sociology, needs to come to terms with the new "essentialisms."

5. Which is the title of an essay of mine (1983) on a Robert Duncan poem. In it I describe a painful scene in my mother's bedroom when, full of adolescent angst and resistance, I prevented my mother from slapping me for a now-forgotten transgression by grasping her frail, arthritic wrists. We both winced.

References

Bakhtin, M. 1934–35. Discourse in the Novel. In *The Dialogic Imagination: Four Essays*, trans. C. Emerson and M. Holquist. Austin: Univ. of Texas Press, pp. 259–422.

Kristeva, J. 1974. Revolution in Poetic Language. In *The Kristeva Reader*, ed. T. Moi. Oxford: Blackwell, 1986, pp. 89–136.

————. 1976–77. Place Names. In *Desire in Language*, trans. T. Gora, A. Jardine, and L. Roudiez. New York: Columbia Univ. Press, 1980, pp. 240–71.

————. 1986. Freud and Love: Treatment and Its Discontents. In *The Kristeva Reader*, pp. 240–71.

Pinker, S. 1994. *The Language Instinct: How the Mind Creates Language*. New York: Columbia Univ. Press.

Rose, J. 1985. Sexuality and the Reading of Shakespeare: *Hamlet* and *Measure for Measure*. In J. Drakakis, ed., *Alternative Shakespeares*. London: Methuen, pp. 95–118.

Willbern, D. 1979. Freud and the Interpenetration of Dreams. *Diacritics* 9:98–110.

————. 1983. MURTHER: The Hypocritic and the Poet. In G. Garvin and S. Mailloux, eds., *Rhetoric, Literature, and Interpretation*. Lewisberg, Pa.: Bucknell Univ. Press, 1983, pp. 80–94.

————. 1994. Pushing the Envelope: Supersonic Criticism. In R. MacDonald, ed., *Shakespeare Reread: The Texts in New Contexts*. Ithaca, N.Y.: Cornell Univ. Press, pp. 170–90.

Winnicott, D. W. 1953. Transitional Objects and Transitional Phenomena. In *Playing and Reality*. London: Tavistock, 1971, pp. 1–25.

————. 1967. The Location of Cultural Experience. In *Playing and Reality*, pp. 95–110.

Chapter Twelve

Trauma, Gender Identity, and Sexuality: Discourses of Fragmentation

Lynne Layton

This essay emerges from my attempt to make some sense of how two of the areas in which I am engaged do and do not intersect. I work both in literary/cultural studies and in psychoanalytic psychotherapy. In the past several years, a number of discourses—among them cultural criticism, psychoanalytic theories of the self, trauma research, and avant-garde art—have arisen to discuss the fragmentation of the self, and these discourses can be quite contradictory. In literature departments, Lacan's critique of the ego and his dictum that the self is essentially fragmented were taken over into culture criticism in the 1970s. Early on, in work such as that of *Screen* theorists, this criticism focused primarily on the pain of fragmentation. A core assertion of Laura Mulvey's groundbreaking Lacanian film criticism (1975) was that film and other apparatuses of culture conspire to allow a male subject to fantasize that he is not essentially fragmented, allow him to take an imaginary unified ego for the whole of his being. While maintaining this fantasy guarantees that he not have to face his pain, the price of his unity and sovereignty is paid by women and other Others, whose subjectivity goes unrecognized. The theory, which posits male narcissism as a societal norm, suggests that the only way to assure respect for difference and diversity is to acknowledge that we are fragmented beings, that no one has the Phallus (Rose 1985; Silverman 1992).

More recently, other strains of poststructuralist thought (such as Derrida's and Barthes' notions of the free play of signifiers) have crossed with Lacanian theory or with British cultural studies to produce cultural

---

This chapter was originally published in *American Image* 52 (1995):107–25, and is reprinted here by permission of The Johns Hopkins University Press.

criticism that celebrates diversity, ambiguity, and fragmentation. Theorists as different as Judith Butler, Constance Penley, E. Ann Kaplan, and Ellen G. Friedman posit the fragmentation of the subject as a strategy of resistance or a guarantee of indeterminacy, especially gender indeterminacy. Whereas Mulvey and Rose argue that the symbolic system violently fragments the female subject, in much recent cultural criticism the pain of this fragmented subject is forgotten or bracketed and she is rather figured as able to subvert the system by enjoying, rearranging, and playing with her fragments.[1]

Much of contemporary Anglo-American psychoanalytic theory focuses on self disorders (see, for example, Kohut and Kernberg). So, in psychology departments, too, people are discussing fragmentation (although, to my knowledge, they are not discussing Lacan). In these discussions, fragmentation is not posited as a feature of normal development. And the agent of fragmentation is neither metaphysical nor linguistic systems, but rather specific interactions with other people, primarily early caretakers.

In Kohut's work (1971, 1977), the self fragments when not properly mirrored or when traumatically disappointed by an idealized other. In Kernberg's work (1975), the self fragments when frustrated in its attempts to negotiate needs for independence and dependence, separateness and attachment. The mechanism central to fragmentation is splitting, an early defense that operates to keep separate good and bad affects, good and bad self-representations, and good and bad object representations. In an environment that is not too unpredictable or harsh, a child comes to integrate good and bad experiences, can tolerate ambivalent feelings, ambivalent cognitions, can experience the self and other as primarily good though at times disappointing. If the environment is harsh, particularly with regard to interactions around dependence and independence, the child continues splitting in order to preserve enough of a sense of a good object to keep developing. In this situation, the child's inner and outer world fragment, become black and white in all arenas. There are rigidly good and rigidly bad self representations: the person oscillates between self-deprecation and grandiosity. There are rigidly good and rigidly bad object representations: the person alternately idealizes and devalues the other. Cognitions tend to be absolute and extreme. Good moods alternate with very dark bad moods, and each seems to come out of the blue. When in one state about the self or other, the person can barely remember having ever felt differently.

High correlations have been found between diagnoses of self disorder and histories of abuse (Herman, Perry, and van der Kolk 1989). The literature on those who have been repeatedly traumatized describes an internal world peopled by victims, abusers, and saviors, of expectations of the world that can only echo what exists in the internal world, and of a life marked by splitting and fragmentation. Judith Herman writes of victims of child abuse: "the child victim's inner representations of her primary caretakers, like her images of herself, remain contradictory and split," and, "under conditions of chronic childhood abuse, fragmentation becomes the central principle of personality organization" (1992, 106–7).

The focus of the work discussed above is the pain suffered and inflicted by those who do not feel cohesive, who feel always threatened by a loss of self. Repeated narcissistic and abusive modes of interaction are the designated causes of fragmentation. In this discourse, the norm posited as both desirable and possible is one of mutual interdependence, in which each person recognizes the other as a separate (that is, diverse) center of initiative (see, for example, Mitchell 1988; Benjamin 1988). A clear focus on relationship distinguishes this conversation from the Lacanian one (where the primary relation is between the subject and the Phallus).

Because of the different ways these two discourses figure fragmentation, I find that, often, after reading a brilliant piece of cultural criticism, my clinical self feels very uncomfortable. For in this work fragmentation is essentialized, universalized, and celebrated in a way that seems not to acknowledge what it feels like to experience fragmentation. Fragments are not seen as arising from specific relational interactions or specific historical circumstances but rather are seen as the condition of selfhood.[2] While such texts demean any notion of a unified self, any wish for an integration of fragments, they paradoxically leave the reader with the sense that their protagonists are in total control of their fragments, that they are auteurs who pick and choose how they wish to represent themselves at any given moment (Harris 1992). In this work, the unconscious is evoked when it is convenient and ignored when it is not.

Often, the protagonists of these texts—the lesbian, the transvestite, the sadomasochist, the hermaphrodite—are made emblems of a third space, a space outside of various forms of cultural oppression. In this status, they perform an important cultural service—they challenge heterosexism, reified notions of gender identity, repressed forms of sexual expression, the hypocrisies of a puritan yet violent culture. At the same time, when these figures become postmodern heroes and heroines, the pain of fragmentation, of marginality, of indeterminacy is often overlooked or glossed over. Discussions of the film *Paris is Burning* are a case in point. While most critics were aware of the fascinating way that the film's subjects made of their oppressed position a creative and celebratory experience, few critics spoke of the ways that these creations were marked by pain and by the terms of the oppression (exceptions are hooks

1992 and Butler 1993). For example, few voices wondered why people whose experience of family is so devastating would choose to form nuclear-styled families. *Paris is Burning* clearly suggests that there is more to parody than ironic distance and critique; there is also longing.[3]

Writing about Foucault's study of the hermaphrodite Herculine, Judith Butler has also observed this tendency to gloss over pain (1990a). She notes the way Foucault romanticizes Herculine's multiple pleasures, all the while knowing that sexuality cannot lie in a safe realm outside of power. Butler's own reading of Herculine compels her to write: "In the place of univocity, we fail to discover multiplicity, as Foucault would have us do; instead, we confront a fatal ambivalence, produced by the prohibitive law, which for all its effects of happy dispersal nevertheless culminates in Herculine's suicide" (99). Because power and sex are coextensive, because the law generates sex, there is no way that Herculine could be in a limbo of heterogeneous pleasures.[4] What Butler locates in her critique of Foucault is the postmodern critic's wish, despite his/her knowledge, that the Other or the unconscious be the unproblematic antidote to our pain (see Rose 1987). As a clinician, these texts make me uncomfortable because every day I sit face to face with people who experience fragmentation not as joyful but as tormenting.

Unlike the cultural criticism discussed above, pain is everywhere in such avant-garde texts as Kathy Acker's *Blood and Guts in High School* (1978), and the pain is avowedly a product of trauma. Acker's protagonist, Janey Smith, has been fucked by her father since early childhood, and the whole book is about how women are fucked and fucked over by men. Janey's fragmentation is rendered in the book's fragmented style. At first glance, this seems the very opposite of what I have been discussing. Acker's text in fact mirrors the way many of my clients experience their fragmentation—as divorced from affect, as irreconcilable, as inevitable, as sometimes their fault, sometimes someone else's, sometimes consensual, sometimes driven. But in texts such as Acker's, the pain of fragmentation is universalized and aestheticized in such a way that, before long, one either forgets that Janey is an incest victim or one assumes that all women in a materialist society are incest victims. By suggesting that Janey's pain is woman's condition, Acker blinds the reader to the fact that Janey's fragments and relational capacities are reified in certain distinct ways that result from her being an incest victim. Acker's Janey, for example, can only figure her sexuality in two ways, either as pure pain and exploitation or pure wildness and freedom. In this text, as in many of the texts of contemporary cultural criticism, sexuality is depicted as either a mystical free space or a space of pure power struggle. In both discourses, fragmentation is universalized and essentialized in such a way that our choices boil down to complete despair or joyous celebration, choices symptomatic of the black-and-white thinking that is a product of fragmentation.

Thus, various contemporary discussions of identity center on fragmentation, but they radically differ in how they talk about it. How and whether these disparate discourses on fragmentation can be brought into relation is the question I now want to raise. To begin, I want to look at how my clients describe their experience of fragmentation and what they and researchers say about the nature of the fragments. Although fragmentation can follow from many kinds of early childhood experiences, I want to focus on sexual abuse because its consequences stand in a distorted mirror relation to the gender indeterminacy and sex radicalism celebrated by culture critics. I will therefore draw on the case material of one of my clients, Sheila, a woman who was sexually abused in childhood by multiple perpetrators and who feels she always had a fluid gender identity.[5] Her therapy has dramatically revealed both the pain and promise of fragmentation.

At the very beginning of therapy, Sheila revealed that she had coded different parts of herself male and female. Sheila identified her voice, size, tomboy activities, intellect, and hardness as masculine. She had not felt at all feminine until her first lesbian relationship; she identified her femininity as a "marshmallow" self, totally vulnerable and "weak." Early in treatment, she claimed that at a very early age she had rejected things feminine because of her proclivities (you can't be athletic in a dress and Mary Janes; Sheila never wore a dress after first grade) and because she wanted to be like her older brothers, who appeared to have all the family privileges. This "masculine" identification drew upon her the taunting and even violence of peers who clearly did not allow a space for gender indeterminacy.

Sheila claimed she consciously chose a masculine identity, but in an autobiographical novel that begins with the description of her first sexual abuse, she appears as a sexy, wild, longhaired, alluring seven-year-old girl. This, as well as many of her dreams, suggests that Sheila unconsciously came to associate a certain vision of femininity with something that provokes abuse. Her choice not to wear a dress at age seven was thus in part a rejection of a femininity she deemed dangerous; the choice was clearly overdetermined. As Sheila grew older, she distanced herself from the vulnerable little girl and came to experience herself as rigidly gendered: she identified her intellectual self as male, her rageful, sadistic self as an abusive male, and all her vulnerability and compliance and pain as female. Her wish in therapy was to integrate her "masculine" and "feminine" selves.

According to researchers, Sheila's rigidly gendered identifications are typical of abuse victims. Margo Rivera, a clinician who specializes in multiple personality, writes: "it is very common for their vulnerable child personalities and their seductive and/or compliant personalities to be female and their aggressive protector personalities to be male" (1989, 27). The alter egos, she asserts, usually reflect extreme cultural stereotypes of masculinity and femininity.

Sheila's story illustrates that when the experienced trauma is sexual abuse or rape, splitting and fragmentation operate on gender identity. As psychologist David Lisak has argued in his work on male victims of sexual abuse (1991, 244–46), the process of male gender identity development itself is traumatic and enforces a process of splitting, and this is of course true of female identity development as well (see Brown 1991 on the traumas of "normal" female development). Lisak (1992) cites a story told by one of his subjects, who, as a young boy, was humiliated for crying when he saw a moth killed. Here was a case of one-trial learning: boys don't cry, at least not in front of others. I agree with Lisak that each gender undergoes a "self-mutilation," for, as he puts it, each is forced to extirpate from the self characteristics that are experienced as part of the self yet coded by the culture as belonging only to the other gender. The tomboy, the effeminate male are only the most obvious sufferers of the trauma of gender identity development. When sexual abuse is added to the first trauma, splitting is intensified, fragmentation guaranteed.

In cases of sexual abuse, gender identity fragments and does so in somewhat predictable ways. Sexually abused girls show significantly greater gender identity conflict than those who have not been abused (Aiosa-Karpas et al., 1991). Rather than the flexibility postmodernists might see in a person whose gender identity is indeterminate, what I and other therapists and researchers see are fragments rigidly coded with cultural stereotypes of femininity and masculinity. Each identity is split between highly negative and highly positive traits; identifying with either is fraught with anxiety and pain because each has complex associations to the abuse and the gender of the abuser. Thus, gender indeterminacy usually reflects severe conflict about taking on a gender identity.

For Sheila, femininity feels dangerous and dirty, though longed for and alluring. Masculinity is sadistic, ugly, and violent, though at times this identity makes her feel safe, smart, invulnerable to hurt. Sheila can go back and forth between the two gender identities but each is so rigidly constructed that it engenders pain; she cannot flexibly interweave these identities, nor can she modulate the extreme way that she experiences their traits. Thus, Sheila's problem lies not in missing masculine and feminine identifications but in the rigidity with which each is encoded, in the dangers that attend identification with any one of the fragments, in the incapacity to integrate the marshmallow woman and the man of steel. Further, some of her identifications, such as the young girl, are, against her conscious wishes, split off from what she calls herself, and others are kept at a distance because they are felt to be shameful. One task of therapy is thus to deconstruct the rigid masculine/feminine dichotomy.

Sexual abuse creates rigid binaries not only in its victims' gender identifications but in their relational styles as well. Sheila, like all of us, developed her relational style within a particular matrix of relationships, and her conflicts and current relational patterns reflect, as Stephen Mitchell has put it, her commitment and deep allegiance to past modes of connection. A core experience for Sheila, both as an abuse victim and as the only daughter of her particular family, is that others find her unacceptable and try to compel her to be different from what she is. Sheila's relationships are marked by her longings to be overpowered by an other who will teach her how to be acceptable. What usually occurs in these relationships is that Sheila soon feels coerced, overrun, and misunderstood, and she then sadistically and self-destructively retaliates. Relational conflicts intensify feelings of fragmentation, and these play themselves out in conflicts about desire and about sexual orientation, in volatile moods, and in her split off but frequently experienced rage.

The victim of repeated abuse tends to split the world into victims, abusers, and rescuers, who are locked in a dialectical dance. S/he enacts and reenacts relational patterns wherein s/he is sometimes the victim, sometimes the abuser, and sometimes the rescuer. Traumatization thus splits the experience of power and powerlessness, domination and submission in extremely marked ways, as recent research by Joan Liem (1992) and colleagues indicates. They note that the literature on women sexually abused as children suggests that they are preoccupied with issues of power. These women exhibit a heightened desire or need for power as well as a need to see themselves capable of exerting power. But, at the same time, they are frightened of power. In Liem's research, women construct stories from pictures on TAT cards. Preliminary results showed that women who had been abused created stories about unequal power relations significantly more often than did women who had not been abused. Liem and other researchers find that power becomes an organizing theme of the relationships that women with an abuse history enter into, and the need for/fear of power is central to how they engage in and provoke particular kinds of interactions.

Margo Rivera's work with multiple personalities shows that power/powerlessness is the axis along which alter egos congeal. She notes that for every personality that identifies with, for example, a compliant girl, there is one "who ferociously resists that position" (1989, 27), such as the antisocial boy. Sheila's relational patterns, like her gender identity, are fragmented in these predictable ways because of her history of abuse. Power and powerlessness, domination and submission is the central axis around which her interactions occur—not only with lovers and parents, but with bosses, friends, and, of course, with me as her therapist. Sheila seeks powerful people to heal her; the tragedy is that those drawn to her usually have little capacity or desire to heal or understand but rather are drawn to her because they need to dominate.

The lack of historical and personal specificity in avant-garde and postmodern critical texts often makes it seem that all of us fragment our relations with others predominantly along the axis of domination and submission. While all of us certainly have experiences of helplessness and powerlessness, while all of us constantly negotiate and renegotiate our needs for dependence and independence, it is not evident to me that power and powerlessness are the primary organizing features either of most people's sexuality or of their relationships. The terms with which Sheila codes her fantasies and experiences are dramatic and particular to people who have consistently been rendered powerless—her core waking fantasy, where she is Joan of Arc saving hordes of innocents from sadistic rapists, is not in my experience a typical one. Nor are frequent feelings of rage the norm; rather, these intense feelings are generated, I think, from traumatic histories of power and powerlessness.[6]

In this moment of our ongoing therapy, Sheila is writing the stories of her internal characters, and each story brings her closer to various gendered split-off parts of her self; each story not only makes these parts more known but makes them more acceptable to her. Currently, I see her as oscillating between a painful fragmentation in which she cannot recognize an overarching self that could claim the fragments and a kind of flexibility that brings pleasure and enrichment, wherein she can see herself in each identity and thus feel each is part of her. A goal of therapy is to create an atmosphere that erodes shame so that the fragments of self become available, less reified, and can be claimed as parts of the self. My recognition of her and all her parts as subjects allows the various parts to recognize and enter into dialogue with each other as subjects, which perhaps erodes the power/powerlessness subject/object axis (see Benjamin 1988). Simultaneously, the act of writing itself seems to be providing Sheila a longed for sense of consistency. At first startled to find that certain images keep repeating in her work, she has come to find this comforting, an antidote to her painful awareness of inconsistencies that plague her and those with whom she is involved. Sheila's longing to be consistent is a longing that postmodern discourse cannot accommodate, that it in fact condemns as immanently oppressive.

Sheila's oscillation recalls for me Judith Butler's sense that we need a "typology of fragmentations" (1990b), so that we can distinguish between the kind of fragmentation caused by oppression—in Sheila's case, by sexual abuse, peer homophobia, and parental narcissism—and the kind of fragmentation lauded in postmodern theory, the kind that is meant to challenge the equally oppressive drive of Western culture toward silencing the diversity within us and around us. We must recognize, however, that even our experiences of diversity are rife with pain because there are so many external and internal attempts to silence them. The omission of that pain in much of postmodern theory is meaningful and needs to be explored.

At the moment, I feel torn between commitment to a humanist paradigm of a cohesive self that functions as an agent and a postmodern paradigm of fragmentation (Flax 1990). I think the two can be reconciled at some points or at least held in tension, and I want to conclude by looking at the work of two theorists concerned with a similar problematic, Joel Whitebook and Margo Rivera.

In "Reflections on the Autonomous Individual and the Decentered Subject" (1992), Whitebook argues that Freud saw the project of the scientific age to be not mastery over internal and external nature but rather the need to renounce omnipotence. Linking Freud's and Kant's notions of the maturity of the autonomous subject, Whitebook writes that the path to mature autonomy is one that requires decentering, or, one might say, the surpassing of a narcissistic position. Whitebook's concern is with the subject who frees himself from the dictates of the authoritarian other. As Jessica Benjamin (1988) has argued, however, domination and the subject-object dichotomy from which domination ensues are not incidental to the Western version of the autonomous subject but rather constitutive of it. In her intersubjective frame, the relinquishing of a narcissistic position requires recognition of and by an other experienced as a separate center of initiative—a relational event.

Whitebook criticizes Lacan for essentializing fragmentation, and he questions why the state of fragmentation that precedes development of the ego should be hypostatized into the true state, why the later developmental dimension is dismissed as fictive and violent. Whitebook calls on Winnicott (1965) and Kohut, for whom "the integrating experience of the mother's smile, far from situating the child on an alienated trajectory, provides him with *hope* in a future when he would no longer suffer the pain and anxiety of infantile helplessness" (1992, 103). I agree with Whitebook's assessment; Lacan is not specific enough about what kinds of relational patterns constitute our fragments, he presumes falsely that our first relationship is narcissistic, and he privileges fragmentation over cohesion. Flax's argument, that Lacan describes not human development but narcissistic development, is compelling (1990).

Margo Rivera (1989) has also wondered about the relation between the subject of postmodern theory, particularly its political feminist versions, and the question of, as she puts it, a central consciousness that integrates the fragments of the self. Rivera writes about severely abused people who become multiple personalities. Noting that the multiple personalities clinicians see are about 90 percent women, Rivera calls attention to the cultural causes and sequelae of fragmentation, primarily with respect to gender inequality. As I noted above, Rivera writes that splitting for the trauma victim leaves not arbitrary fragments but fragments gendered in starkly stereotypical ways. Rivera and Liem (1992) both make it clear that the fragments are organized around the axis of power and powerlessness.

Clinical data suggest that fragmentation is one moment in a dialectic that also must include integration. Rivera writes that clinicians have found that those patients with multiple personality who did not move toward integration, who continued "to guard their separations jealously were much more likely to lapse into their earlier state of dysfunctional dividedness and acute suffering" (1989, 28). She contrasts this to the poststructuralist imperative, where "concepts such as a unified self and a well-defined individual identity are not only not viewed as ideals but are considered to be dangerous ideological fictions used to erase the awareness of differences within and between human beings" (28; see also Flax 1987; 1990, 218–20). I agree with Rivera that what is necessary is some way of recognizing the self in these fragments, or, as she puts it, a growing ability to call each voice "I." What you call this "I" has all kinds of ramifications, but some experience of a cohesive "I," of a sense of sameness that unites even the most disparate fragments, seems to be necessary to relieve suffering. This sense of sameness that one identifies as a core self may be no more than a cultural artifact, but it is one that is necessary to good mental health. Whether it is because our culture forces us to constitute ourselves as agents to be recognized at all, politically and personally, or because there could be no morality without a responsible subject (Greifinger 1995), or because the alternative to feeling cohesive is the painful state of psychosis or emptiness, a sense of identity and agency are crucial components of the ability to be good both to the self and to others. Perhaps an error of postmodern theory is to assume that the experience of a core self precludes the possibility that one experience this self as evolving and changing in its interactions with the world and with others. A core self is not necessarily stagnant; neither is it necessarily narcissistic.[7]

Rivera feels that we can learn a lot about development unimpeded by major trauma from looking at what happens to trauma victims. She sees those who have not been traumatized as "capable of pretending to a unified, non-contradictory identity and denying our complex locations amid different positions of power and desire" (1989, 28). Aiosa-Karpas and colleagues (1991) found that females who were sexually abused were more aware of the constructed and contextual nature of sex roles than those not abused. They write that the abused female adolescents in their study "acquired an expertise for modifying sex roles, values, and attributions according to the circumstances of the external environment. What is feminine in school is very different from what is feminine at home, and the sexually abused adolescent is acutely aware of the difference. It is this ability to present a variety of roles that helps maintain the secret of the victimization" (270). The implication here is that a nonabused person who does not experience identity in a fragmented way may have a harder time seeing what there is to see about the social construction of gender, gender identity, and sexuality.

Is the trauma victim the person most able continually to reinvent the self? Is she the quintessential postmodern figure? Perhaps so, but the above study suggests a parallel between the problem facing the trauma victim and the problem I find with postmodern criticism: yes, the trauma victims are aware of being socially constructed, but their enactment of a variety of roles is defensive and meant to keep the trauma secret. So the pain of fragmentation—its roots in trauma—is erased. In denying the unhappy moment of fragmentation, this criticism sometimes reads like the high theory analogue of the Reagan-Bush happy years.

But what does it mean that those who have not been abused may be less aware of the constructed nature of identity, the fragments that make up the self? While these people may suffer less, postmodern critics point to the political ramifications of their blindness, for example compulsory heterosexuality; their blindness becomes part and parcel of the social reality that inflicts trauma. It is clear that cultural criticism that constructs marginalized people as victorious outsiders occupying a third space serves the important political function of challenging mainstream blindness and violence. But I also think it has the effect of healing trauma, and the way that it does so feels more modern than postmodern to me. This criticism, I think, accords people who are usually stuck with only the pain of marginality an avant-garde stature that brings pride and pleasure. The humanist moment lies in the paradox that to achieve this recognition the criticism performs the very unifying function of which it is skeptical, for it endows its subject with a sense of an essential "we" (e.g., the lesbian, the hermaphrodite) and suggests even more rigorously than bourgeois criticism that this subject is in control of how she represents herself.

Sheila is white and middle class; her trauma of sexual abuse fragmented her gender identity and sexuality. Recent research suggests that this level of trauma is not as rare as one might hope. For example, a demographic study of a random sample of young adults in Detroit showed that 39.1 percent were exposed to post-traumatic stress disorder-level stressors and 23.6 percent developed PTSD (Breslau et al. 1991).

The authors concluded that PTSD is among the most common disorders of young adults, surpassed only by phobia, major depression, and alcohol and drug dependence. Trauma is thus almost normative in the culture.

As we have seen in Sheila's case, developmental traumas also arise from the abuses of a racist, sexist, heterosexist culture (Brown 1991). Feminist critics, such as Waugh (1989), have written about the decentered status of women and the strategies women adopt to deal with the fragmentation caused by oppression; Afro-American critics, such as Gates (1988), have written similarly about the signifying strategies of decentered Afro-American subjects. Some of the best postmodern criticism captures the specificity of cultural sources of fragmentation and the effect on an individual psyche; these demonstrate that fragmentation is not merely an existential given but rather that it is inflicted relationally (see, for example, Williams 1991; Pratt 1984). Indeed, the decentered subject of much of postmodern cultural criticism and art is a victim of culturally imposed trauma. As one of my abused clients recognized, if the mirror of the world does not reflect your smile back to you but rather shatters at the sight of you, you, too, will shatter. These victims are agents, too, making meaning out of their traumas. Nonetheless, trauma restricts the possible domain of self-expression and relational expression and restricts them in particular ways.

Thus, I conclude that theory must find some way of holding the modern and the postmodern in tension. The tendency in certain uses of postmodern theory to split off pain from pleasure is what enables a theorist to celebrate a fragmented subject or claim the fragmented subject as the authentic subject. But fragmentation arises historically, from private and public developmental traumas. These traumas lend particular specificity to the fragments, which tend to be coded in rigid binaries, in stereotyped ways that are the opposite of the fluidity longed for by postmodern theorists. Therapy deconstructs these binaries; the process of doing so creates a sense of cohesion in the client that does not obliterate diversity and is not oppressive, but rather is liberating. Most important, a *different experience of the other,* one that is consistent and predictable and does not repeat the sadomasochistic or narcissistic dynamics of early development (or, if it does, subjects the event to analysis) enables the client to see the "self" in each of her parts and thus to undo the rigid boundaries between them. At this point, these parts can no longer be called fragments.

It seems to me that both therapists and cultural critics need not only to identify the fragments that make up identities but to examine their historically specific nature and origins. Further, therapists and critics alike need to be aware of both the defensive and transformative uses to which these fragments are put in various self-representations.

More attention needs to be paid to the tension between cohesion, which yields a sense of agency, and fragmentation, which does not.[8] And finally, many postmodern thinkers would do well to question their unspoken assumption that relations between self and other, self and systems are always narcissistic and grounded along an axis of power-powerlessness, for this assumption perpetuates an ahistorical way of figuring fragmentation and results in strategies of subversion that can only be highly individualistic.[9] For it is indeed narcissistic self-object relations that cause fragmentation, but such relations do not exhaust either political or individual experience, and theories that presume that they do work within a narrow and distorted range of human possibility.

Notes

1. Teresa Ebert has recently labeled the bulk of this work "ludic feminism," by which she means cultural criticism that "tends to focus on pleasure . . .—as in and of itself—a form of resistance" (1992–93, 7–8). In celebrating difference, this criticism, she argues, glosses over how difference comes about within systems of exploitation, how differences are valorized unequally in the culture. Tania Modleski has also criticized the pluralism inherent to many versions of British cultural studies (1986). And, in later work (1991), she has pointed out that the separation of sex from gender in so much contemporary feminist cultural criticism leads to a celebration of diversity that does not take into account real power inequalities between men and women, gays and heterosexuals, blacks and whites.

Kaplan (1987, 1993), and Penley (1992) would fall under Ebert's "ludic feminism" rubric (she also includes Donna Haraway and Jane Gallop); Ellen Friedman (1993), who associates fragmentation with women writers' refusal to constitute an identity in accord with patriarchy, is not a ludic feminist; I include her because her essay evaluates fragmented style as a strategy of resistance and shows little regard for the social and personal roots of the painful state of fragmentation that produces such a style, a style that reveals as much oppression as resistance. I cite Ebert because the celebrations of fragmentation and of diversity (internal and external), while not the same thing, stand in relation to one another, as the ensuing discussion will demonstrate.

2. In this essay I am commenting on a trend in cultural criticism, but I am not arguing that it is impossible to have a cultural criticism mindful of the experience of fragmentation. Indeed, cultural critics Patricia Williams (1991), Cindy Patton (1993), and, at times, Judith Butler (1993) do seem able to synthesize psychoanalytic and postmodern views of fragmentation, precisely because of their focus on the historical specificity of fragmentation and on the pain engendered by those cultural traumas that fragment the individual. These authors accommodate both the pain and possible pleasures of marginality, and, in part, they are able to do so

by holding agency and fragmentation in tension. Likewise, in the realm of experimental writing, I would place against Acker's work, to be discussed below, Toni Morrison's *Beloved* (1987), where historically specific cultural traumas induce fragmentation and the text centers on selves as agents struggling to integrate their fragments without disavowing them. Nonetheless, in doing my own work (1994) on Madonna, for example, I have read numerous postmodern feminist essays that belong to the trend I describe here.

3. I have encountered similar problems doing research on Madonna. Critics who want to make of her a postmodern heroine simply omit all the textual evidence that shows her pain (for example, Kaplan 1993 and Schwichtenberg 1993). These critics laud her continual reinvention of self, seeing in it her refusal to be bound by cultural definitions of the feminine, and they are right to do so. This is one of Madonna's cultural meanings, one way that she is read by such varied groups as young girls and postmodern academic theorists. At the same time, her longings for unity, her abusiveness to herself and others, and the pain that is everywhere in her work are ignored. It is in fact the exclusion of her pain that makes celebration possible. If we were to acknowledge it, we would notice how domination and submission inform everything she does and wonder whether Madonna's continual reinvention of self is a product of joyful choice or of painful and driven necessity.

4. Ebert focuses on pleasure as central to the "ludic feminism" she critiques; the heart of her criticism is the suggestion that only a class that does not have to worry about the body as a source of labor could so focus on the body as primarily a source of pleasure. Here I am arguing that this focus on pleasure entails not a safe haven from pain but a denial of it. That is, I assume that even the class position from which the ludic feminists speak must be marked by its own dialectic of pleasure and pain; for this reason, the omission of pain or labor is not just a sign of privilege but is in some way defensive.

5. In this paper, I will call this client Sheila, protecting her privacy and the confidentiality I offer her. I speak about her with her knowledge and her permission.

6. Within our cultural matrix, which condemns pain and humiliation yet habitually inflicts them, sadomasochistic desire will necessarily have conflictual multiple meanings, and these demand exploration rather than either facile celebration or condemnation. See Tania Modleski's essay "Lethal Bodies" (1991) for a discussion of sadomasochism that transcends simplistic pro- and anti-positions.

7. I am here extending to the experiential psychological level Amanda Anderson's political/ethical argument in "Cryptonormativism and Double Gestures" (1992). Anderson argues that, to maintain a feminist politics, postmodern political theorists have had to perform a double gesture, that is, allow for essentialism or identity politics in practice while asserting what they consider to be a superior antifoundationalism and antihumanism in theory. Anderson presents an inter-

subjective ethical theory (based on Habermas) in which subjects are constituted not by dominating systems but by ongoing relations with others. In this view, the systemic informs intersubjective relations but does not define them, and domination is no more endemic to communication than is mutual respect. What I want to suggest here is that because we are constituted to experience ourselves as substantive and purposeful, psychological theory also must hold in tension the notions/experiences of both a constructed and a substantive self.

8. Butler (1992) argues that there is no necessary contradiction between the assumption of a socially constructed subject and the experience of agency: "We may be tempted to think that to assume the subject in advance is necessary in order to safeguard the *agency* of the subject. But to claim that the subject is constituted is not to claim that it is determined; on the contrary, the constituted character of the subject is the very precondition of its agency" (12).

9. The intersubjective stance (versus the narcissistic subject-object stance) obviates the need for what Anderson calls the double gesture. I am arguing that a nonnarcissistic subject experiences the self as continuous and coherent but as constituted in and by its relations to others, others also conceived as separate centers of initiative. A breakdown in these relations is what leads to the experience of the other and the self as primarily dominating or submissive (Benjamin 1988). And it is in this situation of breakdown that agency and cohesion (and thus ethics, politics, etc.) become problematic.

References

Acker, K. 1978. *Blood and Guts in High School.* New York: Grove Press.

Aiosa-Karpas, C. J., R. Karpas, D. Pelcovitz, and S. Kaplan. 1991. Gender Identification and Sex Role Attribution in Sexually Abused Adolescent Females. *J. Am. Acad. Child and Adolescent Psychiat.* 30:266–71.

Anderson, A. 1992. Cryptonormativism and Double Gestures: The Politics of Post-Structuralism. *Cultural Critique* 21:63–95.

Benjamin, J. 1988. *The Bonds of Love. Psychoanalysis, Feminism, and the Problem of Domination.* New York: Pantheon.

Breslau, N., G. C. Davis, P. Andreski, and E. Peterson. 1991. Traumatic Events and Posttraumatic Stress Disorder in an Urban Population of Young Adults. *Arch. Gen. Psychiat.* 48:216–23.

Brown, L. S. 1991. Not Outside the Range: One Feminist Perspective on Psychic Trauma. *Am. Imago,* 48: 119–33.

Butler, J. 1990a. *Gender Trouble: Feminism and the Subversion of Identity.* New York: Routledge.

———. 1990b. Gender Trouble, Feminist Theory, and Psychoanalytic Discourse. In L. J. Nicholson, ed., *Feminism/Postmodernism.* New York: Routledge, pp. 324–40.

——. 1992. Contingent Foundations: Feminism and the Question of "Postmodernism." In J. Butler and J. W. Scott, eds., *Feminists Theorize the Political.* New York: Routledge, pp. 3–21.

——. 1993. *Bodies that Matter.* New York: Routledge.

Ebert, T. L. 1992–93. Ludic Feminism, the Body, Performance, and Labor: Bringing Materialism Back into Feminist Cultural Studies. *Cultural Critique,* 23:5–50.

Flax, J. 1987. Re-membering the Selves: Is the Repressed Gendered? *Mich. Quart. Rev.* 26:92–110.

——. 1990. *Thinking Fragments: Psychoanalysis, Feminism, and Postmodernism in the Contemporary West.* Berkeley: Univ. of California Press.

Friedman, E. G. 1993. Where Are the Missing Contents? (Post)Modernism, Gender, and the Canon. *PMLA* 108:240–52.

Gates, H. L., Jr. 1988. *The Signifying Monkey.* New York: Oxford Univ. Press.

Greifinger, J. 1995. Therapeutic Discourse as Moral Conversation: Psychoanalysis, Modernity, and the Ideal of Authenticity. *Communication Rev.* 1:53–81.

Harris, D. 1992. Make my Rainy Day. *The Nation,* June 8, pp. 790–93.

Herman, J. L., J. C. Perry, and B. A. van der Kolk. 1989. Childhood Trauma in Borderline Personality Disorder. *Am. J. Psychiat.* 146:490–95.

Herman, J. L. 1992. *Trauma and Recovery.* New York: Basic Books.

hooks, b. 1992. Is Paris Burning? In *Black Looks: Race and Representation.* Boston: South End Press, pp. 145–56.

Kaplan, E. A. 1987. *Rocking around the Clock: Music Television, Postmodernism, and Consumer Culture.* New York: Routledge.

——. 1993. Madonna Politics: Perversion, Repression, or Subversion? Or Masks and/as Master-y. In Schwichtenberg 1993, pp. 149–65.

Kernberg, O. 1975. *Borderline Conditions and Pathological Narcissism.* New York: Aronson.

Kohut, H. 1971. *The Analysis of the Self.* New York: International Universities Press.

——. 1977. *The Restoration of the Self.* New York: International Universities Press.

Layton, L. 1994. Who's That Girl? A Case Study of Madonna. In C. Franz and A. J. Stewart, eds., *Women Creating Lives: Identities, Resilience, and Resistance.* Boulder, Colo.: Westview, pp. 143–56.

Liem, J. 1992. Need for Power in Women Sexually Abused as Children. Presented at the conference, *Trauma and Its Sociocultural Context.* University of Massachusetts, Boston. Unpublished paper.

Lisak, D. 1991. Sexual Aggression, Masculinity, and Fathers. *Signs* 16:238–62.

——. 1992. Gender Development and Sexual Abuse in Lives of Men. Presented at the conference, *Trauma and Its Sociocultural Context.* University of Massachusetts, Boston. Unpublished paper.

Mitchell, S. A. 1988. *Relational Concepts in Psychoanalysis.* Cambridge: Harvard Univ. Press.

Modleski, T. 1986. Introduction. In T. Modleski, ed., *Studies in Entertainment.* Bloomington: Indiana Univ. Press, pp. ix–xix.

————. 1991. *Feminism without Women*. New York: Routledge.

Morrison, T. 1987. *Beloved*. New York: Knopf.

Mulvey, L. 1975. Visual Pleasure and Narrative Cinema. *Screen* 16:6–18.

Patton, C. 1993. Embodying Subaltern Memory: Kinesthesia and the Problematics of Gender and Race. In Schwichtenberg 1993, pp. 81–105.

Penley, C. 1992. Feminism, Psychoanalysis, and the Study of Popular Culture. In L. Grossberg, C. Nelson, and P. Treichler, eds., *Cultural Studies*. New York: Routledge, pp. 479–500.

Pratt, M. B. 1984. Identity: Skin Blood Heart. In E. Bulkin, M. B. Pratt, and B. Smith, eds., *Yours in Struggle: Three Feminist Perspectives on Anti-Semitism and Racism*. Brooklyn, N.Y.: Long Haul Press, pp. 11–63.

Rivera, M. 1989. Linking the Psychological and the Social: Feminism, Poststructuralism, and Multiple Personality. *Dissociation* 2:24–31.

Rose, J. 1985. Introduction II. In J. Mitchell and J. Rose, eds., *Feminine Sexuality. Jacques Lacan and the école freudienne*. New York: Norton, pp. 27–57.

————. 1987. Introduction. Feminism and the Psychic. In *Sexuality in the Field of Vision*. London: Verso, pp. 1–23.

Schwichtenberg, C., ed. 1993. *The Madonna Connection*. Boulder, Colo.: Westview.

Silverman, K. 1992. *Male Subjectivity at the Margins*. New York: Routledge.

Waugh, P. 1989. *Feminine Fictions: Revisiting the Postmodern*. New York: Routledge.

Whitebook, J. 1992. Reflections on the Autonomous Individual and the Decentered Subject. *Am. Imago* 49:97–116.

Williams, P. 1991. *The Alchemy of Race and Rights*. Cambridge: Harvard Univ. Press.

Winnicott, D. W. 1965. *The Maturational Processes and the Facilitating Environment*. Madison, Conn.: International Universities Press.

CONTRIBUTORS

Ranita Chatterjee holds a Ph.D. from the University of Western Ontario and is an instructor in English and Women's Studies at the University of Utah. She has published essays on William Godwin, Mary Shelley, and *Sammy and Rosie Get Laid*.

Patricia Reid Eldredge teaches English and Liberal Studies at Hamline University in St. Paul, Minnesota. She has published articles using a Horneyan approach to works by Richardson, Dickens, and Doris Lessing.

David Galef is Associate Professor of English at the University of Mississippi. He is the author of *The Supporting Cast: A Study of Flat and Minor Characters* (Penn State, 1993), several novels, including *Flesh* (Permanent Press, 1995), and essays on modern British literature. He has edited *Second Thoughts: A Focus on Rereading* (Wayne State, 1998).

Andrew Gordon is Associate Professor of English and Director of the Institute for Psychological Study of the Arts at the University of Florida. He is author of *An American Dreamer: A Psychoanalytic Study of the Fiction of Norman Mailer* (Fairleigh Dickinson, 1980) and essays on contemporary American literature and film.

Claire Kahane is Professor of English and a member of the Center for the Study of Psychoanalysis and Culture at SUNY Buffalo. She is the author of *Passions of the Voice: Hysteria, Narrative, and the Figure of the Speaking Woman, 1850–1915* (Johns Hopkins, 1996), coeditor of *In Dora's Case: Freud, Hysteria, Feminism* (Columbia, 1985) and *The (M)Other Tongue: Essays in Feminist Psychoanalytic Interpretation* (Cornell, 1985), and editor of *Psychoanalyse und das Unheimliche: Essays aus der amerikanischen Literaturkritik* (Bouvier, 1981).

Lynne Layton is Assistant Clinical Professor of Psychology at Harvard Medical School and in private practice in Brookline, Massachusetts. She is the author of *Who's That Girl? Who's That Boy? Negotiating Gender between Postmodern Theories and Clinical Practice* (Aronson, 1998) and coeditor, with Barbara Schapiro, of *Narcissism and the Text: Studies in Literature and the Psychology of Self* (NYU, 1986).

Véronique Machelidon, a native of Belgium, is a Ph.D. candidate at the University of North Carolina, Chapel Hill, where she is writing a dissertation on George Sand and Charlotte Brontë.

Michelle A. Massé is Associate Professor of English at Louisiana State University. She is the author of *In the Name of Love: Masochism, Women, and the Gothic* (Cornell, 1982) and at work on *Great Expectations: Men, Narcissism, and the Bildungsroman.*

Peter L. Rudnytsky is Professor of English at the University of Florida. He is the author of *Freud and Oedipus* (Columbia, 1987), *The Psychoanalytic Vocation: Rank, Winnicott, and the Legacy of Freud* (Yale, 1991), and two forthcoming books, *Reading Psychoanalysis: Freud, Rank, Ferenczi, and Groddeck* and *Psychoanalytic Dialogues: Ten Interviews.* He has previously coedited *Contending Kingdoms: Historical, Psychological, and Feminist Approaches to the Literature of Sixteenth-Century England and France* (Wayne State, 1991), *Freud and Forbidden Knowledge* (NYU, 1995), and *Ferenczi's Turn in Psychoanalysis* (NYU, 1996).

Barbara Schapiro, Professor of English at Rhode Island College, is author of *The Romantic Mother: Narcissistic Patterns in Romantic Poetry* (Johns Hopkins, 1983), *Literature and the Relational Self* (NYU, 1994), and *D. H. Lawrence and the Paradoxes of Psychic Life* (SUNY, 1999). She is also coeditor, with Lynne Layton, of *Narcissism and the Text: Studies in Literature and the Psychology of Self* (NYU, 1986).

Madelon Sprengnether is Professor of English at the University of Minnesota, where she teaches creative and critical writing. She is the author of *The Spectral Mother: Freud, Feminism, and Psychoanalysis* (Cornell, 1990) and coeditor of *The (M)Other Tongue: Essays in Feminist Psychoanalytic Interpretation* (Cornell, 1985), *The House on Via Gombito: Writing by North American Women Abroad* (New Rivers, 1991), and *Shakespearean Tragedy and Gender* (Illinois, 1997). She has published a collection of poems, *The Normal Heart* (New Rivers, 1981), and a book of autobiographical essays, *Rivers, Stories, Houses, Dreams* (New Rivers, 1983).

Maureen Turim is Professor of Film and Cultural Studies in the English Department of the University of Florida. She is the author of *Abstraction in Avant-Garde Films* (UMI Research, 1985), *Flashbacks in Film: Memory and History* (Routledge, 1989), and *The Films of Nagisa Oshima: Images of a Japanese Iconoclast* (California, 1998). She has also published essays on cinema and video using feminist and psychoanalytic theory.

David Willbern is Professor of English and a member of the Center for the Study of Psychoanalysis and Culture at SUNY Buffalo. He is the author of *Poetic Will: Shakespeare and the Play of Language* (Pennsylvania, 1996) and essays on Freud, Renaissance drama, and contemporary literature.

INDEX

233

7984